A Constructive Semantics of the Lambda Calculus

A Thesis Submitted
In Partial Fulfilment of the Requirements
for the Degree of

Doctor of Philosophy

by

Kalyan Shankar Basu

to the

DEPARTMENT OF COMPUTER SCIENCE AND ENGINEERING

INDIAN INSTITUTE OF TECHNOLOGY, KANPUR

April 1994

CERTIFICATE

It is certified that the work contained in the thesis titled *A Constructive Semantics of the Lambda Calculus*, by *Kalyan Shankar Basu* has been carried out under our supervision and that this work has not been submitted elsewhere for a degree.

H Karnick
Associate Professor
Department of Computer Science and Engineering
Indian Institute of Technology, Kanpur

R. Sangal
Professor
Department of Computer Science and Engineering
Indian Institute of Technology, Kanpur

April, 1994

ABSTRACT

Name of student· **Kalyan Shankar Basu** Roll No: **8921161**

Degree for which submitted **Doctor of Philosophy**

Department **Computer Science & Engg.**

Thesis Title **A Constructive Semantics of the Lambda Calculus**

Name(s) of thesis supervisor(s)

Dr H. Karnick

Dr R. Sangal

Month and year of thesis submission **April 1994**

The Heyting-Semantics of propositions is constituted on the basis of an isomorphism between the proofs of a proposition and the terms of an appropriate typed λ-Calculus It represents a profound alternative to the traditional Tarskian semantics, in that it models *proof* rather than *truth* In this dissertation, we propose a generalization of this conception to the (untyped) λ-Calculus—a calculus for which a Tarskian semantics already exists The critical abstraction involved is an appropriate formal notion of a *proof-object* (of λ-terms) we arrive at this by suitably refining the notion of a *partial evaluation* of a λ-term The collection of the sets of proof-objects of the terms is inductively structured into dependent and impredicative theory of constructive types, under certain operations corresponding to the standard type-theoretic ones The constructions are carried out within the framework of fibered categories, and remarkably, the (internal) category of types is seen to be a (full) sub-category of the partial equivalence relations (on the closed term model)—thus yielding an embedding into the Realizability topos model of impredicative calculi. We obtain the standard denotational semantics of the terms in the topos, and show the resulting class of domain-theoretic objects to be internally cartesian closed We also show that the "external" (partial) ordering on the proof-objects may be formulated as intrinsic *synthetic* structure on the basis of a classifier of recursively enumerable sub-objects.

SYNOPSIS

Name of student: **Kalyan Shankar Basu**   Roll No **8921161**

Degree for which submitted **Doctor of Philosophy**
Department: **Computer Science & Engg**
Thesis Title **A Constructive Semantics of the Lambda Calculus**
Name(s) of thesis supervisor(s):

Dr. H. Karnick

Dr. R Sangal

Month and year of thesis submission **April 1994**

This dissertation is an essay within the tradition of formal semantics Its intellectual descent may be traced to the works of principally three major thinkers Frege, Tarski and Heyting At the basis of Frege's identification of *Sense*--as that part of meaning that determined reference completely, there was a critical, yet not very precise notion of ***structure*** For instance, it was the *logical* structure of propositions (or sentences), induced on the basis of the rules of inference (of a specific logical theory), that was relevant for the determination of their truth—and *not* the *grammatical* structure (or syntax) In Tarski's subsequent re-formulation of the theory in terms of the (necessary and sufficient) conditions of ***validity***, the role of structure is taken over by the algebraic properties of certain universal models However the theory forced a complete (or "global") evaluation because of which only certain kinds of object-language expressions could have a well-defined meaning ([83]), thus its scope was restricted on the basis of a strong referential discipline

It was with A Heyting that a radical alternative to Tarskian semantics became available. Working on the basis of a re-formulation of the notion of *proof* provided by the Brouwer-Heyting-Kolmogorov interpretation ([87]), he proposed that one model the *proofs* of propositions instead of their truth Under this interpretation, the proofs were formalized as the terms of a theory of Types, thus, to each proposition corresponded the *Type* of its proofs—also known as the Curry-Howard Type—and we had the genesis of constructive type theory ([53, 27, 87]) The Types epitomized operational information and the theory provided an effective formal notion of intensional isomorphism that entailed semantic equivalence

Our study is animated by the perspective that a truly general conception of semantics--as was that of Tarski--must take every linguistic system as its field If that is accepted then we ask whether the notion of a constructive semantics admits a valid application to another linguistic domain—namely the λ-Calculus *itself*—for which there exists already a Tarskian semantics ([70]) In the case of propositions, it may be recalled that the constructive theory of types could only be formulated on the basis of a fundamental re-formulation of the notion of a *proof* according to the Brouwer Heyting-Kolmogorov interpretation Hence, we are led to believe that the critical abstraction underlying any answer to the current claim would be some formal notion of a *proof-object* of the λ-terms In this quest we are guided principally by three criteria

1 We would need to capture the information corresponding to "local" (or partial) evaluation, on the basis of which we may individuate some notion entailing semantic equivalence ([89])

2 We should be able to induce, on the basis of the sets of proof-objects of the pure λ-terms, and under some suitable notion of operations defined on them corresponding to the rules of Type dependency and quantification, a full constructive theory of Types (specifically, a Theory of Constructions) ([38])

3 We should be able to exploit the partial-order structure inherent in the notion of a partial evaluation (of the pure λ-terms), towards the construction of a class of objects that could sustain the constitution of the standard denotations of the λ-expressions ([5, Chapter 18 §3]) Moreover, we sophisticate the last criterion by requiring that the construction of (canonical) denotations from the proofs should be carried out within a higher-order intuitionistic universe, in which the denotational objects would essentially be sets (with standard function spaces), this could be taken then to represent a rudimentary abstract logic of programs denotations (*cf* [2])

We note that the last criterion gives us a framework to relate the Tarskian semantics to the Heytingian for propositions, this relationship—between the semantics of *proofs* to that of *provability* (or (intuitionistic) truth)—shows up in the topos interpretation(s) of constructive types ([62, 34])

The crux of our work is the identification of a single general and formal notion which satisfies each of the criteria listed above We arrive at the notion through successive refinements starting from certain topological considerations relating to the convergence of infinite β reductions of *solvable* terms, we identify a certain formal object called a *residue* (of a term) The notion had been identified earlier on other considerations ([5, Chapter 14 §3]), and is similar to that of an *approximate normal form* of a term For any λ-term x, the set of residues of all terms y such that $x \rightarrow_\beta y$ can be shown to determine the computational behavior of a term completely terms with identical such sets are ***semantically equivalent*** and accordingly we take the set as a first approximation to the notion of a (Curry-Howard) Type of ***proof-objects*** of a λ-term

We attempt to set up a (first-order) theory of dependent Types on the basis of the (bi-) categorical equivalence between *relatively cartesian closed categories* and Martin-Lof Type theories (without equality types, [38]) Critical to this construction is the refinement of the notion of a residue—as representing an equivalence class of the relation induced by that of mutual η-subsumption among Bohm trees of terms ([5, Chapter 10 §3]) Thus, the Type of a term is understood as a *partial equivalence relation*, we *induce*, on this basis, a theory that entails those judgements of dependency that are sanctioned by the (sub-) term structure of the calculus, and recursively generalized from this basis Thus, on this formulation, a proof-object is conceived as any such equivalence class of λ-terms, and this is the conception we retain throughout the sequel

Subsequently and on the basis of this notion, we extend the first-order theory to a full impredicative and dependent calculus—essentially a Theory of Constructions ([38]) The significant aspect of the argument is to model the Order of Types, and impredicative quantification over it The constructions are intricate and carried out within the framework of *fibered categories*, more precisely, the theory of *comprehension categories* developed recently in the study of generalized type systems ([40]) We prove that the object of Types forms a *full internal sub-category* ([34]) of the base category of our fibration, and characterize its limit structure as relative cartesian closure (in a suitable internal sense) We take the induction of this higher-order Type theory to constitute a viable program of the constructive semantics of the λ-Calculus

From this point, we turn towards exploring the constitution of the denotational domains of the terms, within an intuitionistic universe We show that our notion of a proof-object permits an elegant embedding of the internal category of Types into the Moggi-Hyland Realizability Topos—as a *full internal sub-category* ([33, 34])—in fact, as a full sub-category of the (internal categorical form of the) partial equivalence relations over the closed term model of the λ-Calculus ([48]) We demonstrate the order-theoretic structure on the objects of this category, and devise a method of completion (with respect to recursively enumerable directed sets) that yields an internal category of directed complete partial orders in the topos ([68]) This category is a generalization of the corresponding Heyting-algebra object of the denotations of propositions and we carry through the analogy formally by showing that the category is (internally) *cartesian closed* Finally we remedy the extrinsic character of this construction by re-formulating the order-structure *synthetically*—*i.e.* on the basis of an intrinsic order induced by a certain classifier of recursively enumerable sub-objects ([35, 58]). We show that the object of all possible proof-objects constitutes a *dominance* ([67]) and hence an object of computable truth-values Our final result is that our category of domain-theoretic objects is actually a sub-category of the *replete* objects ([35, 86]) identified recently as a canonical category of domains internal to the topos

ACKNOWLEDGEMENT

I am grateful to my supervisors for the latitude afforded me in this essay over a fairly abstract and frequently speculative terrain I appreciate deeply their untiring willingness to give a patient hearing to ideas, however intangible. I am grateful to Dr. H. Karnick for accompanying me enthusiastically through the undergrowth of category theory, fibrations, toposes, type theory and domains

I record my appreciation of Dr S Biswas' perceptive comments on my open seminar, they led me to detect an error in the formulation of the definition of the class of Orders in the theory I am indebted to Dr N Mukherjee for his constant encouragement towards the progress of my thesis, and his penetrating observations on the various foundational aspects of my work It was he who made me aware of the great importance of summarizing and presenting my ideas continually I thank Dr B. N Patnaik for his support and encouragment· those delightful discussions with him and Dr N Mukherjee on liguistics and philosphy contributed in many ways to the deepening of my ideas I thank Dr V R Sule for his readiness to share with me his extensive knowledge of mathematics

I acknowledge gratefully the support and facilities extended by the Department of Computer Science and Engineering

Certain individuals gain significance precisely by virtue of rendering redundant every acknowledgement of their value sanil, srikanth, nagarjuna and ravindra constitute a very special memory of these few years It is to the memory of those passionate and unsettled discussions—memories that would be vibrant long after the ideas and words in this thesis are quite faded—that I dedicate this thesis

Contents

List of Figures

List of Tables

Chapter 1

Introduction

This dissertation is an essay within the tradition of formal semantics; and true to its nature as an essay, it is exploratory rather than ampliative. It does not seek an answer to any question that it poses, or that is already posed: it argues for the validity of posing a certain question at all. It suggests the generalization of a certain conception of semantics to a domain for which it is not even clear, *ab initio*, whether the conception makes any sense. A thesis of this nature requires justification—for its conception as well as for its method—and the purpose of this introduction is to provide this. While the justification for its method may reasonably be sought within the technology available in the discipline, that for its conception has to delve deeper—to the philosophical lineage of its foundational concepts; accordingly, we shall spend a fair amount of time in this explication. The intellectual descent of the conception that I propose to generalize, derives from the works of principally three major thinkers in the semantic tradition—Frege, Tarski and Heyting, and we discuss critically, some of their seminal ideas in the sequel.

1.1 Frege and the concept of *Sense*

It may justifiably be said of Frege that his most radical contribution to philosophy was the definition of its foundational question to be the theory of meaning (or *logic* in his terminology)—and not epistemology as posited by Descartes ([17, pages 665–670]). This was his basic intellectual project and it was articulated through his philosophical commitment to free Kant's conception of *a priori* knowledge from every trace of the pure intuition that had been conceived as its ground. This articulation was itself achieved through a subtle shift in focus: in Kant's conception, analytic *a priori* knowledge was rather trivial—it was the synthetic *a priori* which was really a profound matter, and which required the ground of pure intuition

Frege reversed the emphasis by re-defining the analytic, thus displacing the synthetic from its pre-eminent place, and pursued the former within the domain of mathematics—specifically arithmetic ([12, pages 62–82], [17, pages 628–632])

Most of this thinking took place in the phase of Frege's work epitomized in the publication of his *Die Grundlagen der Arithmetik* in 1884, in the subsequent phase(s), the prior conceptualization of the analytic, as well as the general project of rendering a completely objective account of the nature of *a priori* knowledge, was deepened with regard to both pre-supposition and entailment Analyticity was, for Frege, a cognitive status for sentences a sentence was analytic by virtue of the *objective* and *cognitively available* methods for establishing its truth The consideration of such methods led to that of the information embedded within the sentence (and its constituents) on the basis of which such methods could be constructed and justified, and this led to the discovery of the seminal concept of *Sense* (as distinct from reference, or denotation) ([17, pages 631–632])

For Frege, the Sense of a sentence or any complex referring expression was its "mode of designation (or presentation)," it is that part of the meaning of an expression that is relevant to determination of what it designates (in Frege's conception, a sentence was simply a complex term which designated a truth value), it is that part of the information, *objectively* available in a sentence (or referring term), a grasp of which enable, *in principle*, the determination of its truth (respectively, reference) Apprehension of the meaning of a sentence implies apprehension of its Sense—while *empirically* it is possible of course that this apprehension entails in no way the knowledge of its truth or reference It is precisely on this account that the theory of meaning requires the concept of Sense over and above that of reference ([17, pages 81–109, 631–636])

Paradoxically, both the significance *and* the weakness of this concept lay in the stipulation that it be objectively cognitively available The stipulation was significant in that it underscored Frege's basic project of rendering an analysis of meaning free of every psychological or subjective element, it was weak because neither Frege, nor his followers were ever really explicit about the precise site and form of the Sense – nor the conditions of its recovery from the surface syntax of expressions

It was intuitively clear that the Sense-information could only be given on the basis of some notion of the *structure* of expressions ([23]) it was not very clear how one was to understand this notion of structure with any conceptual economy For instance, it was seldom the case—and definitely not so for the formalized logical language that Frege had constructed—that the *grammatical* structure (or the syntax) of expressions coincided with the *logical* structure (that by virtue of which the truth of sentences was determined) One could surely be generous in this instance and identify the Sense with grammatical structure—but the resulting theory would lack conceptual economy, in any case, it was not even necessary that grammatical structure should subsume the logical. While it is clear that the notion of logical structure is inscribed within the inferential rules of the language (if such a concept is applicable), it is not clear if we can infer, on their basis, something like the Sense of *individual* expressions: for, the inferential rules are typically framed in terms of *sets* of (meta-)expressions, and there does not seem to be an easy way to *localize* this information to individual expressions.

It can fairly be said that this critical problem is not adequately understood even now[1], and our essay is profoundly animated by it. In order to understand the problem in its generality, we propose an extension of its scope to calculi other than logical—specifically the λ-Calculus, which is a functional calculus with an expressiveness adequate to represent every computable function. In the context of such calculi we shall use the concept of Sense interchangeably with that of *intension*—strictly speaking, a narrower and more specialized notion—and that of reference interchangeably with that of extension.

The relevant issues are thrown into sharper perspective once we generalize them to functional calculi. Intensions in the case of programming languages may be taken to be the "computational information" encoded in the syntax of the programs, while extensions, the (partial) functions the programs compute. Yet, ambiguity threatens even this: the computational information has to be distilled from its syntax obviously, and as such, this could only take the form of a (sufficiently) abstract operational semantics: unfortunately, Computer Science lacks such a notion[2]. On the other hand, it is known, that the *denotation* of an algorithm is by no means captured through any standard (set-theoretic) notion of a function: some notion of *sequentiality* is inherent to the idea of an algorithm, and standard denotational models in functional domains lose the full abstraction property[3] ([10, 81]) on this account.

The conception of Sense was undoubtedly radical, and it was only on its basis that the theory of meaning could be studied *analytically*. Its imprecision is not to be taken to be symptomatic of its ill-posedness, but an indication of its informativeness. As it turned out, much of the history of the philosophy of language after Frege was a response to him, and an effort to clarify the problems inherent in his conception of meaning. In our context,

[1] In fact, recent writings of J.-Y. Girard suggests a revision of the notion of Sense towards what he calls the "Geometry (of interaction)"—roughly, the factoring out from syntax, all information redundant to the essential finite processes through which the semantics (operational as well as denotational) of complex expressions is determined ([25]).

[2] as noted by Girard ([27, page 14]), structural operational semantics in the style of Plotkin is manifestly *ad hoc* and would not do for this purpose.

[3] whereby exactly those terms are equated in the referential domain as may be exhibited to be *semantically equivalent* (see definition in the sequel).

the next major punctuation of this intellectual territory was effected by Alfred Tarski, after whom the term "semantics" acquired an entirely different—and what can be said to be its modern—connotation.

1.2 Tarski and the concept of *Truth*

The paradigm of model-theoretic truth inaugurated by Tarski underlies all subsequent extensional theories of meaning. The basic idea was simple and far-reaching: define truth as *validity*—that is satisfiability in all interpretation structures. Once this is done we may abolish the troublesome intensions (Senses) altogether, and define meaning to be the set of ***necessary and sufficient conditions for the truth of every sentence of the language*** ([84, 83]). The crux of the argument for the validity of this definition lies in the fact that the truth-conditions (we shall refer to them as T-rules or T-conditions in the sequel) are framed precisely in terms of the structural descriptions on the basis of which, on the Fregean account, extensions were determined in the first place. Moreover, a technical distinction was made between the language for which a theory of meaning was being supplied—the *object language*—and one in which the T-conditions were expressed: the *meta-language*. Thus, the structural information that went into the constitution of the Sense could be entirely incorporated (within the T-conditions), while its conceptual burden was delegated to an extensional referential realm through the mediation of the meta-language; this did render a regressive theory, but only in the last instance. In any case, Tarski advanced a powerful argument for the meta-language, saying that only thus may we avoid the semantic paradoxes (*e.g.* the Liar paradox). In fact, on his account, the question of meaning for a language which could function as its own meta-language was not really a well-posed one: such languages would always generate paradoxical expressions for which no meaning could be assigned—and hence the theory may not be complete ([83]).

The theory generalizes easily to functional calculi: taking truth to be the denotation of logical sentences, we may formulate an analogous theory for, say the λ-Calculus, by defining meaning as the set of conditions governing the denotation of the terms in *universal* models—that is, models into which, roughly speaking, all other models may be embedded.[4] It is important to note that at no stage does Tarski equate meaning with denotation—or even the set of denotations in all possible models: he defines meaning in terms of the (set of) *conditions governing validity*. Yet the weakness of the formulation lies precisely in the requirement that these conditions be expressed in a meta-language. This construct is no mere technical

[4] A similar concept is available for logic—namely, the Herbrand structure.

it is a point at which the entire validity of the argument is hinged. We cannot evade the fact that without a meta-language the theory may never be complete, that only by virtue of some rather drastic constraints on the object-language can we expunge an infinity of sentences that we indubitably understand, but to which the theory can assign no (non-trivial) meaning. This fundamental weakness manifests itself in certain other concrete ways which we elucidate below—especially since it is only *vis-a-vis* them that the theoretical advantages of the subsequent proposal of Heyting may be clearly apprehended.

The T-rules reveal themselves to be be uninformative—both operationally, and, surprisingly enough, denotationally. We take the latter case first. An adequate theory of meaning has to characterize that part of the information *ideally* available in an expression, governing its denotation (across specific interpretation structures): such is the understanding we inherit from Frege and I take this to be reasonably beyond controversy. The Tarskian theory lacks this conception and hence can provide no such general characterization: typically, the process through which denotations (in some canonical sense corresponding to validity, or to universal models) are determined on the basis of the structural descriptions, is an induction in the meta-language over some general algebraic structure[5] ([84]). It may justifiably be argued that the meaning of an expression should consist only in the structural information intrinsic to a language, and should in no way contain any reference to algebraic properties of extrinsic structures. On the other hand the operational aspect of the deficiency is that the T-rules remain opaque to *semantic equivalence*: roughly speaking, two terms are said to be semantically equivalent if they have an identical "behavior" in every term context—under some notion of behavioral equivalence—typically, based on minimal (*i.e.* to the point of definedness) or complete evaluations. It is reasonable to expect that such pairs of terms should have *isomorphic* intensions (or Senses). The T-rules give us no method to compute such isomorphisms.

The opacity of the T-rules to the operational aspect of term semantics is very much more evident in respect of the inference or rewrite rules of the language. While it is true that term structure determines denotations, it does so only in the last instance; in truth, it is the inference or rewriting process which does so directly, and it is in this that an operational semantics—*i.e.* the specific contributions of terms to the semantics of the contexts they come to be embedded in—is to be sought. We have already made some remarks on this point in the section on Frege. Remarkably, these contributions constitute information that is "local" in nature: in general terms need only to be partially evaluated in the computation of the

[5] This might be a boolean lattice for the propositional case, cylindric algebras for higher-orders, or a domain (isomorphic to its function space—say D^{∞}) for the λ-Calculus.

overall semantics of the embedding term contexts ([89]) The T-rules on the other hand, force complete evaluation in every case, and consequently, provide only "global" semantic information As a result, the rules lose application in certain cases of perfectly meaningful sentences (for instance, the Liar paradox in the case of Logic)—a point which we have remarked earlier This deficiency is in fact symptomatic of the unconstrained *infinitary* nature of the T-rules—a point noted by Girard in [25]

In view of the points listed above, we may say that the semantic information content of a term is epitomized within the set of its contributions to the overall semantics of possible term contexts, and that this set consists of information which is finitary and of a "local" nature, moreover, a system of aggregation which can capture this information, may, in all possibility, provide a basis on which term intensions may be represented and intensional isomorphisms (entailing semantic equivalences) be computed. We shall see, in the subsequent theory of Heyting, a system that can claim to do precisely this

1.3 Heyting and the concept of *Proof*

At around the time that Tarski was advancing his semantic conception of Truth, an alternative conception of semantics was emerging in another distinct conceptual tradition This was Constructive tradition—itself a ramification of Intuitionism, and the notion of semantics it engendered received its first clear articulation in the work of A Heyting ([8, 87]) The essential idea was simple and radical *model the proofs, instead of the truth*—with proof understood in an appropriate constructive sense Thus, in this theory of semantics—which we would henceforth refer to as Heyting Semantics—to every proposition would correspond the collection of its proofs Moreover with the appropriate constructive formulation of the notion of proof, these collections would be structured into a system of syntactic entities, and inscribed within a calculus of inferencing (*cf* [48, 27] for excellent studies) This system could thus be thought of as constituting a theory of *Types* (after the formulations of Russell and Godel) and it was as such that this constructive theory of semantics developed under Martin-Lof ([51, 53]) and Girard ([27])(amongst others)

The pivotal notion involved here was that of proof, classical proofs were deficient in two major respects first, they had an infinitary formulation, second, they behaved non-deterministically when sought to be reduced to a canonical form on the basis of Gentzen's Hauptsatz ([27, Appendix B]) Actually, both were aspects of a specific problem in the formulation of the structural rules of classical logic (the Weakening and Contraction rules to be precise ([25, pages 77-81])) The precise details are unimportant here, the significant point is that classical proofs could only have degenerate models Thus, the point of departure of the constructive theory was a re-formulation of the notion of proof itself The relevant conceptual shift was provided by the Brouwer-Heyting-Kolmogorov interpretation of the logical connectives ([87, Section 3]), and the natural deduction style of presentation of the inference rules valid under the interpretation ([27, Chapter 2]). The remarkable point in this conceptualization was that every constructive proof was isomorphic to a term of a typed λ-Calculus—and thus we had an isomorphism between the proofs of a proposition and the terms of the Type corresponding to it—an isomorphism that has come to be known in Computer Science as the Curry-Howard isomorphism ([27, Chapter 3])

It is important to note that the constructive paradigm of semantics still retained the Tarskian conception, though at one order removed from its traditional point of application We still give a Tarskian semantics to the theory of Types, since without that, the latter would merely syntactic objects possibly lacking even consistency The point is that we retain it just as a *criterion* for the formal consistency of the theory of Types—which latter represents the actual semantics under the current paradigm Conceived of in this way, the theory overcomes much of the defects of the earlier one

We shall argue that the theory of Types constructed on the basis of the Curry-Howard isomorphism (and modulo the logical equivalences of Constructive Type theory) may very well claim to be a system of representation of the intensions of propositions As such, the Type of a proposition can be seen to be informative both denotationally and operationally—remedying a major deficiency of the Tarskian theory The logico-syntactic structure of a Type yields directly a formal and effective procedure for the construction of a term of that Type: any such term being a proof of the corresponding proposition, we have an immediate criterion of its (intuitionistic) truth—independent of any reference to extrinsic algebraic structures On the other hand, the inferential structure of the judgements of Constructive Type theory provide a formal procedure for defining and demonstrating Type isomorphisms moreover provably isomorphic Types imply that the corresponding propositions are semantically equivalent—under the notion of equivalence based on the complete evaluation of (the truth of) embedding propositional contexts[6] Thus, a Type functions as a kind of an "interface specification" (*cf.* [25, Section IV 5]) and furnishes a formal informative criterion for operational (and denotational) equivalence

The significant aspect of the notion of a constructive Type, is its pure operational nature.

[6]The converse problem—i e if semantically equivalent propositions have isomorphic Types—is a more complex question, however, in the case of the λ-Calculus as developed in this thesis, we have a straightforward affirmative answer

The terms of a Type are but (the representations of) proofs—which are themselves the transformations and analyses of sentences according to the inference rules of the language Every proof of a proposition being available as a term of the corresponding Type, we have information about every possible way in which the proof of an embedding complex proposition may incorporate one of the embedded proposition. Thus, the Type of a term may be seen as the complete representation of its operational semantics The essence of the Brouwer-Heyting-Kolmogorov understanding of a proof was its strictly finitistic nature, and this is embodied in the constructive conception of semantics, what is not that emphatic is the "local" aspect of the operational information, and this is in fact a significant point of divergence between the intuitionistic Tarskian semantics formulated in terms of sheaf models ([87, Chapter 14]) and constructive Type semantics We shall make a more explicit comment on this in our conclusion however, in the subsequent development, we shall make a case for a more general understanding of the notion of proof, and one which is sensitive to this aspect of "local" (or partial) information Arguably, the most significant aspect of the theory of Constructive Types is its finitistic, constructive nature consequently, constructive proofs, unlike classical ones, are *effective*—in other words, they are representations of computable functions and have non-degenerate models[7] Moreover, the infinitary nature of the T-rules, which resulted in their loss of application in certain valid cases, may be redressed (to a great extent) in the constructive formulation

The fundamental re-conceptualization attempted in this paradigm is undoubtedly revolutionary, even though in its current form, it still leaves a great scope for deepening and abstraction For one, the syntax of the Type expressions is still too close to the syntax of the propositions themselves—close enough to identify a easy syntactic isomorphism between the two. If indeed the Types are to play the role of Fregean Senses, the notion of structure would have to be re-formulated with a greater degree of abstraction On the other hand, the concept of partial evaluation is virtually absent within the current formulation, the concept of a Type is still too closely tied to the notion of provability (or intuitionistic truth)—which again is a matter of global or complete evaluation This manifests itself in the uninhabited Types for paradoxical expressions, which are indubitably meaningful It is here that the concepts of intuitionistic model theory—that is typically articulated as the Kripke-Joyal semantics in sheaf categories ([19])—could play a deepening role Girard's conception of a realm of "geometric" objects underlying the syntactic proof-expressions ([25, pages 69, 91–98]) is extremely suggestive Both the finitism of constructive proofs, and the partiality represented in

[7] Though recent research indicates that under certain conditions, algorithms may be extracted from classical proofs too (*cf* [55])

the intuitionistic sheaf formulations point to the need for localized formulations– typical of geometric objects This is a provocative line of thought which we reserve for further comment in the conclusion

1.4 A Constructive semantics of the λ-Calculus

With the preceding discussion, we may appreciate the intellectual context of our proposal—which is, the generalization of Heyting's conception of semantics to *functional* calculi—specifically the λ-Calculus The proposal carries a serious import semantics, and specifically formal semantics, is salient to any language and only to language; the λ-Calculus is a formal language and has already, a Tarskian (or denotational) semantics formulated principally by D S Scott ([72, 73, 70]) It is thus evidence for the true generality of Heyting's conception, to have a well-defined application to the formal semantics of the λ-Calculus

As we have remarked in the very first paragraph, it is not even clear at this stage, what could precisely be meant by the proposed notion Thus, before we may progress with the substantive theory, we have to clarify, in fact define, terms The central concept in the constructive semantics of propositions is that of *proof* as we have remarked, it was only through the re-formulation of this notion on the basis of the Brouwer-Heyting-Kolmogorov interpretation, that we could arrive at a non-trivial theory of Types Thus, we would expect that some notion of a *proof-object* would be the principal abstraction behind the proposed theory In the quest for this abstraction, we choose to be guided by principally three considerations, which are discussed below.

We have already remarked that a system of aggregation designed to capture the information corresponding to the contributions of the terms to the semantics of various embedding term contexts, would provide us a basis on which term intensions could be represented and intensional isomorphisms (entailing semantic equivalences) computed. Such contributions being generally of the nature of partial evaluations, we come across precisely such a notion in the theory of the λ-Calculus This is the notion of an *approximate normal form* ([5, Chapter 14 §3]), used extensively in the theory of continuity and in the local structure analyses of λ-models It is also known that if a pair of terms have identical sets of approximate normal forms, they are *semantically equivalent*—in the sense of yielding equivalent head normal forms of embedding contexts ([5, Chapter 10 §4, Chapter 19 §2], [89, Section 6]) Accordingly, we take this (actually a slight refinement of this which we call a *residue*) as the first approximation to the notion of a proof-object This decision commits us to the view that *semantically equivalent* terms should have the same Type—in other words, that for such terms, intensional isomorphism would be conceived as intensional *identity* In fact, in the development of the theory, we would define Types (intensions) for terms *modulo* semantic equivalence

The second consideration stems from the requirement that the sets of proof-objects be structured into a certain kind of constructive Type theory, known as the *Theory of Constructions* To appreciate this, we may review the precise format in which the Heyting semantics of propositions is realized The process consists of two steps first, the construction of a Type theory on the basis of the isomorphism between proofs of a proposition and the terms of its corresponding Type; second, the Tarskian semantics of *this* theory in an appropriate (sub-)category of sets and functions The second step is essential, since without it we have merely a system of syntactic objects of which we may not even assert formal consistency Variations in the initial logic of the propositions entails variations in the kind of Type theory which we obtain For our purpose, we shall consider a very general kind of constructive Type theory known as the Theory of Constructions (*cf* [38] for an excellent study), and which corresponds to higher-order intuitionistic logic The salient aspects of this theory is the representations of dependent Types (and thus, dependent sums and products), and of impredicatively quantified (or polymorphic) Types The theory is impredicative, and thus consists of two strata—the *Types* and *Orders* The Types correspond to the propositions (under the Curry-Howard isomorphism), while the Orders represent the hierarchy of the domains of impredicative quantification, and other sortal domains

Thus, the first step of the constructive semantics may be characterized roughly as the induction, on the basis of the propositional constants of the logical theory (and their constructive proofs), of a canonical system of formal objects (namely, the Theory of Constructions), under the rules of quantification over impredicative and other sortal domains The second step, in which we give a Tarskian semantics to the Theory of Constructions is mathematically more delicate A rigorous logical view of models commits us to provide the interpretation in an universe of sets and functions—or to put it categorically, in a suitable full sub-category of the category of sets with *full* function spaces[8] Unfortunately, the interpretation of impredicative quantification requires that the sub-category be closed under internal limits, and the classical logic of sets dictates that we may not have any such non-trivial full sub-category As is well-known, the remedy is to shift to intuitionistic logic, and thus from the boolean topos of Sets to a general elementary topos This does yield non-trivial models, and a canonical construction towards this end is the topos of presheaves over the categorical form of the initial Type theory ([62]) However, we are still in the realm of the abstract, and historically, a "con-

[8]This was motivation behind the attempts of both D S Scott ([74]) and A M Pitts([62]) to fully embed (categorical) models of the pure and the polymorphic λ-Calculus, respectively, in their pre-sheaf toposes

crete" instance of an elementary topos model was discovered by Hyland and Moggi, and came to be known as the Effective Topos (more generally, as a Realizability topos) ([33, 34, 36, 61]). In this interpretation, the strata of Types was interpreted as the full sub-category of partial equivalence relations over the combinatory algebra underlying the topos—and known as the *modest sets*[9] ([61, 69]).

The constructive semantics of the λ-Calculus is realized within an identical format. The first step would be the induction, on the basis of the pure λ-terms (actually equivalence classes of terms, and the sets of their proof-objects), of a Theory of Constructions (in an appropriate categorical form, known as a *CC*-Category (*cf.* [40])), and under the rules of Type dependency and quantification. We should emphasize the fact that these rules are eventually spelt out in terms of certain operations on the sets of proof-objects, and as such, it is a criterion of the adequacy of the latter notion, that it admits such operations as well-defined. In the resulting Type theory, the λ-terms yield the constant Types; the rest of the Types and Orders come from the induction process.

The third consideration is to have a framework within which a perspicuous connection may be exhibited between the constructive semantics and the traditional denotational semantics of the λ-Calculus: for, in view of our remarks on the nature of intensional information represented in the Types, the former should permit a complete determination of denotational information. We recall that such a connection in the case of propositions was clearly articulated in the topos interpretation itself: the proofs were structured into a small and complete category of Types, while the denotations—i.e. the truth values were available as the global sections of the sub object classifier. In the case of λ-expressions, denotations are traditionally taken in domains—which are essentially algebraic complete partial orders. The use of domains is profoundly related to the fact that the set of what we have called *residues* admits a partial order structure and the set of such forms for any λ-term is a directed set under this order ([5, Chapter 14 §3]). Moreover, it can be shown that the set of all possible such forms yields a domain under directed completion, and hence the directed set of residues of any term has a least upper bound in this domain ([5, Chapter 10 §2]): this bound is precisely what may be taken as the denotation of the term in the canonical Bohm tree model of the Calculus ([5, Chapter 18 §3]). Since the notion of a proof-object for a pure λ-term is essentially derived from that of a residue, we would want a framework where this process of obtaining the canonical denotation of a term, from the Type of its proof-objects, would be

[9] To be more precise, the sub-system of Types was structured as a *full internal sub-category* (with the requisite completeness properties): meaning thereby, an internal category in the topos, isomorphic to a full sub-category of the latter (in an appropriate *fibered* sense ([82, 34, 61])).

perspicuously displayed—*and in the rigorous logical sense of interpretation*—i e. *in an universe of (possibly non-standard) sets* with full function spaces This would yield a properly logical account of extracting denotations from intensions, as well as make available to us, a standard (set-theoretic) logic to reason about the domains of these denotations.

A precise account of the intended methodology may be described as follows We would fully embed our category of Types as a full internal sub-category of the Moggi-Hyland Realizability Topos obtained from the closed term model of the λ-Calculus The resulting internal category is then essentially a small category of sets, and we would identify a certain internal (or *synthetic*) structure—essentially on the basis of a suitable object of *computable* truth values (*cf.* [35, 86])—around which we may perform the domain-theoretic construction which yields us the denotations (of the pure λ-terms) in the standard sense—as least upper bounds of the corresponding sets of proof-objects The whole construction would be carried out *internally* in the topos, and we are thus rendered a small category of *synthetic* domain-theoretic objects (directed complete partial orders, or dcpos) which can sustain the usual notion of the denotation of terms, moreover, this small category is *logically* one of sets, and we may reason about them in the standard intuitionistic logic of sets

It turns out that a simple refinement of the notion of a residue enables us to satisfy all the considerations discussed above The basic idea is to conceive of a residue as the representative of an equivalence class of λ-terms, under the relation induced by the mutual η-subsumption relation among Böhm trees ([5, Chapter 10 §3]) The final notion of a proof-object then, is that of an equivalence class under this relation. and thus, every λ-term, and in fact every Type, can be thought of as a *partial equivalence relation* on the closed term model of the Calculus Consequently, our category of (pre-)domains may be seen to be a full sub-category of the (internal) category of the modest sets—a fact of considerable theoretical significance An exploration of the properties of this category reveals that it is (internally) cartesian closed—in a remarkable analogy to the propositional case, where the corresponding object of truth-values (denotations) was a Heyting algebra object

With this, we may turn to the substantive development of the ideas discussed here In our understanding, the program of a general constructive semantics is a novel conception, with deep mathematical and philosophical implication: it is a theory with a great scope for abstraction, and whereby it may open up a truly general conception of information and language. In this, our efforts may be seen as the carving out of some initial territory.

1.5 Overview

The development of the thesis is as follows

Chapter 2. In this chapter we try to identify a first approximation to the formal notion of a proof-object We approach the problem from an apparently unrelated direction: namely, we seek a purely topological criterion that will distinguish infinite β-reduction sequences of *solvable* terms as *convergent*, as opposed to the those of unsolvable ones. We refine and adapt certain notions developed in the context of rewriting systems to the λ-Calculus (which is *not* one, in the technical sense), and come up with a notion of a *residue* of a term, on the basis of which such a criterion can be formulated We propose to associate with any term, the set of its residues, anticipating that these sets would subsequently be structured into a theory of Types We explore the order-theoretic properties of these sets, and prove that a pair of terms possessing identical sets of residues would have the same Bohm trees, and thus be *semantically equivalent* in an appropriate sense

Chapter 3. In this chapter explore the dependency structure of the theory of Types generated, eventually, on the basis of the sets of residues of the pure λ-terms We present first a version of Martin-Lof Type theory (without equality Types), that is essentially the first-order fragment of the Theory of Constructions, and discuss its standard categorical interpretation in relatively cartesian closed categories Next, we present a formulation within which our sets of residues may (inductively) generate a relatively cartesian closed category—and thus a specific first-order dependent Type theory—under suitably defined operations corresponding to dependent sums and products In this formulation, we conceive a residue as the representative of an equivalence class of a certain canonical relation on the set of pure λ-terms—this being the conception we shall retain eventually, of a proof-object

Chapter 4. In this chapter we present some of the theoretical tools we shall need to represent the later results in an elegant and abstract way Dependency structure is ideally interpreted in the framework of fibered categories, and we present this theory in a form that is well-adapted to the interpretation of Type structures—namely, the *Comprehension Category* framework extensively studied by B Jacobs recently We characterize fiber-wise structure needed to model dependent sums and products, and representability conditions needed to model dependency judgements We prove some of the main results we would utilize in the sequel

Chapter 5 In this chapter, we continue the explication of the theory behind the categorical interpretation of (full) constructive Type theories It is impredicative quantification (or polymorphism) which is the most delicate to model, and we present the framework of *internal categories* within which the forms of completeness required for the interpretation may be elegantly represented We explicate the complementarity between internal categorical and fibered modes of representation, and emphasize the usefulness of being able to shift from one to the other We present the remarkable notion of a full internal sub-category and underscore the close relation between its limit structure, and that of the ambient category, we use it to define structure in internal categories We spend some time in relating fibered and internal modes for base categories which do not have all pullbacks, but only a basic display map structure Finally, we present the full Theory of Constructions, and an elegant categorical model described by B Jacobs, and known as a CC-Category

Chapter 6. In this chapter, we complete the development of Chapter 3 we present the induction of a (full) Theory of Constructions on the basis of the sets of residues (of equivalence classes) of the pure terms, under operations corresponding to dependent and impredicative forms of quantification Methodologically, this is accomplished by generating a CC-Category under the operations mentioned This entails, on account of the theory explicated in the previous chapter, that the sub-system of the Types may be conceived as a full internal sub-category of the base category (of the CC-Category), in fact what may be described as a ***full internal relatively cartesian closed category*** This accomplishes to a great extent, our objective of developing what we have characterized as the constructive semantics of the calculus The interpretation of the Theory of Constructions in some suitable topos is quite standard, and we do not labour it Instead, in the sequel we address the question of developing some of the standard denotational theory on the basis of our category of Types

Chapter 7. In this chapter we present some of the theory behind a "concrete" topos model of dependent and impredicative Type theory—namely the interpretation in the Moggi-Hyland Realizability Topos We present some of standard structures involved in the interpretation specifically the (sub-)categories of the ω-sets and the modest sets. We explicate the completeness structure needed to model polymorphism and dependency—switching between internal and fibered modes of description We explicate the notion of the internal logic of the topos, and the interpretation of intuitionistic logic in the latter Finally, we embed the relevant categorical structures identified in the last chapter into this standard framework we prove that thereby our category of Types is embedded as a full internal sub-category of the ω-sets (and hence of the realizability topos), that it is internally a full sub-category of the category of the modest sets, and finally that it has a certain restricted form of completeness when so embedded (*relative* to a certain sub-category of the ω-sets)

Chapter 8. In this chapter, we shall carry out some of the standard denotational constructions within the topos of the previous chapter Intuitively, the set of residues of a term carries a partial order, and in fact is a directed set under it The set of all residues is a domain under directed completion, and a canonical denotation of a term may be obtained as the least upper bound of its set of residues. We shall show that this intuition is conserved even as we refine the notion of a residue into that of a proof-object (*i e* an equivalence class) and thus in the category of Types embedded in the topos as described in the previous chapter We carry out the directed completion and obtain thereby, a small category of domain-theoretic objects (in the topos), and carrying the canonical denotations of the terms as least upper bounds of the corresponding Types We prove that this category is *internal cartesian closed*, in remarkable analogy to the propositional case Finally, we recast the constructions in a *synthetic* form that is, we identify a suitable object of computable truth-values, on the basis of which the partial-order structure on the objects of our denotational category appears as intrinsic structure Thus, we have a category of (synthetic) domain-theoretic objects that can sustain the standard denotations of the pure terms, and which are *logically*, a small category of sets, with *full function spaces*

Chapter 2

Residues

A formal analogy between the Type represented by a Proposition (under the Curry-Howard isomorphism), and the Type represented by a λ-term (under an analogous notion), can be initiated if we have some idea of the objects that could function as the analogue of proofs of propositions. A fairly simple idea may aid us here: if a pair of propositions represent isomorphic Types, then every propositional context has the same truth value when either of the pair is substituted into it. Taking truth to be the reference of propositions, we would be justified then, in looking for a class of objects correlated with each λ-term, such that if two such classes be isomorphic, the corresponding terms would cause every λ-context to have the same normal form under their substitution. Refining the notion of normal form to *head normal form*—which may be be thought of as a *minimal* notion of reference (i.e. to the point of definedness)—we would have the following precise formulation

$$\int x = \int y \Rightarrow \forall C[\,]\ C[x] =_h C[y] \tag{2.1}$$

where $C[\,]$ is an arbitrary λ context, $m =_h n$ means that the terms m and n have the same head normal form, and $\int x$ is the notation we shall use for the Type of the term x. This formulation indicates that we should look for the objects constituting $\int x$ within the theory of Solvability. Accordingly, we shall address first the conditions under which (a possibly infinite) β-reduction sequence for a term may still be considered to yield a valid semantic value.

2.1 Convergence

Much of the arguments of this section were formulated by Wadsworth ([89]) and Barendregt ([5]). We re-arrange them in order to extract the information that would be significant for our purpose. As we are aware, terms having a normal form admit readily the notion of semantic value—which is simply the normal form itself, or some suitable interpretation of it in a semantic domain. It is well-known, that of the remaining class of terms, not all may be deemed as meaningless the unsolvable terms may consistently be equated to some meaningless token, while there exists a residual class which have no normal form, but may be deemed meaningful[1] Let us try to understand the situation by comparing the following β-reduction sequences:

$$(\lambda x\ xx)(\lambda x\ xx) \longrightarrow (\lambda x\ xx)(\lambda x\ xx) \longrightarrow$$
$$(\lambda f\ (\lambda x\ f(xx))(\lambda x\ f(xx))) \longrightarrow \lambda f\ f(\lambda x\ f(xx))(\lambda x\ f(xx))) \longrightarrow$$

the first is an example of an unsolvable term (which we would denote as Ω), that may be thought of as meaningless, the second is a solvable term (which we would denote as Y), which may be considered meaningful though it has an infinite reduction sequence One of the differences between the two cases which may strike us, is that the latter derivation leads to something like an infinite normal form while the former yields an unsolvable term even in the limit We can take this as the point of departure and try to arrive at a formal characterization of this difference A promising perspective is that of term-rewriting the λ-Calculus is not a term-rewriting system technically (*cf* [11, 31]), but we could try to apply the criteria developed for infinite rewriting sequences and see precisely where they are wanting. Since the analysis would involve infinite reductions (and hence, infinite terms), we make these notions precise (using the formulation of [15])

Definition 2.1.1 *Let Σ denote the set of finite sequences over the set of natural numbers $\aleph$. We denote the prefix order on Σ as $\prec$, sequence concatenation by $*$, and the sub-sequence relation by $\sqsubset$ We shall consider an alphabet consisting of a denumerable set of variables $\mho$, a $\mho$-indexed set of unary operators $\lambda \equiv \{\lambda x\}_{x \in \mho}$, and a binary operator $\cdot$ For any element τ of this alphabet we shall denote by $ar(\tau)$, the arity of τ (with variables considered to be of zero arity) A λ^∞-term χ is defined to be a partial function $\chi : \Sigma \rightarrow \mho \bigcup \lambda \bigcup \{\cdot\}$ subject to the following conditions*

1. $\sigma \in dom(\chi) \Rightarrow \forall \phi \prec \sigma\ \phi \in dom(\chi)$

2. *For any $\sigma \in dom(\chi)$, we define the* out-degree *of σ by*

$$Out(\sigma) = Card(\{\phi \in dom(\chi) \mid \exists m \in \aleph\ \phi = \sigma * (m)\})$$

Then we shall have that

$$\sigma \in dom(\chi) \Rightarrow Out(\sigma) = ar(\chi(\sigma))$$

[1] In fact, it is *inconsistent* (with regard to the theory of β-equality) to equate such terms to the unsolvable terms

We have the usual notion of β-reduction

$$(\lambda x\ M)N \longrightarrow M(N/x)$$

on the set of terms λ^∞. This generates a rewrite relation $\longrightarrow_\beta$ (we may sometimes abbreviate this simply as β) on λ^∞ in the usual way, and we call the resulting rewrite system, the λ^∞-Calculus

The inclusion of infinite terms in the language sanctions infinite reductions, hence we have to formalize the notion of the limits of transfinite reduction sequences We shall follow the methodology of Dershowitz *et al* ([15]), and topologize the set λ^∞ through a metric ∂.

Definition 2.1.2 *For a pair of terms $s, t \in \lambda^\infty$, we define the* distance *between them by*

$$\partial(s,t) = \frac{1}{2^{d(s,t)}}$$

where $d(s,t)$ is defined as follows,

$$\begin{aligned} d(s,t) &= \min\{|\sigma| \,|\, \sigma \in dom(s) \bigcap dom(t), s(\sigma) \neq t(\sigma)\} \qquad for\ s \neq t \\ &= 0 \quad otherwise \end{aligned}$$

in which $|\ |$ denotes the length function for sequences

It is known that with this metric, the set λ^∞ forms a complete ultra-metric space (*cf.* [56]) This allows us to define a notion of convergence of a finite or transfinite sequence of terms

Definition 2 1 3 *For a finite or transfinite sequence of λ^∞-terms $\langle s_\gamma \rangle_{\gamma<\kappa}$ indexed by ordinals γ less than some ordinal κ, we say that a term t is the* limit *of the sequence (equivalently, the sequence* converges *to t—written as*

$$\lim_{\gamma\to\kappa} \langle s_\gamma \rangle_{\gamma<\kappa} = t$$

if, for any neighborhood V of t, there exists an ordinal $\alpha < \kappa$, such that $\forall\gamma \quad \alpha < \gamma < \kappa \quad s_\gamma \in V$ We have the obvious generalization to sequences indexed by ordinals in some range between a pair of ordinals α, γ, which would be denoted as $\langle s_\lambda \rangle_{\alpha \leq \lambda \leq \gamma}$

As we know, this formulation of convergence in terms of countable sequences is fundamentally limited[2]—and our objective in this section is precisely to work towards a more abstract formulation (in terms of *filter bases* or centered collections, see [16]) We may define the notion of a *derivation* in the λ^∞-Calculus, on the basis of this formulation of convergence ([15])

[2]For instance, it is impossible to define and analyze the topology of an uncountable set of topological spaces, or formulations in analysis (classical integration theory), within the framework of countable sequences

Definition 2.1.4 *For the reduction relation β, and an arbitrary ordinal κ, we define the κ-iterate (or the κ-transitive closure) of β—symbolized as $\xrightarrow{\kappa}_\beta$, as follows*

If $\kappa = 0$ *then the κ-iterate $\xrightarrow{\kappa}_\beta$ is simply the identity relation,*

If κ is a successor ordinal $\iota + 1$ *then $\xrightarrow{\kappa}_\beta = \xrightarrow{\iota}_\beta \bigcup (\xrightarrow{\iota}_\beta \circ \longrightarrow_\beta)$,*

If κ is a limit ordinal *then for terms s, t we have $s \xrightarrow{\kappa}_\beta t$ if $s \xrightarrow{\iota}_\beta t$ for some $\iota < \kappa$ or there exists a sequence of terms $\langle s_\mu \rangle_{\mu<\kappa}$ such that $s_\nu \xrightarrow{\mu}_\beta s_\mu$ for all $\nu < \mu < \kappa$ and $\lim_{\mu\to\kappa} s_\mu = t$*

A derivation of length κ with respect to the reduction relation β is sequence of terms $\langle s_\mu \rangle_{\mu<\kappa}$ such that $s_\nu \xrightarrow{\mu}_\beta s_\mu$ for all $\nu < \mu < \kappa$ We say that the derivation converges *to a term t if the limit of the sequence of terms constituting the derivation is the term t*

We may generalize the notion of derivation to arbitrary (binary) relations R over λ^∞ in the obvious manner

This gives us the basic framework to reason about infinite derivations and terms The basic approach within the tradition of term-rewriting systems is to consider, for arbitrary ordinals α, derivations of length α which have a limit—and define such derivations as normalizing or otherwise, if that limit is a normal form, appropriately defined We have the following definition in [15]

Definition 2.1.5 *([15, Definition 4 1]) An α-normal form of a term s in λ^∞, for an ordinal α, and with respect to the reduction relation R, is a term t such that $s \xrightarrow{\alpha}_R t$ and $t \longrightarrow_R t'$ only if $t' = t$*

We see of course that this would not do for us both derivations, for Ω and Y considered above would turn out to end in normal forms on this criterion Hence, we define a normal form in a more direct manner as follows

Definition 2.1.6 *A λ^∞-term t is said to be in β-normal form iff for no sequence $\sigma \in \mathrm{dom}(t)$, is the value of $t(\sigma)$ a β-redex*

A β-redex is, as usual a (sub-) term of the form $(\lambda x.M)N$ thus, a term is in normal form if and only if it has no *finitely accessible* occurrence of a β-redex We may reformulate Definition 2 1 5 as follows

Definition 2.1.7 *An α-normal form of a term s in λ^∞, for an ordinal α, and with respect to the reduction relation β, is a term t in β-normal form, such that $s \xrightarrow{\alpha}_\beta t$*

We shall try to characterize infinite meaningful β-reductions as those which converge (in the most general topological sense) to normal forms We shall work within the topology of the ultra-metric space obtained on the basis of Definition 2 1 2 We need the following auxiliary notions

Definition 2.1 8 *Let $\lambda\perp$ denote the set of (finite) λ-terms augmented with a constant $\perp$ For an λ-term N, we may define a corresponding $\lambda\perp$-term $\lceil N \rceil$ (its* residue*) as follows (the notational conventions used are standard $\lambda\vec{x}$ is used to denote a generic sequence of λ-abstractions, the components variables of which may be taken to be $x_1, \ldots, x_n$)*

$$\lceil N \rceil = \begin{cases} \lambda\vec{x}\ \perp & \text{if } N \text{ is not in hnf, and has the form } \lambda\vec{x}\ M \\ \lambda\vec{x}\ y\lceil M_1 \rceil \cdots \lceil M_n \rceil & \text{if } N \text{ has the hnf } \lambda\vec{x}\ yM_1 \cdots M_n \end{cases}$$

where "hnf" is an abbreviation for head normal form

The same notion appears in Barendregt in connection with a discussion on continuity ([5, Definition 14 3 6 (ii)]) $\lambda\perp$-terms may be thought of as denoting sets of λ-terms by the following convention

Definition 2.1 9 *For any term $t \in \lambda^\infty$, and a $\lambda\perp$-term X, we say that t* extends *X, (written as $t > X$) iff*

$$\mathrm{dom}(X) \subset \mathrm{dom}(t) \bigwedge \forall\sigma \in \mathrm{dom}(X)\ X(\sigma) \neq \perp \Rightarrow t(\sigma) = X(\sigma)$$

thus, in an intuitive sense, if we understand that the occurrence of $\perp$ to denote "undefined", then $t > X$ simply means that as functions, t extends X We shall use $\geq$ for the obvious partial order obtained on this basis We define the extent *$[\ ]$ of a $\lambda\perp$-term X as follows*

$$[X] = \{t \in \lambda^\infty \mid t > X\}$$

In the sequel, we would be extending the extension relation to $\lambda\perp$-terms, defined in the same way as above Note that for $\lambda\perp$-terms X and Y, if $X \geq Y$, then $[X] \subseteq [Y]$

Now consider a β-reduction sequence (that is, a derivation) $\langle X \rangle$ of length α

$$\langle X \rangle \equiv \langle X_0 \longrightarrow X_1 \longrightarrow \cdots \rangle$$

We have the sequence of $\lambda\perp$-terms $\langle \lceil X_i \rceil \rangle_{i<\alpha}$, and thence the sequence of sets of λ^∞-terms $\langle [\lceil X_i \rceil] \rangle_{i<\alpha}$ We can easily verify the following property

Lemma 2 1.10 *For all $0 < i < \alpha$, we have that $[\lceil X_{i+1} \rceil] \subseteq [\lceil X_i \rceil]$*

Proof: For any term X_i in the sequence, we must have that the succeeding term X_{i+1} is obtained by contracting a β-redex in X_i. The residue $\lceil X_i \rceil$ would have had a $\perp$ at the occurrence of this redex, while $\lceil X_{i+1} \rceil$ would either have a β-redex at the same node, or a non-redex. Hence $\lceil X_{i+1} \rceil \geq \lceil X_i \rceil$, and thus $[\lceil X_{i+1} \rceil] \subseteq [\lceil X_i \rceil]$.

Let us review briefly some notions of convergence from Topology: an excellent reference is [16, Chapter X §2].

Definition 2.1.11 *A collection of subsets of a Topological space is said to be* centered *if the intersection of any finite number of them is non-empty. A centered collection of subsets converges to a point $x \in X$ (in a topological space $(X, \mathcal{O})$) if for each neighborhood $\mathcal{O}_x$ of the point x, there exists a member of the collection contained in $\mathcal{O}_x$.*

It is quite clear that the collection $\langle [\lceil X_i \rceil] \rangle_{i<\alpha}$ of sets obtained from the β-reduction sequence $\langle X \rangle$ above is a centered collection of sets. We have the following proposition.

Proposition 2.1.12 *If the derivation $\langle X \rangle$ converges (in the sense of Definition 2.1.3) to a term $x \in \lambda^\infty$ in β-normal form then the centered collection of sets $\langle [\lceil X_i \rceil] \rangle_{i<\alpha}$ converges to x.*

Proof: Suppose x is finite: then the last term of the derivation $\langle X \rangle$ must be x (apply definition of convergence, and note that finite terms are isolated in the topology), and in that case $\lceil x \rceil = x$ or $[\lceil x \rceil] = \{x\}$, hence any neighborhood $\mathcal{O}_x$ contains $\{x\}$ and the proposition is trivially true. Now suppose x is infinite, let the length of the derivation be α, then, the definition of convergent sequences tells us that for any neighbourhood $\mathcal{O}_x$ of x, there exists some ordinal $\kappa < \alpha$, such that $\forall \gamma . \kappa < \gamma < \alpha . X_\gamma \in \mathcal{O}_x$. In other words, for any depth $d \in \aleph$ characterizing $\mathcal{O}_x$, there exists an ordinal $\kappa < \alpha$, such that all terms in the derivation after X_κ agree with x up to depth d. Since x has no finitely accessible β-redexes, this means that for any such neighbourhood, there exists an ordinal $\kappa < \alpha$, such that all terms in the derivation after X_κ have all β-redexes at a depth greater than the corresponding depth d. In that case $\forall \gamma . \kappa < \gamma < \alpha$, the extent of the residue of X_γ must be contained in $\mathcal{O}_x$. Hence the proposition.

We also have the converse.

Proposition 2.1.13 *The derivation $\langle X \rangle$ (of length α) converges (in the sense of Definition 2.1.3) to a term $x \in \lambda^\infty$ in β-normal form if the centered collection of sets $\langle [\lceil X_i \rceil] \rangle_{i<\alpha}$ converges to x.*

Proof: By hypothesis, every neighborhood of $\mathcal{O}_x$ of x contains an element of the centered collection Now, for any neighborhood $\mathcal{O}_x$, we have a depth d such that $\mathcal{O}_x$ contains all terms which agree with x up to depth d Hence, our hypothesis tells us that for every such neighborhood, and thus every depth d, the class of terms that agree with x up to this depth contains a set from the centered collection: in particular, we may say that for every depth d, the class of $\lambda\perp$-terms that agree with x up to that depth include the residue of a term of the derivation But any residue has the property that it has no occurrence of a β-redex Thus we have that at no (finite) depth does x have a β-redex—which gives us the proposition

Thus we can see that the notion of the residues of a term allow us to arrive at a completely general criterion for the meaningfulness of those infinite derivations which end in an (infinite) normal form (as distinct from those which don't) moreover, this criterion is seen, on the basis of the last couple of propositions, to be equivalent to the one formulated in terms of countable sequences We have thus some ground to believe that the sets of residues of a term epitomize, in some way, the contributions to its net semantic definition Accordingly, we shall explore the idea that the class of residues of a term, which we formally define as

$$\int N \equiv \{\lceil N' \rceil \mid N \xrightarrow{*} N'\}$$

(for a λ-term N, and where we use $\xrightarrow{*}$ as the normal transitive-reflexive closure of the β-reduction relation) may be used as the *Type* of a term, in analogy with the Curry-Howard isomorphism for propositions and the Type of their proofs In other words we are proposing formally that the class of residues of a term may be taken to function akin to the class of proofs within a constructive theory of Types which is constructed on their basis This program will be initiated in the next chapter and the denouement shall take up most of the sequel, in the remaining part of this chapter we make good our conjecture made in Equation 2 1—namely that if any two terms have the same class of residues, then for every context, their substitution yields terms with the same head normal form (in some suitable sense under which head normal forms may be deemed to be the "same") The basic theory is worked out in Barendregt ([5, Chapter 10 §4, Chapter 19 §2]), and we offer here, slightly more direct proofs of the relevant theorems

2.2 Semantic Equivalence

We start with a few definitions

Definition 2.2.1 *A term is said to be in* head normal form *if it is of the form $\lambda\vec{x}\, yM_1 \quad M_n$ The head segment of a term in this form is $\lambda\vec{x}\, y$ Let k be an element of the finite non-empty sequences over the natural numbers. The k-reduct of M, written as $(M\downarrow)_k$ is defined inductively as follows*

$$(M\downarrow)_k = \begin{cases} M_i & \text{if } k \equiv \langle i\rangle,\ i \leq n, \text{ and principal hnf of } M \text{ is } \lambda\vec{x}.yM_1 \cdots M_n \\ (M'\downarrow)_{\langle i\rangle} & \text{if } k \equiv k' \bullet \langle i\rangle, \text{ and } M' = (M\downarrow)_{k'} \end{cases}$$

where the principal hnf is the last term of the head reduction sequence of M, the k-reduct is undefined if any of the clauses of the definition is not defined If k is an element of finite sequences over the natural numbers, then we define the k-head segment of a term M, written as $(M\downarrow)^k$, inductively as follows

$$(M\downarrow)^k = \begin{cases} \text{head segment of the principal hnf of } M & \text{if } k \equiv \langle\rangle \\ (M'\downarrow)^{\langle\rangle} & \text{where } M' = (M\downarrow)_k \end{cases}$$

Definition 2.2.2 *The Böhm representation of a term M, written as $\mathcal{B}(M)$ is the following inductively characterized tree if M is not in head normal form then $\mathcal{B}(M)$ is simply the single-node tree $\perp$, otherwise, let M have the form $\lambda\vec{x}\, yM_1 \quad M_n$ then $\mathcal{B}(M)$ is defined to be the tree given in Figure 2-1*

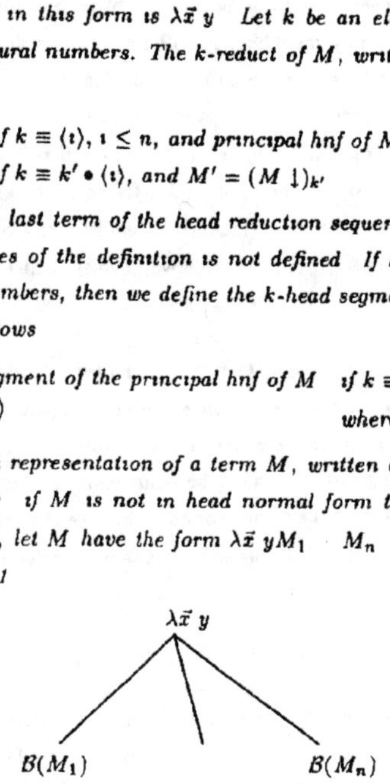

Figure 2-1 The Bohm representation

This definition generalizes in the obvious way to the Bohm representation of residues, and contexts We state a few simple propositions, some of which would be useful in proving the main theorem

Lemma 2.2.3 *For terms M and M', such that $M \stackrel{\bullet}{\longrightarrow} M'$, we have that $\mathcal{B}(\lceil M\rceil) \subseteq \mathcal{B}(\lceil M'\rceil)$, where $\subseteq$ is the containment order on trees with $\perp$ considered as representing an undefined value*

Proof: This holds trivially if M is not in hnf Otherwise M is of the form $\lambda\vec{x}\, yM_1 \cdots M_n$, and we must have that $M' \equiv \lambda\vec{x}\, yM_1' \quad M_n'$, where $M_i \stackrel{\bullet}{\longrightarrow} M_i'$ for all i in the appropriate range Hence the Bohm representations are identical up to depth 0 Now applying the reasoning inductively to the reductions $M_i \stackrel{\bullet}{\longrightarrow} M_i'$, we have the proposition

Remark 2.2.4 *We shall use the extension order $<$ (cf Definition 2 1 9) interchangeably with the containment order $\subseteq$ It is easy to see that $\mathcal{B}(\lceil M \rceil) \leq \mathcal{B}(\lceil M' \rceil)$ if and only if $\lceil M \rceil \leq \lceil M' \rceil$, for terms M and M'*

Lemma 2.2.5 *For terms M, M_1, M_2 such that $M \xrightarrow{*} M_1$ and $M \xrightarrow{*} M_2$, we would have that $\mathcal{B}(\lceil M_1 \rceil)$ and $\mathcal{B}(\lceil M_2 \rceil)$ are compatible*

Proof: By the Church-Rosser theorem we have that $\exists M_3\ M_1 \xrightarrow{*} M_3 \wedge M_2 \xrightarrow{*} M_3$, By the Lemma 2 2 3 we have that $\mathcal{B}(\lceil M_1 \rceil) \subseteq \mathcal{B}(\lceil M_3 \rceil)$ and $\mathcal{B}(\lceil M_2 \rceil) \subseteq \mathcal{B}(\lceil M_3 \rceil)$, and hence the proposition

Lemma 2.2.6 *The set of residues $\int M$ for any term M is structured as a directed set under the extension order $\leq$ for residues*

Proof: Consider any two elements $\lceil M_1 \rceil, \lceil M_2 \rceil$ in the set $\int M$, we have of course that $M \xrightarrow{*} M_1$ and $M \xrightarrow{*} M_2$, by the Church-Rosser theorem we have that $\exists M_3 .\ M_1 \xrightarrow{*} M_3 \wedge M_2 \xrightarrow{*} M_3$, and Lemma 2 2 3 tells us that $\lceil M_3 \rceil \geq \lceil M_1 \rceil$ and $\lceil M_3 \rceil \geq \lceil M_2 \rceil$, and of course $\lceil M_3 \rceil \in \int M$ and hence the proposition

Definition 2.2.7 *A $\lambda\bot$-term is said to be in partial normal form if it has no occurrence of a $\beta\bot$-redex A $\bot$-redex is a sub-term of the form $\bot M$, with $M \in \lambda\bot$*

Lemma 2.2.8 *Consider the following poset $\lceil \lambda \rceil = \{\lceil M \rceil \mid M \in \lambda\}$, with the extension order $\leq$ It has the following properties*

1 *every compatible pair $x, y \in \lceil \lambda \rceil$ has a least upper bound in $\lceil \lambda \rceil$,*

2 *every finite directed subset has a least upper bound in $\lceil \lambda \rceil$.*

Proof. Since x and y are both $\lambda\bot$ terms, and we know that under the extension order, the poset $\lambda\bot$ is (finitely) consistently complete, we have that lub of x and y exists in $\lambda\bot$ It is also easy to see that for x and y in partial normal form, their lub too would be in partial normal form, also, for any term z in partial normal form, there exists a λ-term z' such that $\lceil z' \rceil = z$ (just replace every occurrence of $\bot$ in z with Ω) Hence the lub of x and y is in $\lceil \lambda \rceil$ As for two, we use the fact that $\lambda\bot$ is directed-complete under the extension order, and the lub of a finite set of terms in partial normal form is a finite term in partial normal form

Lemma 2.2.9 *For a term $M \in \lambda$, and $k \in \mathrm{dom}(\mathcal{B}(\lceil M \rceil))$ we have that*

$$\mathcal{B}(\lceil M \rceil)(k) = \begin{cases} (M \downarrow)^k & \text{if } (M \downarrow)_k \text{ is in head normal form} \\ \bot & \text{otherwise} \end{cases}$$

Proof By induction on the length of k The proposition can easily be seen to hold for $|k| = 0$ and $|k| = 1$ Let us suppose it is true for $|k| = n$, and consider an appropriate $k = k' \bullet \langle i \rangle$ where $|k'| = n$ Let $(M \downarrow)_{k'} = \lambda \vec{x}\, yM_1 \quad M_n$, by induction hypothesis, $\mathcal{B}(\lceil M \rceil)(k') = (M \downarrow)^{k'}$, now if M_i is not in hnf, then we would have that $\mathcal{B}(\lceil M \rceil)(k) = \bot$ (by definition of $\lceil M \rceil$); otherwise we would have that $\mathcal{B}(\lceil M \rceil)(k) =$ the head segment of M_i; hence the proposition.

Let $\lceil \lambda \rceil^{\infty}$ denote the directed lub-completion of the poset $\lceil \lambda \rceil$ that is $\mathcal{B}^{\infty}(\lambda)$ is obtained by formally adjoining to $\lceil \lambda \rceil$, the (possibly infinite) terms corresponding to the least upper bounds of directed sets of $\lambda\bot$-terms It can easily be seen that $\lceil \lambda \rceil^{\infty}$ is a consistently-complete algebraic cpo

Definition 2.2.10 *For any λ-term M, let $\infty(M)$ denote the lub $\bigvee(\int M)$ in $\lceil \lambda \rceil^{\infty}$, by Lemma 2 2 6 we have that $\int M$ is structured as a directed set, and must have an lub in $\lceil \lambda \rceil^{\infty}$*

We reproduce without proof, a simple though important proposition from Barendregt.

Lemma 2 2 11 *([5, Lemma 8 3 16]) Let $M \equiv \lambda \vec{x}\, yM_1 \cdots M_n$, if $M \xrightarrow{\bullet} N$ then*

$$N \equiv \lambda \vec{x}\, yN_1 \quad N_n \text{ and } M_i \xrightarrow{\bullet} N_i \text{ for } 1 \le i \le n$$

Corollary 2.2.12 *([5, Corollary 8 3 17])*

1. *Let M be in head normal form, and $M \xrightarrow{\bullet} N$ then N is in head normal form*
2. *Let M have the head normal forms*

$$\lambda x_1 \cdot x_n\, yN_1 \quad N_m \quad \text{and}$$
$$\lambda x_1 \quad x_{n'}\, y'N'_1 \quad N'_{m'}$$

then $n = n'$, $y \equiv y'$, $m = m'$ and $N_i =_\beta N'_i$ for $1 \le i \le m$

Lemma 2.2.13 *For terms $M_1, M_2 \in \lambda$, if $\exists N\; M_1 \xrightarrow{\bullet} N \wedge M_2 \xrightarrow{\bullet} N$ then M_1 and M_2 must have the same $\langle\rangle$-head segment*

Proof: If either is already in hnf, then N must also be in hnf and must have the same head segment as the former, hence the other must have the same head segment too Otherwise, if N is in hnf then the proposition follows immediately, otherwise, let N' be a hnf of N, then the proposition follows by the previous consideration

Corollary 2.2.14 *Interconvertible terms have the same $\langle\rangle$-head segment*

For λ-terms M, N such that $M \xrightarrow{*} N$, we shall in the sequel, by abuse of notation, write $M \xrightarrow{*} \lceil N \rceil$. Thus, for some $\lambda\bot$-term P, we would write $M \xrightarrow{*} P$ to mean that for some λ-term N, $M \xrightarrow{*} N$ and $P = \lceil N \rceil$ We would extend this usage to cover the following: for $P \in \lambda\bot$, $M \in \lambda$, we shall write $M \xrightarrow{*} P$, if for some extension $N \geq P$, we have that $M \xrightarrow{*} N$.

Lemma 2.2.15 *Let $X \in \lceil \lambda \rceil^\infty$, and $X = \bigvee\{X_i \mid i \in I\}$ (for some indexing set I), then, for some $k \in \mathrm{dom}(\mathcal{B}(X))$, we have that $\mathcal{B}(\lambda)(k) = s$ iff $\exists i \in I\ \mathcal{B}(X_i)(k) = s$*

Proof: Immediate, from the properties of trees and their least upper bounds

In the sequel, we shall take contexts $C[\,]_k$ to be in their Bohm representation, this implies that the occurrence k is determined by this representation We have the following important proposition

Lemma 2.2 16 *We have the following equivalence for $k \in \mathrm{dom}(\mathcal{B}(\infty(M)))$*

$$\mathcal{B}(\infty(M))(k) = \lambda\vec{x}\ y \Leftrightarrow \exists C[\,]_k\ \exists N \in \lambda\ M \xrightarrow{*} C[N]_k \bigwedge (N\downarrow)^{\langle\rangle} = \lambda\vec{x}.y$$

with the context $C[\,]_k$ in its Bohm representation

Proof: $\Rightarrow$: By definition, we have that $\infty(M) = \bigvee\{\lceil M' \rceil \mid M \xrightarrow{*} M'\}$, by the previous Lemma, there must exist some M', such that $M \xrightarrow{*} M'$ and $\mathcal{B}(\lceil M' \rceil)(k) = \lambda\vec{x}\ y$; which means that the Bohm representation of M' must be of the form $C'[\lambda\vec{x}\ yN_1 \quad N_m]_k$ for some context $C'[\,]_k$ (in its Bohm representation)

$\Leftarrow$: Suppose $M \xrightarrow{*} C[N]_k$ for some context $C[\,]_k$ in its Bohm representation, without loss of generality, we may assume that N is in the head normal form, and of the form $\lambda\vec{x}\ yN_1 \quad N_m$, then we would have an element in $\int M$ with the k-th node of its Bohm representation labeled by $\lambda\vec{x}\ y$; hence, by Lemma 2 2 15, the proposition

Lemma 2.2.17 *Suppose there exists context $C[\,]_k$ (in the Böhm representation), such that for some $N \in \lambda$, $M \xrightarrow{*} C[N]_k$, then, for any other context $C'[\,]_k$ (in the Bohm representation) and $N' \in \lambda$ such that $M \xrightarrow{*} C'[N']_k$, we must have that $N =_\beta N'$.*

Proof: We can see that $C'[N]_k$ is the Bohm representation of some term P, and all redexes of P occur in sub-trees that do not overlap with k, similarly there would be some term Q such that $C''[N]_k$ is its Bohm representation, and all redexes of Q occur in sub-trees that do not overlap with k Thus $M \xrightarrow{*} P$ and $M \xrightarrow{*} Q$, then by the Church Rosser Theorem, and using the fact that sub-trees are not affected by reductions in other sub-trees, the proposition follows

Corollary 2.2.18 *Suppose*

$$\begin{aligned} &\exists C[\ ]_k\ \exists N \in \lambda\ N \equiv \lambda \vec{x}\, y N_1 \cdots N_m \quad \textit{and} \\ &\exists C'[\ ]_k\ \exists N' \in \lambda\ N' \equiv \lambda \vec{z}\, w N'_1 \cdots N'_{m'} \quad \textit{and} \\ &M \xrightarrow{*} C[N]_k \wedge M \xrightarrow{*} C'[N']_k \end{aligned}$$

then we must have that $\vec{x} = \vec{z}, w = y, m = m'$ *and for* $1 \le i \le m$ *we have* $N_i =_\beta N'_i$; *the contexts* C, C' *are assumed to be in the Böhm representation*

Proof: By the same reasoning as above, and Corollary 2.2.12

We have the main theorem

Theorem 2.2.19 *For any* $M \in \lambda$ *and* $k \in \mathrm{dom}(\infty(M))$ *we have*

$$\mathcal{B}(\infty(M))(k) = (M \downarrow)^k$$

Proof: We proceed by induction on the length of k

Case $|k| = 0$: thus $k = \langle\rangle$, if M is unsolvable then the proposition holds trivially; now all N in hnf such that $M \xrightarrow{*} N$ must have the same head segment (cf Corollary 2.2.14)—say $\lambda\vec{x}\, y$, then we have $\mathcal{B}(\infty(M))(\langle\rangle) = \lambda\vec{x}\, y = (M \downarrow)^{\langle\rangle}$

Case $|k| = 1$: let $k = \langle i\rangle$ for some i, consider any hnf of M—say $\lambda\vec{x}\, yM_1 \cdots M_n$: any other hnf would be of the form $\lambda\vec{x}\, yM'_1 \cdots M'_n$, with $M_i =_\beta M'_i$ for all appropriate i, in particular, for any of the head normal forms $\lambda\vec{x}\, yM_1 \cdots M_n$, any M_i would have the same $\langle\rangle$-head segment (across the head normal forms of M) (by Corollary 2.2.14) Hence the proposition holds in this case

Hypothesis: Assume the proposition true for all (appropriate) sequences k with $|k| \le n$

Case $|k| = n + 1$: Suppose $k = k' \bullet \langle i\rangle$ by hypothesis $\mathcal{B}(\infty(M))(k') = (M \downarrow)^{k'}$, by the Lemma 2.2.16 we would have a context $C[\ ]_{k'}$ (in the Bohm representation) and some term N in head normal form ($N \equiv \lambda\vec{x}\, yN_1 \cdots N_m$) such that $M \xrightarrow{*} C[N]_{k'}$ (and thus $\mathcal{B}(\infty(M))(k') = (M \downarrow)^{k'} = \lambda\vec{x}\, y$, if such an N in hnf did not exist, we would have had $\mathcal{B}(\infty(M))(k') = \bot$), also, for any other context $C'[\ ]_{k'}$ (in the Bohm representation) and term N' in hnf such that $M \xrightarrow{*} C'[N']_{k'}$, we would have by Corollary 2.2.18 that N' is of the form $\lambda\vec{x}\, yN'_1 \cdots N'_m$ with $N_j =_\beta N'_j$ for all appropriate j Hence for all such j, we would have that N_j and N'_j have the same $\langle\rangle$-head segment (by Corollary 2.2.14), and hence, in particular, $\mathcal{B}(\infty(M))(k) = (M \downarrow)^k$

Now recall the definition of the Bohm tree of a term, which we reproduce below.

Definition 2.2.20 (*cf* [5, *Definition 10 1 4*]) *The Böhm tree of a term M, written $\mathcal{BT}(M)$ is a single node labeled by $\perp$ if M is unsolvable, otherwise, if the principal head normal form of M is $\lambda\vec{x}\,yM_1 \quad M_n$, it is the inductively defined tree shown in Figure 2-2*

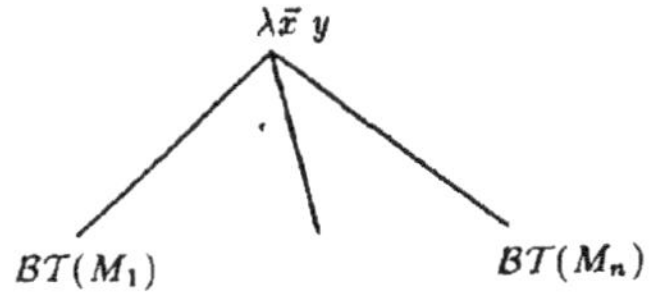

Figure 2-2 The Bohm Tree

From this definition and the relevant results above, we have the following proposition and its corollary

Proposition 2.2.21 *For $k \in \mathrm{dom}(\mathcal{BT}(M))$, we have that $\mathcal{BT}(M)(k) = (M\downarrow)^k$*

Proof: Immediate

Corollary 2.2.22 *If two terms M and N are such that $\int M = \int N$, then $\mathcal{BT}(M) = \mathcal{BT}(N)$*

Proof: Immediate, from Theorem 2 2 19

Hence, the set $\int N$ for any term N– which we shall henceforth call the λ-Type of N—has all the information from which the Bohm tree may be constructed: and in fact it has more What we call the λ-Type and symbolize as $\int N$ (for any term N), goes in Barendregt under the symbol $C'(N)$ (*cf* [5, Definition 14 3 6 (iii)]), we have the following proposition (from Barendregt) which indicates how this set governs the semantic behavior of the corresponding term in arbitrary contexts

Theorem 2.2.23 ([5, *Corollary 14 3 20*]) *For an arbitrary context $\mathcal{D}[\,]$, and a term M, we have that*

$$\mathcal{BT}(\mathcal{D}[M]) = \bigvee\{\mathcal{BT}(\mathcal{D}[x]) \mid x \in C'(M)\}$$

Hence, we have the easy corollary

Corollary 2.2 24 *For terms M and N, if $\int N = \int M$ then for any context $C[\,]$ we shall have that $\mathcal{BT}(C[M]) = \mathcal{BT}(C[N])$*

Hence referring back to Equation 2.1, and the considerations we started with, we can claim that the λ-Types epitomize all the salient semantic information for the corresponding terms, and we may consider further the possibility of constructing a system of (Curry-Howard) Types on their basis. This is the subject of the next chapter, where we structure the λ-Types into a system admitting an interpretation of a theory of Dependent Types.

Chapter 3

The Theory of Dependent Types

This chapter is structured as follows in the first section we have a brief description of an Intuitionistic Theory of Types this is essentially Martin-Lof's Type theory (without equality judgements), or in other words, the dependent first-order fragment of Hyland-Pitts' presentation of the Theory of Constructions We present the syntax of the Types and terms, and the rules for the inference for *judgements*, we also discuss the various issues in its interpretation, and present a categorical model for it In the next section, we structure the λ-Types of the previous chapter into a relatively cartesian closed category—which is a general framework for the interpretation of a theory of dependent Types In this, we conceptualize the residues as (representing) equivalence classes for a certain equivalence relation (on the set of λ-terms) Thus, in general, a λ-Type is structured as a collection of equivalence classes—and can be thought of as a *partial equivalence relation* on the set of λ-terms The precise motivation behind this formulation would become clear in the later chapters, when the category of Types would be structured as an *internal* category within a standard categorical model for polymorphic calculi

3.1 Intuitionistic Type Theory and its Interpretation

In this section we provide an overview of a theory of dependent Types—the term syntax and the structure of judgements and the significant aspects of its categorical interpretation.

3 1.1 A Theory of Dependent Types

As the preliminary step in the construction of a full theory of constructive Types, we shall extract the fragment on dependent Types from Martin Lof's Intuitionistic Type Theory ([53, 50, 51]), but not including equality Types The relevant fragment is taken from the fine study of Hyland and Pitts on the Theory of Constructions ([38]) The theory consists of ***judgements*** J made in ***contexts*** Γ and symbolized as

$$J\,[\Gamma]$$

The judgements we shall be concerned with in this chapter have the forms

$$\begin{array}{rcl} A & & \\ s & \in & A \\ A & = & B \\ s & = & t \in A \end{array}$$

The first expresses that A is Type, the second, that the term s is a term of the Type A, the third, that A and B are equal Types, and the fourth, that s and t are equal terms of the Type A

We shall use upper-case letters (or greek letters) for Types, and lower-case letters for terms, variables would be denoted generically by the letters x, y, z, w Contexts are sets of variable declarations, partially ordered by the pre-supposition relation, which we explain below Judgements are always made in contexts, which declare the Types of all the free variables occurring in it. Variable declarations have the form

$$x \in P$$

which can be seen to be a particular kind of judgement A variable declaration is said to presuppose another if the former has an occurrence of a free variable, which the latter declares For any variable declaration J, we shall denote the variable declared, generically, as ξ_J, and its Type as P_J More formally, we define a context as follows

Definition 3.1.1 *A context* $\Gamma \equiv (\Gamma, \leq)$ *is a poset of variable declarations satisfying*

1 *The elements of* Γ *are variable declarations and distinct variables have distinct declarations*

2 *If* $J \in \Gamma$ *then* $J\,[\Gamma|_J]$ *is a judgement of the theory, where* $\Gamma|_J = \{J' \mid J' \leq J\}$

We shall write $[J, \Gamma]$ to denote the context with J as its maximal element, and given two disjoint contexts Γ, Γ', we write $[\Gamma, \Gamma']$ for the context formed by their union ordered such that everything in Γ' is greater than anything in Γ, finally if $J \notin \Gamma$, then $[J > \Gamma]$ denotes the context formed by adding J to Γ as the maximal element

The general rules of the Type theory would be familiar from a study of Martin-Löf systems Other than the rules of reflexivity, transitivity and symmetry for the equality relation, we have the derivational rules as in Table 3 1 Along with them, we also have a general principal of substitution, which is as follows

Definition 3.1.2 *An* interpretation *of a context* Γ *in another context* Δ *consists of a function* p *assigning to each judgement* J *in* Γ, *a term* p_J *such that for each* J *in* Γ,

$$p_J \in P_J(p_{J'}/\xi_{J'} \mid J' < J)\ [\Delta]$$

is also a judgement of the theory, then the general principle of substitution *is, that whenever* $J\ [\Gamma]$ *is a judgement of the theory, and* p *is an interpretation of* Γ *in* Δ, *then*

$$J(p_{J'}/\xi_{J'} \mid J' \in \Gamma)\ [\Delta]$$

is also a judgement of the theory

The rules in Table 3 1 are labelled according to the following conventions a typical label is of the forms X Y-N or X-N, where X is a symbol from the set $\{1, \Sigma, \Pi, C, E, S, A, W\}$ and interpreted respectively as Unit, Sum, Product, Constant, Equality, Substitution, Assumption and Weakening, Y shall be from the set $\{F, I, E, =\}$ and interpreted respectively as Formation, Introduction, Elimination and Equality, the number N would be optional and label multiple versions of a clause

As we can see from Table 3 1, we have eliminated equality types these constrain the class of models, and particularly, the model we shall be considering does not support them. Following Hyland Pitt's adaptation, we have used constants *fst* and *snd* for projection rather than elimination constants This can be done as long as we consider a single "level" of Types adding a second level of Orders, and requiring rather strong closure conditions on the quantification of Types over Orders leads to paradoxical situations, and we must use rules given in terms of elimination constants rather than projection constants (*cf* [38, §1 9]). The Σ rules are the ones for existential quantification and are known as the "Sum" rules; the Π rules are for universal quantification and are known as "Product" rules The rule Constant Introduction allows the introduction of (non-logical) constants into the theory This theory can be shown to be the theory of the proofs of (intuitionistic) first-order logic ([48]).

3.1 2 The Categorical Interpretation

Historically, the categorical interpretation of Type theory, takes its cue from the work of Lawvere who used indexed categories, with some additional structure (these are known as

E	$\frac{s \in A \quad A = B}{s \in B}$	$\frac{s = t \in A \quad A = B}{s = t \in B}$
S-1	$\frac{p \in P\,[\Gamma] \quad q \in Q\,[\Gamma', x \in P > \Gamma]}{q(p/x) \in Q(p/x)\,[\Gamma'(p/x) > \Gamma]}$	$\frac{p = p' \in P\,[\Gamma] \quad q = q' \in Q\,[\Gamma', x \in P > \Gamma]}{q(p/x) = q'(p'/x) \in Q(p/x)\,[\Gamma'(p/x) > \Gamma]}$
S-2	$\frac{p \in P\,[\Gamma] \quad Q\,[\Gamma', x \in P > \Gamma]}{Q(p/x)\,[\Gamma'(p/x) > \Gamma]}$	$\frac{p = p' \in P\,[\Gamma] \quad Q = Q'\,[\Gamma', x \in P > \Gamma]}{Q(p/x) = Q'(p'/x)\,[\Gamma'(p/x) > \Gamma]}$
A	$\frac{A\,[\Gamma]}{x \in A\,[x \in A > \Gamma]}$	
W	$\frac{A\,[\Gamma] \quad J\,[\Gamma' > \Gamma]}{J\,[\Gamma', x \in A > \Gamma]}$	
U–F	$\frac{}{1_T}$	
U–I	$\star \in 1_T$	
U–E	$\begin{array}{c} t \in 1_T \\ t = \star \in 1_T \end{array}$	
Σ–F	$\frac{B\,[x \in A, \Gamma]}{\Sigma x \in A\; B\,[\Gamma]}$	$\frac{A = A'[\Gamma] \quad B = B'\,[x \in A, \Gamma]}{\Sigma x \in A\; B = \Sigma x \in A'\; B'\,[\Gamma]}$
Σ–I	$\frac{s \in A \quad t \in B(s/x)}{\langle s, t \rangle \in \Sigma x \in A\; B}$	$\frac{s = s' \in A \quad t = t' \in B(s/x)}{\langle s, t \rangle = \langle s', t' \rangle \in \Sigma x \in A\; B}$
Σ–E-1	$\frac{u \in \Sigma x \in A\; B}{fst(u) \in A}$	$\frac{u = u' \in \Sigma x \in A\; B}{fst(u) = fst(u') \in A}$
Σ–E-2	$\frac{u \in \Sigma x \in A\; B}{snd(u) \in B(fst(u)/x)}$	$\frac{u = u' \in \Sigma x \in A\; B}{snd(u) = snd(u') \in B(fst(u)/x)}$
Σ–=-1	$\frac{s \in A \quad t \in B(s/x)}{fst(\langle s, t \rangle) = s \in A}$	$\frac{s \in A \quad t \in B(s/x)}{snd(\langle s, t \rangle) = t \in B(s/x)}$
Σ–=-2	$\begin{array}{c} u \in \Sigma x \in A\; B \\ \langle fst(u), snd(u) \rangle = u \in \Sigma x \in A\; B \end{array}$	
Π–F	$\frac{B\,[x \in A, \Gamma]}{\Pi x \in A\; B\,[\Gamma]}$	$\frac{A = A'[\Gamma] \quad B = B'\,[x \in A, \Gamma]}{\Pi x \in A.B = \Pi x \in A'.B'\,[\Gamma]}$
Π–I	$\frac{t \in B\,[x \in A, \Gamma]}{\lambda x \in A\; t \in \Pi x \in A\; B\,[\Gamma]}$	$\frac{A = A'\,[\Gamma] \quad t = t' \in B\,[x \in A, \Gamma]}{\lambda x \in A\; t = \lambda x \in A'\; t' \in \Pi x \in A.B\,[\Gamma]}$
Π–E	$\frac{u \in \Pi x \in A.B \quad s \in A}{us \in B(s/x)}$	$\frac{u = u' \in \Pi x \in A\; B \quad s = s' \in A}{us = u's' \in B(s/x)}$
Π–=	$\frac{s \in A\,[\Gamma] \quad t \in B\,[x \in A, \Gamma]}{(\lambda x \in A\; t)s = t(s/x) \in B(s/x)\,[\Gamma]}$	$\frac{u \in \Pi x \in A\; B}{\lambda x.ux = u \in \Pi x \in A\; B}$
C-I	$\frac{A\,[\Gamma]}{f(x_1, \ldots, x_n) \in A\,[\Gamma]}$	

Table 3.1 The System of Dependent Types

Hyperdoctrines) to interpret first-order logic ([47, 76]) The fundamental insight that the syntactic properties of quantification are such as to make it possible to represent them as adjoints to substitution, is a basic theme that runs through almost every kind of subsequent categorical interpretation of logic ([46, 76, 78]) Martin-Lof's theory of intuitionistic Types added a nuance to this predicates on a Type were also Types (dependent on the former), and hence objects of the base category, proofs, which had previously been relegated to the fibers (as morphisms) in models of classical logic, returned as first-class citizens of the base category– as terms of the base Types, the models of this kind of Type theory was a compact object known as a *locally cartesian closed category*—essentially a cartesian closed category with cartesian closed slices These were shown to be models of Martin-Lof Type theory with equality Types ([77]) Certain other considerations—such as the need to have full recursion in these models, and hence fix-points—led to their generalization essentially, the existence of equalizers in cartesian closed categories does not go well with the requirements of fix-points The removal of fix-points necessitates the designation of a class of morphisms in the category as representing Type dependency Such morphisms were called ***display*** maps by Taylor, in his pioneering work on such systems ([85]), and the resulting categorical structures were axiomatically studied by Hyland and Pitts under the name of ***relatively cartesian closed categories*** ([38])

As the title of this chapter indicates, we shall use the framework of Hyland and Pitts to assimilate our theory of λ-types (and other sets of residues) In the rest of this section we shall briefly indicate the main features of these structures and how they allow the modelization of the Type theory given in Table 3 1 In categorical model theory, we usually work on the basis of an equivalence between the category of theories and that of models ([38, pages 162–164]) This allows a theory to be generated from any object in the category of models, and hence, our strategy will be to structure our objects as a category in the category of models We shall make no pretense of being rigorous in this section its purpose is merely to give a description of the various features of the model in light of the syntax of the theory it interprets, and not to demonstrate the fact that it is a model

The paradigm for the interpretation (in a certain category $\mathbf{C}$) is, that the set of Types dependent on a particular Type A, is a (designated) full sub-category of the slice over A. The objects in this slice are morphisms with co-domain A and belonging to a class of morphisms called ***display*** morphisms, we have called them F-morphisms in our work This class of F-morphisms need certain closure properties—which make it a kind of generalized full sub-category of $\mathbf{C}$ (in a *fibered* sense, *cf* [82]) For any object A, the full sub-category of the slice $\mathbf{C}/A$ consisting of F-morphisms, would be denoted as $\mathcal{F}(A)$ A judgement of the form

$B\ [x \in A]$ would be interpreted by a F-morphism $\|B\| \to \|A\|$ (with the co-domain $\|A\|$ being the interpretation of the Type A). this would be an object of $\mathcal{F}(A)$ (we shall confuse the name of a Type with the symbol for its interpretation), in general a judgement of the form $B\ [\Gamma]$ would be interpreted as an object of $\mathcal{F}(\|\Gamma\|)$, where $\|\Gamma\|) \equiv \Pi_j \|A_j\|$—the cartesian product of the interpretations of the *maximal* Types in the context Γ. A judgement of the form $y \in B\ [\Gamma]$ would be interpreted as a morphism $\|\Gamma\| \to \|B\|$ that is a *section* (a right-inverse) for the F-morphism $\|\beta\| \to \|\Gamma\|$ that interprets the judgement $B\ [\Gamma]$. Equality judgements are interpreted by the equality of the corresponding interpretation morphisms in the category.

We can see that this kind of interpretation would need the category to have finite products. We would model the substitution rule by pulling back (along the morphism that interprets the judgement $p \in P\ [\Gamma]$). Moreover, the Weakening rule could also be seen to be interpretable by pulling back (along the F-morphism that interprets the judgement $A\ [\Gamma]$). Hence we must have that our sub-category of F-morphisms be closed under pull-backs over arbitrary morphisms in **C**.

The unit clauses imply that the interpretation of 1_T is an object isomorphic to the terminal object of **C**. Moreover, since any isomorphism in **C** could be thought of as resulting from pulling back this isomorphism (which is a F-morphism) along some morphism, we would have that the class of F-morphisms must contain all isomorphisms in **C**. For certain model-theoretic reasons, we would use a slightly stronger principle—namely, that for any object of **C**, the unique map from it to the terminal object, is a F-morphism. This condition ensures an equivalence between the category of Martin-Löf Type theories and the category of relatively cartesian closed categories, and it obtains in our category of Types.

It is well known that the rules for Sums allow it to be interpreted as a left adjoint to the pullback functor $\psi^* : \mathcal{F}(A) \to \mathcal{F}(B)$ for any F-morphism $\psi : B \to A$ ([47, 76, 77]). This can be easily verified using the general principle of substitution. The specific form of these rules in terms of projection constants, entails that the co-unit of this adjunction is actually part of an isomorphism (the other part is the morphism interpreting the constant ***snd***). This is taken care of by using the fact that ***(left) composition*** with a map yields a left-adjoint to pulling back along it. Hence we would require that our class of F-morphisms be closed under composition.

Finally, it is also known that the rules for Products allow it to be interpreted as a right adjoint to the pullback functor $\psi^* : \mathcal{F}(A) \to \mathcal{F}(B)$ for any F-morphism $\psi : B \to A$ ([***ibid***]). Hence we would require that every such pull-back functor have a right adjoint, which we shall denote as $\psi_{\dashv}$. Moreover there is a technical requirement that the model satisfies the criterion (known as the Beck-Chevalley condition) that "quantification commute with substitution."

This holds automatically for the interpretation of Sums, since in this case the left-adjunction was given by composition. In the case of products we have to impose this explicitly

Definition 3.1.3 (The Beck-Chevalley condition) *Let us have a pullback in* **C**, *of a* $\mathcal{F}$-*morphism* f *along a morphism* g, *and let the pullback cone have morphisms* h *and* k *(whose co-domain is the domain of* g*), with* k *(necessarily) in* $\mathcal{F}$. *Given this context, the canonical natural transformation:*

$$k_{\dashv} \circ h^{*} \stackrel{\cdot}{\rightarrow} g^{*} \circ f_{\dashv}$$

is an isomorphism

We may summarize all these requirements in the following definition

Definition 3.1.4 *A Category* **C** *is said to be a* relatively cartesian closed category, *if it satisfies the following conditions*

1. *It has finite products*

2. *It has a designated class of morphisms, denoted by the symbol* $\mathcal{F}$, *which satisfies the property that the class is closed under pullbacks along arbitrary morphisms in* **C**

3. *For any object, the unique morphism from it to the terminal object is in the class* $\mathcal{F}$.

4. *The class* $\mathcal{F}$ *is closed under composition*

5. *For any morphism* $f : B \rightarrow A$ *in the class* $\mathcal{F}$, *there is a right-adjoint* $f_{\dashv}$ *to the pullback functor* $f^{*} : \mathcal{F}(A) \rightarrow \mathcal{F}(B)$ *where* $\mathcal{F}(X)$ *denotes, for any object* X, *the full sub-category of the slice category over* X, *whose objects are in the class* $\mathcal{F}$. *This right-adjoint satisfies the Beck-Chevalley condition*

This is the kind of category that we shall prove our category of λ-types to be. In categorical model theory, we usually understand theories to be categories themselves, and hence in particular, a model for itself. Under the conditions of Definition 3.1.4, we can prove a (bi-) categorical equivalence between the category of Martin-Lof Type theories (without equality Types), and the category of relatively cartesian closed categories. Under this equivalence, every such category, yields a certain theory, whose judgements are exactly those satisfied in the category ([38, pages 162-164]). Hence, to show that the sets of residues interpret a certain Martin-Lof Type theory, it is enough to prove that the category constructed is relatively cartesian closed. We note the equivalence without proof

Theorem 3.1.5 *([38, Corollary, page 161]) There is a categorical equivalence between the category of Martin-Löf Type theories (with interpretations of one theory in another as morphisms) and the category of Relatively Cartesian Closed Categories (with morphisms, functors that preserve finite products, the class $\mathcal{F}$ of morphisms, pullbacks of morphisms in $\mathcal{F}$ along arbitrary morphisms, and right adjoints to pullback functors along morphisms in $\mathcal{F}$)*

3.2 A Relatively Cartesian Closed Category of λ-Types

In this section we show that the class of λ-Types of the last chapter may be (inductively) structured into a relatively cartesian closed category (under the rules of dependency and quantification) The critical construction involved in this is to conceive a residue as representing an equivalence class for a certain equivalence relation over the set of λ-terms Thus, a λ-Type can be thought of as representing a certain *partial equivalence relation* over λ, the significance of which shall become clearer in the later chapters The formulation shall take a syntactic form—that is, every Type would have a *name* within a certain term syntax, and interestingly, under this representation, the dependency structure of our Types would be seen to be engendered by syntactic sub-term relationships—which is quite natural, perhaps, to the intuition

Let us define first the equivalence relation that we shall use throughout the construction This is the familiar relation between terms used in the theory of solvability—and according to which, terms are in this relation if their Bohm trees are can be "made compatible" through (possibly infinite) η-expansions We shall explicate this relation this relation precisely in a later chapter for now, the following statement would suffice

Definition 3.2.1 *The binary relation $\simeq$ on the set of λ-terms is characterized by the following statement*

$$x \simeq y \Leftrightarrow \forall C[\,]\ (C[x] \text{ is solvable} \Leftrightarrow C[y] \text{ is solvable})$$

where $C[\,]$ is an arbitrary λ-context

Note that this is *not* to be taken as a definition, but as a characterization equivalent to it, this serves our purpose for the present We can easily see that $\simeq$ is a *congruence*—a fact that we shall use heavily in our formulations in the sequel

The class of Types which we shall structure into a category, is given on the basis of a certain syntax defined as follows

Definition 3.2.2 *Let us have a distinguished set of variables $\mho$, and let us denote by λ, the set of terms of the λ-Calculus, generated on this set of variables The set Λ is the smallest*

set of expressions satisfying the following rules

1. $\lambda \subset \Lambda$
2. $\Sigma x \cdot \alpha\, \beta \in \Lambda$, *for* $\alpha, \beta \in \Lambda$
3. $\Pi x \cdot \alpha\, \beta \in \Lambda$, *for* $\alpha, \beta \in \Lambda$

We have, in this language, binding operators $\Sigma x \cdot \alpha$ and $\Pi x \cdot \alpha$, in addition to the standard one λx. The rules for bound and free variables are given as follows.

Definition 3.2.3 *The variable x occurring in a Λ-term M is said to be* bound *under the following inductive rules*

1. *If M is in the pure λ-fragment, then x is bound if it occurs in the scope of an operator λx (cf. [30, Definition 1.10])*
2. *x is bound in the scope of the operator $\Sigma x \cdot \alpha$ (equivalently, $\Pi x \cdot \alpha$) if it occurs in a (sub-) term of the form $\Sigma x \cdot \alpha\, \beta$ (respectively, $\Pi x \cdot \alpha\, \beta$), and is* free *(i.e. not bound) in the sub-term β*

We shall denote by Λ_0 the class of *closed* Λ-terms—that is, terms containing no occurrence of a free variable—according to the conditions defining bound variables just stated. In addition to the syntax presented above, we shall sometimes emphasize application by enclosing the applicand in parenthesis: this shall be the rule when we represent λ-definable functions as combinators—for instance as the pairing combinator $\langle\ ,\ \rangle$, projection combinators π_0 and π_1, and combinations of these with other arbitrary λ-definable functions. We would also embed combinator expressions in the terms, whenever there is no risk of ambiguity.

We define, on the basis of the equivalence relation $\simeq$, an equivalence relation—which we shall denote as $\simeq$ too—on the class of Λ-terms. $\simeq$ on the latter class is nothing but the congruence generated by $\simeq$; we state this formally.

Definition 3.2.4 *For arbitrary Λ-terms A, a, we define by $A(a/x)$ the result of substituting the free occurrences of x in A, by a. The equivalence relation $\simeq$ on the class of Λ-terms is defined to smallest relation satisfying the following set of inductive rules:*

1. *$\simeq$ on the sub-class $\lambda \subset \Lambda$ is the relation $\simeq$ as defined in Definition 3.2.1,*
2. *for Λ-terms A, B, we have that $A \simeq B$ iff there exist a Λ-term C with variables $x_1, \ldots, x_n$ free, such that $A = C(a_1/x_1, \ldots, a_n/x_n)$ and $B = C(b_1/x_1, \ldots, b_n/x_n)$, for Λ-terms $a_1, \ldots, a_n$ and $b_1, \ldots, b_n$, with $a_i \simeq b_i$ for $1 \leq i \leq n$*

We shall denote the $\sim$ equivalence class of a Λ term x as $[x]_\sim$, omitting the subscript $\sim$ when there is no possibility of confusion with any other equivalence relation

For each $\simeq$-equivalence of Λ-terms, say $[x]$, we shall construct a Type and denote it as $\oint[x]$ the elements of this Type would be $\simeq$-equivalence classes of λ-terms We define the notion as follows.

Definition 1 2.5 *For any $\lambda\bot$-term b, we denote by $[b]$ the $\simeq$-equivalence class of $b(\Omega/\bot)$ where Ω is the standard unsolvable λ-term $(\lambda x\ xx)(\lambda x\ xx)$ The (partial) operator $\oint$ on the class of $\simeq$-equivalence classes of Λ-terms is defined as follows*

$$\oint[x] = \{[b] \mid b \in \int(y) \text{ for some } y \simeq x\}, \text{ for } x \in \lambda \tag{1 1}$$

$$\oint[\Sigma x\ \ \alpha\ \beta] = \{[\langle a,b\rangle] \mid [a] \in \oint[\alpha], [b] \in \oint[\beta(a/x)]\} \tag{1 2}$$

$$\oint[\Pi x\ \ \alpha\ \beta] = \{[f] \mid [a] \in \oint[\alpha] \Rightarrow [fa] \in \oint[\beta(a/x)]\} \tag{1 3}$$

With these notions precise, we can define our category of Types, for which we shall use the symbol $\Im$ Prior to that we need to understand the rather special way in which morphisms would be defined in our category

Definition 1.2.6 *For the sets $X \equiv \oint[x]$ and $Y \equiv \oint[y]$ with $x, y \in \Lambda_0$, we shall say that a set-theoretic map $F\ \ X \to Y$ is* tracked *by a λ-term f, if for all $[a] \in X$ we have that $F([a]) = [fa]$*

This notion can be seen to be well-defined since the relation $\simeq$ is a congruence As we can see, there would, in general, be many λ-terms tracking the same set-theoretic map The morphisms in our category would essentially be maps which are tracked by λ-terms We have the following definition

Definition 1.2.7 *The category $\Im$ has the following constitution*

Objects: *Objects are sets of the form $\oint[\alpha]$ for $\alpha \in \Lambda_0$,*

Morphisms: *Morphisms are of two types*

F-morphisms: *F-morphisms are set-theoretic maps tracked by some λ-term, and isomorphic to a map of the form $\pi_0\ \ \oint[\Sigma x\ \ \alpha\ \beta] \to \oint[\alpha]\ \ [\langle a,b\rangle] \mapsto [a]$ tracked by the λ-term (corresponding to the combinator) π_0,*

s-morphisms: *s-morphisms may be defined on the basis of the following clauses*

1 The identity map on any object, tracked by the λ-term $\lambda x\ x \equiv I$, is a s-morphism,

2 *An s-morphisms F $\oint[\Sigma x\ \alpha\ \beta] \to \oint[\Sigma y \cdot \gamma\ \delta]$ is a map tracked by some λ-term f, and such that for some s-morphism $G \cdot \oint[\alpha] \to \oint[\gamma]$ the diagram shown in Figure 3-1 commutes*

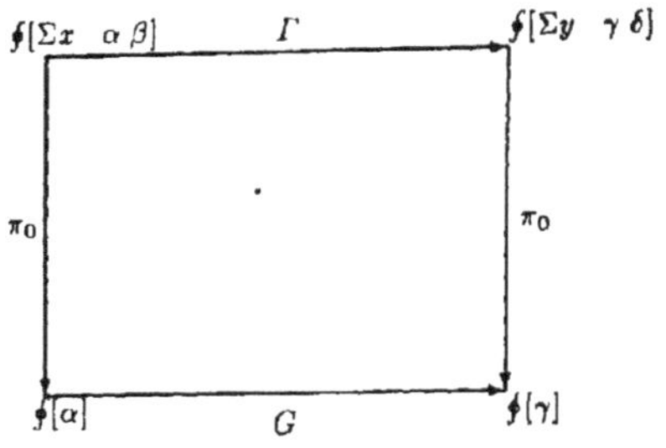

Figure 3-1 s morphisms

We shall claim that this category is relatively cartesian closed To verify this we would go through the list of defining properties of such a category

Proposition 3.2.8 *The category $\Im$ has a terminal object, and finite products*

Proof: It can be easily seen that the object $1 = \oint[\Omega]$, where Ω is, as usual, the standard unsolvable term, is the terminal object (up to isomorphism) Every object X has an unique map 1_X to 1, tracked by the term $\lambda y\ \Omega$, moreover 1_X is a F-morphism: it is isomorphic to the map π_0 $\oint[\Sigma x\ 1\ X] \to 1$ Any other object, containing a single $\simeq$-equivalence class is isomorphic to 1, and may be thought of as a terminal object too

As for finite products, it can easily be verified that the (cartesian) product of the objects $\oint[X]$ and $\oint[Y]$ is the object $\oint[\Sigma x\ X\ Y] \cong \oint[\Sigma y\ Y\ X]$ To see this, note that

$$\oint[\Sigma x\ \ X\ Y] = \{[\langle a, b\rangle] \mid [a] \in \oint[X], [b] \in \oint[Y]\}$$

and hence the proposition

We may note at this point that since a F-morphism is always *isomorphic* to map π_0 · $\oint[\Sigma x\ \alpha\ \beta] \to \oint[\alpha]$, we may assume it to have this general form for most purposes We use this convention in the succeeding proofs We would also abuse language and say "the F-morphism ϕ $\Sigma x\ \alpha\ \beta$" when we actually mean the first projection

Proposition 3.2.9 *The class of F-morphisms is closed under composition*

Proof: We consider the following configuration a F-morphism $F \quad \oint[\Sigma x \cdot \delta\, \gamma] \rightarrow \oint[\delta]$, where $\delta \equiv \Sigma y \cdot \alpha\, \beta$, and a F-morphism $G \quad \oint[\Sigma y \quad \alpha\, \beta] \rightarrow \oint[\alpha]$ Of course, both F and G are tracked by the λ-term π_0 We claim that the composition $G \circ F$ is isomorphic to the morphism $\pi_0 \cdot \oint[\Sigma y \quad \alpha\, \Sigma x' \quad \beta\, \gamma(\langle y, x' \rangle / x)] \rightarrow \oint[\alpha]$ To see this, let us verify the isomorphism $\oint[\Sigma x \cdot (\Sigma y \quad \alpha\, \beta)\, \gamma] \cong \oint[\Sigma y \cdot \alpha\, \Sigma x' \cdot \beta\, \gamma(\langle y, x' \rangle / x)]$ Consider a typical element of the left hand side term in the isomorphism, from the Equation 3 2 it can be seen to be $[\langle\langle a, b \rangle, c \rangle]$, with

$$[c] \in \oint[\gamma(\langle a, b \rangle / x)] \tag{3 4}$$

$$[b] \in \oint[\beta(a/y)] \tag{3 5}$$

$$[a] \in \oint[\alpha] \tag{3.6}$$

On the other hand, a typical element of the right hand side may be seen to be $[\langle d, \langle e, f \rangle\rangle]$, with

$$[f] \in \oint[\gamma(\langle y, x' \rangle / x)(d/y)(e/x')] \text{ that is}$$

$$[f] \in \oint[\gamma(\langle d, e \rangle / x)] \text{ simplifying} \tag{3.7}$$

$$[e] \in \oint[\beta(d/y)] \tag{3.8}$$

$$[d] \in \oint[\alpha] \tag{3.9}$$

comparing Equations 3 4–3 6 with Equations 3 7–3 9, we can see that the part of the isomorphism from lhs → rhs is tracked by the λ-term (using pairing and projection combinators) $\langle \pi_0 \circ \pi_0, \langle \pi_1 \circ \pi_0, \pi_1 \rangle\rangle$, while the other part is tracked by the λ-term $\langle\langle \pi_0, \pi_1 \circ \pi_0 \rangle, \pi_1 \circ \pi_1 \rangle$ Hence the proposition

Proposition 3.2.10 *The class of F-morphisms is closed under pull-backs along itself, and along the class of s-morphisms*

Proof: Consider F-morphisms $\phi \quad \oint[\Sigma x \quad \alpha\, \beta] \rightarrow \oint[\alpha]$ and $\psi \cdot \oint[\Sigma y \quad \alpha\, \gamma] \rightarrow \oint[\alpha]$, we claim that the pullback of ϕ along ψ is given by the F-morphism

$$\psi^*(\phi) \quad \oint[\Sigma z\, .\, (\Sigma y \quad \alpha\, \gamma)\, \beta(\pi_0(z)/x)] \rightarrow \oint[\Sigma y \quad \alpha\, \gamma]$$

To see this, note that a typical element of the domain is $[\langle\langle a, b \rangle, c \rangle]$ with

$$[\langle a, b \rangle] \in \oint[\Sigma y \quad \alpha\, \gamma]$$

$$[c] \in \oint[\beta(\pi_0(z)/x)(\langle a, b \rangle / z)] \text{, or simplifying}$$

$$[c] \in \oint[\beta(a/x)]$$

Hence the domain is essentially the set-theoretic pull-back (over the equivalence classes of the relation $\simeq$) and the maps making up the pullback cone are given by $\psi^*(\phi)$ tracked by the term π_0, and the map $\psi' \; \oint[\Sigma z \; (\Sigma y \,.\, \alpha\; \gamma)\; \beta(\pi_0(z)/x)] \to \oint[\Sigma x \cdot \alpha.\beta]$ tracked by the term $\langle \pi_0 \circ \pi_0, \pi_1 \rangle$

As for pullbacks along s-morphism, consider again the F-morphism ϕ and an s-morphism $U \;\; \oint[\gamma] \to \oint[\alpha]$ tracked by the term u, the same considerations as in the paragraph above tell us that the pullback of ϕ along U is given by the morphism $U^*(\phi)$ $\oint[\Sigma y \cdot \gamma\; \beta(u(y)/x)]$ The maps making up the pullback cone are, as in the previous case, $U^*(\phi)$ tracked by the term π_0 and the map $U' \;\; \oint[\Sigma y \;\; \gamma\; \beta(u(y)/x)] \to \oint[\Sigma x \;\; \alpha.\beta]$ tracked by the term $\langle u \circ \pi_0, \pi_1 \rangle$

As we have seen in the last section, closure of the class of F-morphisms under pullbacks allows us to think of any morphism $\phi \;\; X \to Y$ as giving rise to a pullback functor ϕ^* $\mathcal{F}(Y) \to \mathcal{F}(X)$ where $\mathcal{F}(X)$ denotes the full subcategory of the slice category $\Im/X$ consisting of F-morphisms The action of this functor on objects is as stated in Proposition 3 2 10; its action on morphisms is quite easy to see it is exactly as we would expect for the corresponding set-theoretic case, and we express it as follows

Definition 3.2 11 *For an object $\oint[\alpha]$, and any morphism $F \;\; \oint[\Sigma x \;\; \alpha\; \beta] \to \oint[\Sigma x \,.\, \alpha\; \gamma]$, tracked by a term f, and an arbitrary morphism $U \;\; \oint[\delta] \to \oint[\alpha]$, tracked by the term u, the action of U^* on F is the morphism*

$$U^* \;\; \oint[\Sigma z \;\; \delta\; \beta(u(z)/x)] \to \oint[\Sigma z \;\; \delta\; \gamma(u(z)/x)] \quad [\langle d, b\rangle] \mapsto [\langle d, (\pi_1 \circ f)\langle ud, b\rangle\rangle]$$

tracked by the term $\langle \pi_0, (\pi_1 \circ f) \circ \langle u \circ \pi_0, \pi_1\rangle\rangle$, using standard combinator notation

The significant point is that for U in the class of F-morphisms, this functor has a right adjoint

Proposition 3.2 12 *For a F-morphism $\psi \;\; \oint[\Sigma x \;\; \alpha\; \beta] \to \oint[\alpha]$, the pullback functor ψ^* has a right adjoint Π_ψ*

Proof: The proof goes pretty much as for a sub-category in **Sets** Assume that ψ is tracked by the term s Consider a F-morphism $\phi \;\; \oint[\Sigma y \;\; (\Sigma x \;\; \alpha\; \beta)\; \gamma] \to \oint[\Sigma x \;\; \alpha\; \beta]$, we claim that the right adjoint Π_ψ has the following action on ϕ

$$\Pi_\psi(\phi) = \pi_0 \quad \oint[\Sigma x \;\; \alpha\; \Pi y' \;\; \beta\; \gamma(\langle x, y'\rangle/y)] \to \oint[\alpha]$$

To verify this, consider a F morphism $D \;\; \oint[\Sigma z \;\; \alpha\; \delta] \to \oint[\alpha]$, and a map

$$U \;\; \oint[\Sigma y \;\; (\Sigma x \;\; \alpha\; \beta)\; x(s(y)/\delta)] \to \oint[\Sigma y \;\; (\Sigma x \cdot \alpha\; \beta)\; \gamma]$$

tracked by the term u, the domain of U is, of course, the domain of $\psi^*(D)$. We shall claim that there exists an unique map

$$U^* : \oint[\Sigma x : \alpha\ \delta] \to \oint[\Sigma x : \alpha\ \Pi y' : \beta\ \gamma(\langle x, y'\rangle/y)]$$

such that

$$U = \epsilon \circ \psi^*(U^*) \tag{3.10}$$

where ϵ is a certain map specified later on

$$\epsilon : \oint[\Sigma y : (\Sigma x : \alpha\ \beta)\ (\Pi y' : \beta\ \gamma(\langle x, y'\rangle/y))(s(y)/x)] \to \oint[\Sigma y : (\Sigma x \cdot \alpha\ \beta)\ \gamma]$$

The domain of ϵ is the domain of the pullback of $\Pi_\psi(\phi)$ along ψ. We note that a typical element of $\oint[\Sigma x : \alpha\ \Pi y' : \beta\ \gamma(\langle x, y'\rangle/y)]$ is $[\langle a, f\rangle]$ where

$$\begin{aligned} [a] &\in \oint[\alpha] \\ [f] &\in \oint[(\Pi y' : \beta\ \gamma(\langle x, y'\rangle/y))(a/x)] \text{ —that is,} \\ [f] &\in \oint[\Pi y' : \beta(a/x)\ \gamma(\langle x, y'\rangle/y)(a/x)] \qquad (3.11) \\ &= \{[g] \mid [b] \in \oint[\beta(a/x)] \Rightarrow [gb] \in \oint[\gamma(\langle x, y'\rangle/y)(a/x)(b/y')]\} \\ &= \{[g] \mid [b] \in \oint[\beta(a/x)] \Rightarrow [gb] \in \oint[\gamma(\langle a, b\rangle/y)]\} \text{ on simplifying} \qquad (3.12) \end{aligned}$$

Now consider a typical element $[\langle a, d\rangle] \in \oint[\Sigma x : \alpha\ \delta]$, let a typical element of $\oint[\beta(a/x)]$, for some $[a] \in \oint[\alpha]$, be denoted as $[b]$, we have a map

$$\bar{d} : \oint[\beta(a/x)] \to \oint[\Sigma y : (\Sigma x : \alpha\ \beta)\ x(s(y)/\delta)]$$

tracked by a term $\lambda n\ (\langle a, n\rangle, d)$ which has the following action: $[b] \mapsto [(\langle a, b\rangle, d)]$ for general $[a]$, $[b]$ and $[d]$ under the assumptions already stated. Now consider a map obtained as $\pi_1 \circ (U \circ \bar{d}) \cdot \oint[\beta(a/x)] \to \oint[\gamma(\langle a, b\rangle/y)]$ tracked by a term

$$q \equiv \lambda m\ \pi_1(u((\lambda n\ (\langle a, n\rangle, d))m)) \tag{3.13}$$

this has the property that $[b] \in \oint[\beta(a/x)] \Rightarrow [gb] \in \oint[\gamma(\langle a, b\rangle/y)]$, and hence from Equation 3.12 we may say that $[q] \in \oint[\Pi y' : \beta(a/x)\ \gamma(\langle x, y'\rangle/y)(a/x)]$. Hence we have a map

$$\begin{aligned} U^* : \oint[\Sigma x : \alpha\ \delta] &\to \oint[\Sigma x : \alpha\ \Pi y' : \beta\ \gamma(\langle x, y'\rangle/y)] \\ [\langle a, d\rangle] &\mapsto [\lambda m\ \pi_1(u((\lambda n\ (\langle a, n\rangle, d))m))] \end{aligned}$$

tracked by a term whose form is easy to make out (we shall not labour it). Moreover, from the way that this map has been defined from U, we can also see that it is unique for a given U. Now we verify the commutation claimed in Equation 3.10. First note that ϵ is the evaluation map tracked by the term $\langle\pi_0, \mathrm{ap}(\pi_1, \pi_1 \circ \pi_0)\rangle$ using the notation for pairing and projection combinators, and where $\mathrm{ap}(\ ,\ )$ is the application combinator hence $\epsilon : [\langle\langle a,b\rangle, g\rangle] \mapsto [\langle\langle a,b\rangle, gb\rangle]$. Now consider a typical element $[\langle\langle a,b\rangle, d\rangle] \in \oint[\Sigma y : (\Sigma x : \alpha . \beta) . x(s(y)/\delta)]$: the action of $\psi^*(U^*)$ on this is (from Definition 3.2.11) $\langle\langle a,b\rangle, g\rangle$ (where g is as defined in Equation 3.13). The action of ϵ on this is $[\langle\langle a,b\rangle, gb\rangle]$, as we have seen above $gb = \pi_1(u(\langle\langle a,b\rangle, d\rangle))$ and hence the action of the composite may be written as

$$\epsilon \circ \psi^*(U^*) : [\langle\langle a,b\rangle, d\rangle] \mapsto [\langle\langle a,b\rangle, \pi_1(u(\langle\langle a,b\rangle, d\rangle))\rangle]$$

and we can see immediately that

$$[\langle\langle a,b\rangle, \pi_1(u(\langle\langle a,b\rangle, d\rangle))\rangle] = [u(\langle\langle a,b\rangle, d\rangle)]$$

and hence the proposition.

The final point that we have to verify is whether the right adjoint operation detailed above satisfies the Beck-Chevalley condition. An account of this condition has already been given in the last section, in the present context, our task gains simplicity since the corresponding objects are presented on the basis of a syntax.

Proposition 3.2.13 *Given a pullback square in $\mathfrak{I}$ shown in Figure 3-2, the canonical natural transformation $U^* \circ \Pi_{E'} \to \Pi_E \circ U'^*$ is an isomorphism.*

Proof: We have the situation shown in Figure 3-2 (where the pullback square is marked with a right angle at its top left corner) in which we have omitted the $\oint[\cdot]$ decoration on the Λ_0-terms: this is to be taken as implicit. In the proof below, in order to keep the notation simple, we adopt the convention of underlining Λ_0-terms to indicate the $\oint[\ ]$ operation: that is, $\underline{X} \equiv \oint[X]$ for all $X \in \Lambda_0$. We assume that U is tracked by the term u. Referring to the figure, the action of $\Pi_{E'}$ on P has the domain

$$\underline{\Sigma y : \psi . \Pi z : R . S(\langle y,z\rangle/z)}$$

allowing a clash between in substituted variables, since the meaning is obvious. The action of U^* on this has the domain

$$\begin{aligned} & \underline{\Sigma x : \phi . (\Pi z : R . S(\langle y,z\rangle/z))(u(x)/y)} \\ = \; & \underline{\Sigma x : \phi . \Pi z : R(u\{x\}/y) . S(\langle u(x),z\rangle/z)} \qquad (3.14) \end{aligned}$$

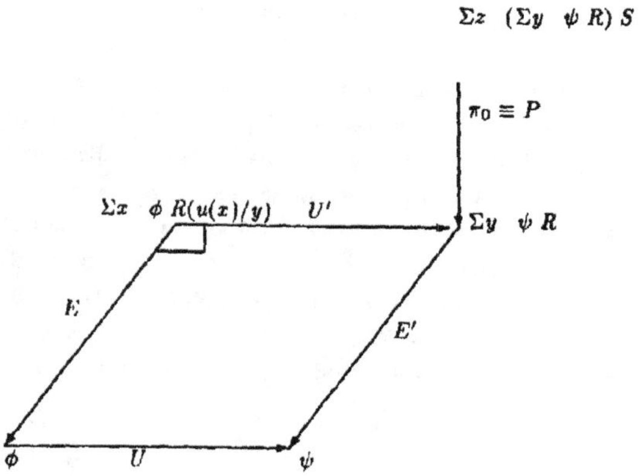

Figure 3-2 The Beck-Chevalley Condition

upon simplifying the substitutions On the other hand, the action of U'^{*} on P has the domain

$$\underline{\Sigma a\ \ (\Sigma x\ \ \phi\ R(u(x)/y))\ S(\langle(u \circ \pi_0)(a), \pi_1(a)\rangle/z)}$$

The action of Π_E on this object can be seen to be

$$\begin{aligned} & \underline{\Sigma x\ \ \phi\ \Pi a\ \ R(u(x)/y)\ S(\langle(u \circ \pi_0)(a), \pi_1(a)\rangle/z)(\langle x, a\rangle/a)} \\ = \ & \underline{\Sigma x\ \ \phi\ \Pi a\ \ R(u(x)/y)\ S(\langle u(x), a\rangle/z)} \end{aligned} \tag{3.15}$$

upon simplifying the substitutions Comparing Equation 3.14 and Equation 3.15, the proposition follows easily

Hence the Beck-Chevalley condition is satisfied, and that completes the circuit of verifications: we have the final theorem

Theorem 3.2.14 *The category $\mathfrak{T}$ is relatively cartesian closed*

Proof: Immediate from Theorem 3 1 5 and Propositions 3 2 8–3 2.13

This validates our claim that we may induce a theory of dependent Types on the basis of a suitable conception of a proof object for λ-terms It is this conception of a proof-object that we shall retain in the sequel We should note that in making this choice, we commit ourselves to the view that *semantically equivalent* terms (in other words, those related by ≃)

have *identical* Types (and hence, we compute Types for terms *modulo* this equivalence)—a position that may be thought to be rather too strong, especially in view of our remarks in the introduction that intensional isomorphism is all that would have been apposite in this regard In any case the resulting theory is adequate for supporting the general program of semantics that we have proposed, and that is what concerns us in primarily in this work.

Chapter 4

Fibrations and Comprehension Categories

We have seen, in the previous chapter, that we can induce, on the basis of the sets of residues of λ-terms (or their equivalence classes), a theory (category) of dependent Types. In this chapter, we shall recast this construction within a framework that is more general, and facilitates the further development of our argument towards the construction of a full (impredicative) constructive Type theory, as well as embed it, in an appropriate way, within a certain standard model of polymorphic calculi The framework which makes this chain of constructions both elegant and abstract is the Theory of *Fibered* Categories; a theory that originated in a fairly distant field, but found recognition in the late eighties in formal semantics as an abstract and general—and perhaps *the* correct abstract framework, for studying the semantics of constructive impredicative Type theories (*cf* [39]) The form in which we shall be using the main insights of the fibrations framework, is a particularly elegant construction of Bart Jacobs, which he called *Comprehension Categories*: the idea originates in considerations on the structure of the judgements of generalized type systems (*cf* [6]) and is particularly well-adapted to the study of their semantics. Moreover, it can be looked upon as an easy generalization of the relatively cartesian closed structure that we have been looking at in previous chapter. In the first section, we shall present the basic features of the theory of fibered categories, while in the second we shall look at the structure of comprehension categories

4.1 Fibered Categories

Fibered Categories provide an abstract notion of a "category varying over another," and thus an interpretation of Types dependent on (other) Types Moreover, as we shall see, it allows a precise formulation of the conditions required for modeling both dependency *and* polymorphism Thus, the notion is foundational for various paradigms for the (categorical) interpretations of Constructive Type theories The classical reference for the basic theory (for the English reader) is [9], other excellent expositions, especially in the context of models for constructive Type theory, include [40, 61, 57]

Definition 4.1.1 *Let p $\mathbf{E} \to \mathbf{B}$ be a functor between arbitrary categories* $\mathbf{E}$ *and* $\mathbf{B}$. *A morphism $g \cdot X' \to X$ in* $\mathbf{E}$ *is said to be* cartesian *over a morphism $u = p(g)$ in* $\mathbf{B}$ *if, given any morphism f $Y \to X$, a factorization $p(f) = u \circ v$ in* $\mathbf{B}$ *uniquely determines a morphism h $Y \to X'$ in* $\mathbf{E}$ *such that $p(h) = v$, and a factorization $f = g \circ h$*

Definition 4.1.2 *In the context of definition 4 1 1 above, the functor p* $\mathbf{E} \to \mathbf{B}$ *is called a* fibration *if for every $X \in \mathbf{E}^o$, and arrow u $I \to p(X)$ in* $\mathbf{B}$, *there exists a cartesian morphism g $X^* \to X$ in* $\mathbf{E}$, *such that $p(g) = u$ We say that X^* is a* re-indexing *of X along*

A few terminological points need to be stated, they would facilitate the discussion in the sequel In the context of Definitions 4 1 1 and 4 1 2, an arrow f in E such that $p(f) = u$ for an arrow u in $\mathbf{B}$, is called an arrow *above* u An arrow in $\mathbf{E}$ above an identity in $\mathbf{B}$ is called *vertical* For any $I \in \mathbf{B}^o$, the collection of objects X of $\mathbf{E}$ such that $p(X) = I$, along with vertical arrows in $\mathbf{E}$ above id_I, is called the *fiber* over I, and denoted by $\mathbf{E}_I$ We note that this is a sub-category of $\mathbf{E}$, and it is useful to think of it as the category of I-indexed families The cartesian morphism g corresponding to u in Definition 4 1 2 is called the *cartesian lifting* of u at X

Definition 4.1 3 *If p* $\mathbf{E} \to \mathbf{B}$ *is a fibration, a* cleavage *for p is a particular choice, for any $u \in \mathbf{B}^m$ and $X \in \mathbf{E}^o$ (such that $p(X) = \mathrm{cod}(u)$), of a cartesian lifting of u at X A fibration equipped with a particular cleavage is called a* cloven *fibration Such a choice of a cartesian lifting for u at X may be denoted as $u(X)$ $u^*(X) \to X$ A collection of such choices for every appropriate u and X—that is, the cleavage—induces for every u $A \to B$ a functor u^* $\mathbf{E}_B \to \mathbf{E}_A$, called the* re-indexing, *or* substitution *functor*

Example 4 1.4 *A simple and well-known example of a fibration is based on arrow categories For an arbitrary category* $\mathbf{B}$, *the arrow category* $\mathbf{B}^{\to}$ *consists of morphisms of* $\mathbf{B}$ *as objects,* *and commuting squares in* **B** *as morphisms. The functor* dom : $\mathbf{B}^{\rightarrow} \rightarrow \mathbf{B}$ *is an example of a fibration. This can be easily seen. Consider an object* $g : A \rightarrow X$ *in* $\mathbf{B}^{\rightarrow}$, *and an arrow* $f : Y \rightarrow A = \mathrm{dom}(g)$. *It can be verified that the cartesian lifting of* f *at* g, *is the commuting square, whose upper boundary is* $Y \xrightarrow{f} A \xrightarrow{g} X$ *and lower boundary is* $Y \xrightarrow{g \circ f} X \xrightarrow{\mathrm{id}_X} X$. *A more interesting case occurs when the category* **B** *has pullbacks. in this case the codomain functor* cod : $\mathbf{B}^{\rightarrow} \rightarrow \mathbf{B}$ *is a fibration. Consider an object* $g : A \rightarrow X$ *in* $\mathbf{B}^{\rightarrow}$; *and an arrow* $f : Y \rightarrow X = \mathrm{cod}(g)$. *It can be verified that the cartesian lifting of* f *at* g, *is the pullback square of* g *along* f.

Example 4.1.5 *Another easy example of a fibration can be defined as follows. For an arbitrary category* **C**, *we define the category* Fam(**C**) *(over* **Sets***) as having the following constituents.*

Objects: *Objects are families* $\{X_i\}_{i \in I}$ *where* $I \in$ **Sets** *and* $X_i \in \mathbf{C}^{\circ}$

Morphisms: *A morphism* $f : \{X_i\}_{i \in I} \rightarrow \{Y_j\}_{j \in J}$ *consist of a function* $\phi : I \rightarrow J$ *in* **Sets**, *along with a family of morphisms* $\{f_i : X_i \rightarrow Y_{\phi(i)}\}$ *in* **C**

The functor p : Fam(**C**) $\rightarrow$ **Sets** *is the obvious one* $p : \{X_i\}_{i \in I} \mapsto I$. *We can verify that it is a fibration. For any map* $u : J \rightarrow I$ *in* **Sets**, *the cartesian lifting of* u *at* $X \equiv \{X_i\}_{i \in I}$ *is the map* $u(X) : \{X_{u(j)}\}_{j \in J} \rightarrow \{X_i\}_{i \in I}$, *consisting of* u, *and the* J*-indexed family of identity maps* $\{\bar{u}_j : X_j \rightarrow X_{u(j)}\}$.

We may generalize this example trivially to the case of families indexed by some subcategory **S** *of* **Sets**: *we designate this as* Fam$_{\mathbf{S}}$(**C**). *In fact the full generalization of this example—in which we would replace* **Sets** *by an arbitrary category* **B**, *leads to the theory of fibrations itself.*

Categorical Type theory is all about structure in the fibers, which is preserved along the re-indexing functors and reflected into the base through certain devices. One usually puts enough structure in the fibers to interpret the type-theoretic operations—for instance, sums and products, and their usual relationships. Hence, an important aspect of most of this fiberwise "structuration", is cartesian closure. Towards that end, the most elementary notion is that of the fibered terminal object. Intuitively, a fibration could be said to have a fibered terminal object if every fiber has an (ordinary) terminal object, which is preserved by the re-indexing functors. In order to present this idea formally, we shall adopt a general framework within which other notions like fibered products and exponents could be naturally expressed.

Definition 4.1.6 *Let $p : \mathbf{E} \to \mathbf{B}$ and $q : \mathbf{D} \to \mathbf{B}$ be fibrations over the same basis $\mathbf{B}$. A functor $H : \mathbf{E} \to \mathbf{D}$ is called cartesian if $q \circ H = p$ and f is p-cartesian implies that Hf is q-cartesian.*

Hence, we may define a category $Fib(\mathbf{B})$ having as objects, fibrations over $\mathbf{B}$, and as morphisms, cartesian functors as defined above. It can be verified that $Fib(\mathbf{B})$ has a terminal object—namely the Identity fibration $Id_B : \mathbf{B} \to \mathbf{B}$. In fact, it is not surprising that $Fib(\mathbf{B})$ is a 2-category: given $G, H : p \to q$ in $Fib(\mathbf{B})$, a 2-cell is a natural transformation $\sigma : G \to H$ having vertical components ($q\sigma_d = id_{pd}$).

A well-known construction in $Fib(\mathbf{B})$ is the 2-pullback (in **Cat**) of a fibration $p : \mathbf{E} \to \mathbf{B}$ along an arbitrary functor $K : \mathbf{A} \to \mathbf{B}$. It is well-known that this yields a fibration again, and we state this formally.

Lemma 4.1.7 *Let $p : \mathbf{E} \to \mathbf{B}$ be a fibration and $K : \mathbf{A} \to \mathbf{B}$ an arbitrary functor, then in the diagram below, $K^*(p)$ is a fibration.*

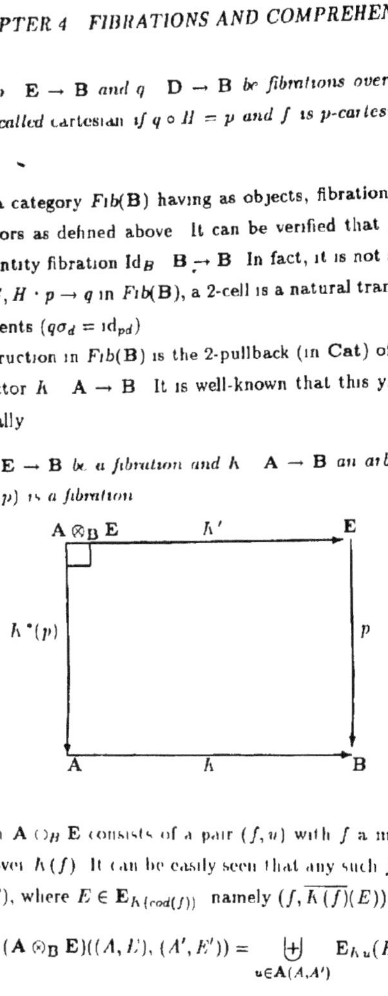

Proof. A morphism in $\mathbf{A} \otimes_B \mathbf{E}$ consists of a pair (f, u) with f a morphism in $\mathbf{A}$ and u a morphism in $\mathbf{E}$, over $K(f)$. It can be easily seen that any such f has a cartesian lifting at any $(cod(f), E)$, where $E \in \mathbf{E}_{K(cod(f))}$, namely $(f, \overline{K(f)}(E))$. We also note

$$(\mathbf{A} \otimes_{\mathbf{B}} \mathbf{E})((A, E), (A', E')) = \biguplus_{u \in \mathbf{A}(A, A')} \mathbf{E}_{Ku}(E, E')$$

where $\mathbf{E}_{Ku}(E, E')$ denotes the class of morphisms $E \to E'$ over the $\mathbf{B}$-morphism Ku.

This construction, whereby a new fibration is derived by pulling back along an arbitrary functor, is known as a *change of base*. In fact, in very much the same way as in the case of "ordinary" category theory, products are obtained by pulling back terminal arrows along terminal arrows, we may derive fibered products in $Fib(\mathbf{B})$ by pulling back

Lemma 4.1.8 *The category* Fib(**B**) *admits finite products which are preserved under change of base*

Proof: Given fibrations p $\mathbf{E} \to \mathbf{B}$ and q $\mathbf{D} \to \mathbf{B}$, their product $p \times q$ can be seen to be $p \circ p^*(q)$ $\mathbf{E} \otimes \mathbf{D} \to \mathbf{B}$ Preservation under change of base follows quite easily The terminal object is the identity fibration as above

The 2-categorical structure of *Fib*(**B**) allows us to define the notion of a (fibered) adjunction.

Definition 4.1.9 *Let p $\mathbf{E} \to \mathbf{B}$ and q $\mathbf{D} \to \mathbf{B}$ be fibrations over the same basis* **B**, *and F $p \to q$ and G $q \to p$ be cartesian functors F is called the* fibered left adjoint *of G if F is an ordinary left adjoint of G, with a vertical unit η (or equivalently, a vertical co-unit ϵ)*

This definition actually yields us a family of *local* adjunctions $F_A \dashv G_A$ for each $A \in \mathbf{B}$, between the fibers $\mathbf{E}_A$ and $\mathbf{D}_A$, by restriction An excellent account of these notions can be found in ([41, 40])

We can now define the notion of fibered terminal objects formally

Definition 4.1.10 *([41, Definition 3 5]) A fibration p $\mathbf{E} \to \mathbf{B}$ admits a terminal object if the unique morphism from p to the terminal object in* Fib(**B**) *has a fibered right adjoint (which we shall denote as* **1***)*

Spelling it out, this entails that the functor **1** yields, for each $A \in \mathbf{B}$, a terminal object $\mathbf{1}A$ in the fiber above A, and the for any map u $A \to B$, the canonical map $u^*(\mathbf{1}B) \to \mathbf{1}A$ is an isomorphism Moreover $p \circ \mathbf{1} = \mathrm{id}_{\mathbf{B}}$

We turn next to the idea of fibered cartesian closure Intuitively, we speak of a fibration being a *fibered cartesian closed category* when each of the fibers is cartesian closed, and the re-indexing functors preserve this structure (up to isomorphism of course) Recall from Lemmas 4 1 7 and 4 1 8, that given a fibration p $\mathbf{E} \to \mathbf{B}$, we may form in *Fib*(**B**) the self-product $p \times p$ $\mathbf{E} \otimes \mathbf{E} \to \mathbf{B}$ There is the obvious fiber-wise diagonal morphism Δ $p \to p \times p$ in *Fib*(**B**) The definition of fiber-wise cartesian products is now quite simple· recall that cartesian products in the basic theory is defined as right adjoints of diagonal functors in **Cat**.

Definition 4.1.11 *([41, Definition 3 6]) A fibration p $\mathbf{E} \to \mathbf{B}$ admits cartesian products if the morphism Δ $p \to p \times p$ in* Fib(**B**) *has a fibered right adjoint*

This data amounts to the following for every $A \in \mathbf{B}$, there is a cartesian product in the fiber category $\mathbf{E}_A$ and this product is preserved by the re-indexing functor u^* corresponding to any u $B \to A$ in **B**

The condition for fiberwise exponential is somewhat more complicated The standard definition through a parametrized right adjoint has to be transplanted in the fibrational setting with some care We furnish the following characterization, and an alternate account may be found in [41]

Definition 4.1.12 *Given the cartesian functor* F $\mathbf{E} \otimes \mathbf{E} \rightarrow \mathbf{E}$ *in* Fib($\mathbf{B}$), *that is the fibered right adjoint to the functor* Δ, *as in Definition 4 1 11, we say that the fibration p has* **fibered exponents**, *if there is a cartesian functor* $G : p \times p \rightarrow p$ *in* Fib($\mathbf{B}$), *such that the mediating morphism* $\langle G, \pi \rangle$ $p \times p \rightarrow p \times p$ *(in the context of the pullback diagram in Figure 4-1) is a fibered right adjoint to the corresponding mediating morphism (for F)* $\langle F, \pi \rangle$ $p \times p \rightarrow p \times p$ *in* Fib($\mathbf{B}$), *and such that all (relevant) triangles in the right hand figure commute*

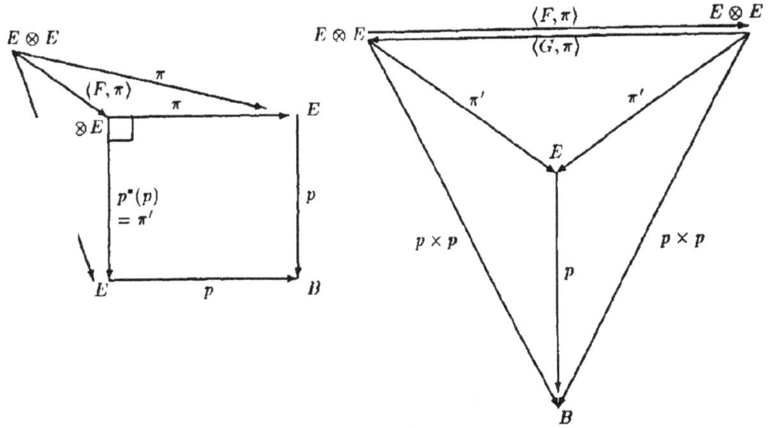

Figure 4-1 Fibered Exponents

It may be verified that this data amounts to the following for every $A \in \mathbf{B}$, there is an exponent in the fiber category $\mathbf{E}_A$ and this exponent, (and the usual cartesian identities) are preserved by the re indexing functor u^* corresponding to any u $B \rightarrow A$ in $\mathbf{B}$ The above set of definitions gives us the notion of a *fibered cartesian closed category* that is, a fibration having a terminal cartesian products and exponents in every fiber, and such that all the structure is preserved by the re indexing functors

While the notion of a fibered cartesian closed category is significant from the point of view of interpreting some of the operations involved in theory of dependent types, a full interpretation involves at least two more essential features: one is the possibility of forming generally, for any object $I \in \mathbf{B}^o$ (the base), I-indexed products and co-products, the second is the possibility of being able to *reflect* (or recover) the structure of the fibers in the base. As is well-known, this in itself is a form of the question of representability—specifically of the fiberwise global sections functor (cf. [40, Chapter 4 §5], [61, Chapter 2 §4]), and more generally of fiberwise hom-sets. With this in mind we have the following general definition.

Definition 4.1.13 *([61, Definition 2.4.9]) Let $p : \mathbf{E} \to \mathbf{B}$ be a cloven fibration (see Figure 4-2). We say that p is* locally small *if for each $I \in \mathbf{B}$, and $X, Y \in \mathbf{E}_I$, there is an object $[X,Y] \in \mathbf{B}$, an arrow $\pi : [X,Y] \to I$ in $\mathbf{B}$, and an arrow $\pi^X_Y : \pi^*(X) \to \pi^*(Y)$ in $\mathbf{E}_{[X,Y]}$, such that the following holds:*

> *for any $\alpha : J \to I$ in $\mathbf{B}$, and an arrow $f : \alpha^*(X) \to \alpha^*(Y)$ in $\mathbf{E}_J$ there is an unique arrow $\hat{f} : J \to [X,Y]$ in $\mathbf{B}$, such that $f = \hat{f}^*(\pi^X_Y)$.*

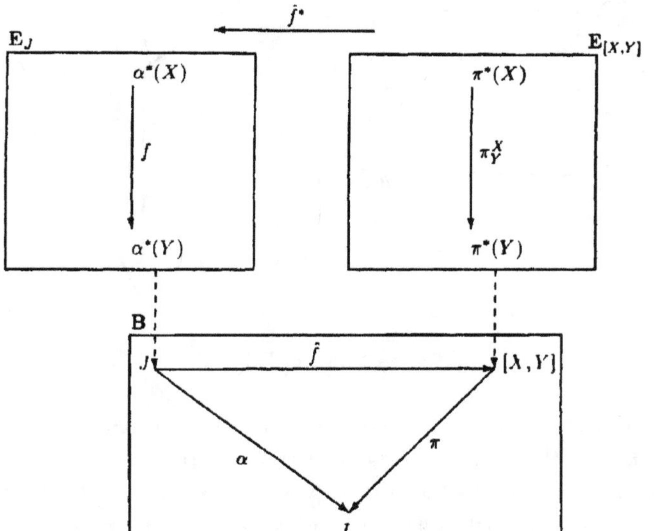

Figure 4-2

An equivalent formulation is to be found in [40], we state it here for reference.

Definition 4.1.14 *([40, Lemma 4 5 2]) Let p* $\mathbf{E} \to \mathbf{B}$ *be a cloven fibration, p is locally small if and only if for each* $I \in \mathbf{B}$ *and* $X, Y \in \mathbf{E}_I$*, the functor* $(\mathbf{B}/I)^{op} \to \mathbf{Ens}$ *given by*

$$J \xrightarrow{\alpha} I \mapsto \mathbf{E}_J(\alpha^*(X), \alpha^*(Y))$$

(where **Ens** *is a "suitably large" universe) is* representable

Locally small fibered cartesian closed categories have all the structure required to interpret a theory of dependent Types The precise details of the interpretation may be consulted in [61]

Our final point in this section has to do with the notion of a *generic object* for a fibration, essential for the interpretation of a free Type variable in impredicative systems (which we shall take up in the sequel) This idea of a "small set of objects" relative to the base is captured in the notion of "the family of all objects" of the fibration, in the sense that any object of any fiber may be "obtained" by re-indexing the generic object along an appropriate morphism Generic objects along with fibered products give us models of the polymorphic λ-Calculus, and hence is of interest to semanticists (*cf* [61, Sections 2 3 and 2 4])

Definition 4 1.15 *Consider a fibration p* $\mathbf{E} \to \mathbf{B}$*, an object* Λ *in the fiber over* $p\Lambda \equiv \Omega_0$ *is known as a* generic object *(for p) if for any object* $E \in \mathbf{E}$*, we are given (the choice of) a cartesian map* $\bar{E}$ $E \to \Lambda$

This definition implies that any object E in the fiber over $pE \equiv I$, can be regarded as the re-indexing of the generic object Λ along a specified map $\underline{E}$ $I \to \Omega_0$ Thus, the generic object may be considered as the family of all objects in the category **E** In a great many respects this condition is an analogue of that of local smallness in the latter, we had the notion of the (representations) of the family of all morphisms between any two objects in the total category We shall see, in the next chapter, that this correspondence is not merely figurative locally small fibrations are formally pretty close to fibrations with a generic object

In the next section, we shall present a structure that consummates the features of a locally small fibered cartesian closed category salient to an interpretation of a theory of dependent Types, and in a more perspicuous manner—being defined in close correspondence with the structure of the judgements of the theory

4.2 Comprehension Categories

The notion of a Comprehension Category was introduced ([10]), to capture, essentially, the structure of judgements in a Constructive Type Theory The significant aspects to be interpreted are "context comprehension," expressed in the assumption rule $((A \in \mathit{Type}\ [\Gamma]) \mapsto$

$[x \; A > \Gamma]$), and dependency (expressed in the projection $[x \; A > \Gamma] \mapsto [\Gamma]$) The structure is abstracted in the following definition

Definition 4.2.1 *([40, Definition 4 1 1]) A* comprehension category *is a functor of the form* $\mathcal{P} \;\; \mathbf{E} \to \mathbf{B}^{\to}$ *satisfying the conditions*

1. $\mathrm{cod} \circ \mathcal{P} : \mathbf{E} \to \mathbf{B}$ *is a fibration*

2. f *is cartesian in* $\mathbf{E} \Longrightarrow \mathcal{P}(f)$ *is a pullback in* $\mathbf{B}$

where cod *refers to the co-domain functor* $\mathrm{cod} \;\; \mathbf{B}^{\to} \to \mathbf{B} \;\; (f \;\; X \to Y) \mapsto Y$*.* $\mathcal{P}$ *is called a* full *comprehension category in case* $\mathcal{P}$ *is a full and faithful functor It is said to be* cloven *in case the corresponding fibration is cloven*

Following Jacobs, for a comprehension category $\mathcal{P} \;\; \mathbf{E} \to \mathbf{B}^{\to}$, we would denote the composition ($\mathrm{cod} \circ \mathcal{P}$) as p, and the composition ($\mathrm{dom} \circ \mathcal{P}$) by $\mathcal{P}_0$ The components $\mathcal{P}E$ are known as *projections*, and re-indexing functors of the form $\mathcal{P}E^*$ are known as *weakening* functors For an object $E \in \mathbf{E}$ we write $|E| = \{u \;\; pE \to \mathcal{P}_0 E \,|\, \mathcal{P}E \circ u = \mathrm{id}\}$, and call this set— the set of *sections* of E We would call $\mathbf{E}$ the *total* category

It is now quite easy to see that the apparatus of display maps in the constitution of a relatively cartesian closed category generalizes to the notion of projections in a comprehension category Given the category $\mathbf{B}^{\to}$, we denote by $\mathbf{B}^{\to}(\mathcal{F})$, the full sub-category of $\mathbf{B}^{\to}$ with display maps as objects Then the inclusion $\mathbf{B}^{\to}(\mathcal{F}) \hookrightarrow \mathbf{B}^{\to}$ gives us a full comprehension category While this is an elementary result, we spell out the proof (in tutorial detail!) as an example of the intricacies involved in reasoning in the context of fibrations

Proposition 4.2 2 *Given the category* $\mathbf{B}$*, along with a subcategory (of* $\mathbf{B}^{\to}$*) of display maps* $\mathbf{B}^{\to}(\mathcal{F})$*, the inclusion* $\mathbf{B}^{\to}(\mathcal{F}) \hookrightarrow \mathbf{B}^{\to}$ *gives us a full comprehension category*

Proof: We shall use the following conventions the category $\mathbf{B}^{\to}(\mathcal{F})$ shall be denoted as $\mathbf{E}$, ($\mathrm{cod} \circ \hookrightarrow$) as p, ($\mathrm{dom} \circ \hookrightarrow$) as $\mathcal{P}_0$ and $\hookrightarrow$ as $\mathcal{P}$ It is easy to see that p is a fibration for any object $A \;\; \mathcal{P}_0 A \to pA$ in $\mathbf{E}$, and any arrow $u \;\; b \to a \equiv pA$, the cartesian lifting of u at A is the pullback square of PA along u, the closure property of display maps guarantees that the domain of the lifting is in the appropriate fiber

For the second condition, we shall refer to Figure 4-3 Let us suppose that we have a cartesian morphism $f \;\; B \to A$ in $\mathbf{E}$, above $u \;\; a \to b$ (we denote pA by a and pB by b) We have the pullback of PA along u as shown, Since we have a full sub-category, this is the image under $\mathcal{P}$ of a morphism $\pi \;\; A_b \to A$ in $\mathbf{E}$ The square $\mathcal{P}f$ (which is the embedding square in the lower frame) is commuting; hence we have the mediating

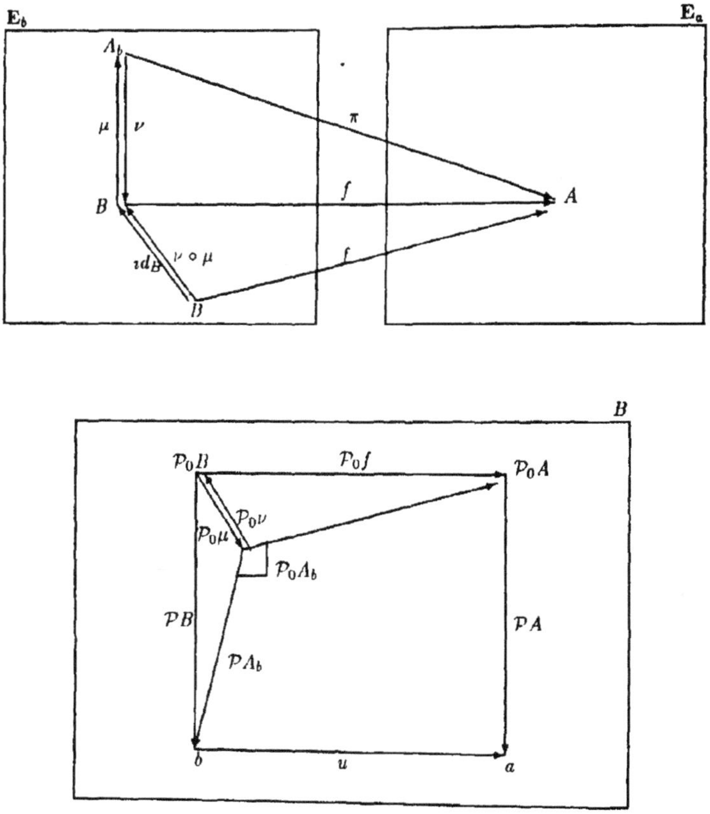

Figure 4-3. Display map categories

morphism from $\mathcal{P}_0 B$ to $\mathcal{P}_0 A_b$, this is the image, under $\mathcal{P}_0$ of a morphism $\mu : B \to A$ in $\mathbf{E}$, and such that $f = \pi \circ \mu$. Now due to the cartesian-ness of π, we have an unique morphism $\nu : A_b \to B$, such that $\pi = f \circ \nu$. Now, the universal property of the pullback qualifies π too as a cartesian lifting of u at A. Since both π and f are cartesian liftings of u, we may assert that they are isomorphic, and hence the proposition. The reader may see this more explicitly in the situation depicted in the lower triangle in the top frame(s). The cartesian-ness of f allows us an unique morphism such that this lower triangle commutes, hence we must have that $\mathrm{id}_B = \nu \circ \mu$. Reasoning by parity about the other cartesian lifting π, we derive that $\mathrm{id}_{A_b} = \mu \circ \nu$. Hence $A_b \cong B$, which implies that $\mathcal{P}f$ is [isomorphic to] the pullback.

Finally the fullness of the comprehension category is obvious by virtue of the fullness of the corresponding sub-category.

On the other hand, we can show that every comprehension category determines a category of display maps: we shall return to this after a few technical lemmas have been established. All of them are elementary and are to be found in Jacob's thesis ([40]), we restate the ones (in the form) that we would need in the sequel, and lay out their proofs more explicitly.

Lemma 4.2.3 *([40, Lemma 4.1.7]) Let $\mathcal{P} : \mathbf{E} \to \mathbf{B}^{\to}$ be a comprehension category. For every $E \in \mathbf{E}$ and $u : A \to pE$ in $\mathbf{B}$, one has a pullback of $\mathcal{P}E$ along u of the form shown in Figure 4-4.*

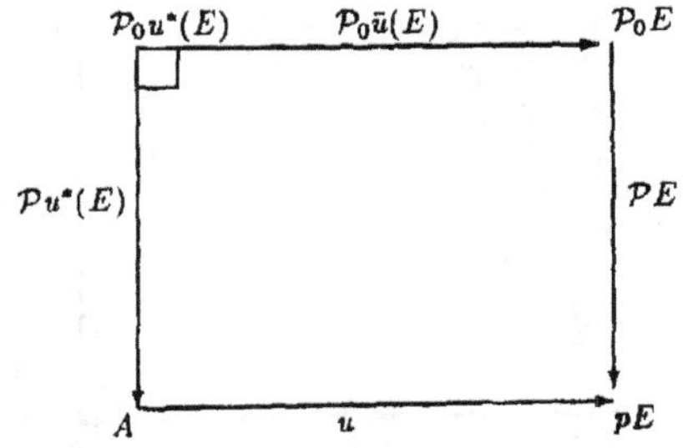

Figure 4-4: General form of Pullbacks for Comprehension Categories

Proof: Since $p \equiv \mathrm{cod} \circ \mathcal{P}$ is a fibration, we must have a cartesian lifting of u at E—that is, a cartesian morphism $\bar{u}(E) : u^*(E) \to E$ in $\mathbf{E}$ above u. But then by definition, $\mathcal{P}\bar{u}(E)$ must be a pullback in $\mathbf{B}$, and hence the proposition.

Lemma 4.2.4 *([10, Lemma 4.1.8]) Let $\mathcal{P} : \mathbf{E} \to \mathbf{B}^{\to}$ be a comprehension category, then, for every $u : A \to pE$ in $\mathbf{B}$, we have that $|u^*(E)| \cong \mathbf{B}/pE(u, \mathcal{P}E)$*

Proof: By definition

$$
\begin{aligned}
|u^*(E)| &= \{v : p(u^*(E)) \to \mathcal{P}_0(u^*(E)) \mid \mathcal{P}u^*(E) \circ v = \mathrm{id}\} \\
&= \{v : A \to \mathcal{P}_0(u^*(E)) \mid \mathcal{P}u^*(E) \circ v = \mathrm{id}\}
\end{aligned}
$$

since $p(u^*(E)) = A$. Now, by Lemma 4.2.3 any such v yields $w = \mathcal{P}_0\bar{u}(E) \circ v : A \to \mathcal{P}_0 E$. Also, $\mathcal{P}E \circ w = \mathcal{P}E \circ \mathcal{P}_0\bar{u}(E) \circ v = u \circ \mathcal{P}u^*(E) \circ v$ since $\mathcal{P}E \circ \mathcal{P}_0\bar{u}(E) = u \circ \mathcal{P}u^*(E)$; but then $\mathcal{P}u^*(E) \circ v = \mathrm{id}_A$ by definition. Hence we may write

$$
\begin{aligned}
|u^*(E)| &\cong \{w : A \to \mathcal{P}_0 E \mid \mathcal{P}E \circ w = u\} \\
&\cong \mathbf{B}/pE(u, \mathcal{P}E)
\end{aligned}
$$

by definition of morphisms in the slices

Corollary 4.2.5 $\mathbf{B}(A, \mathcal{P}_0 E) \cong \biguplus_{u : A \to pE} |u^*(E)|$

Proof: We can see that $\mathbf{B}(A, \mathcal{P}_0 E) \cong \biguplus_{u : A \to pE} \mathbf{B}/pE(u, \mathcal{P}E)$. Hence, using this lemma, the proposition

We can see now that any comprehension category renders us a display map category

Proposition 4.2.6 *Any Comprehension category $\mathcal{P} : \mathbf{E} \to \mathbf{B}^{\to}$ yields us a class of maps $\{\mathcal{P}E \mid E \in \mathbf{E}\}$ in $\mathbf{B}$ that is one of display maps*

Proof: The class $\{\mathcal{P}E \mid E \in \mathbf{E}\}$ can be thought of as a class of display maps, since the pullback of any of them along an arbitrary morphism remains in the class (Lemma 4.2.3)

Hence comprehension categories have the basic structure needed to model the constructions within display map categories

We can develop all the notions of fiberwise structure we have mentioned earlier. Consider the notion of a fibered terminal object: we follow Jacobs in formulating this concept in terms of Erhard's *D-categories* ([18])

Definition 4.2.7 *([40, Definition 4.1.5]) A* comprehension category with unit *is given by a fibration $p : \mathbf{E} \to \mathbf{B}$, provided with a terminal object functor $1 : \mathbf{B} \to \mathbf{E}$ which has a right adjoint $\mathcal{P}_0 : \mathbf{E} \to \mathbf{B}$*

We may spell out precisely how this gives rise to a comprehension category

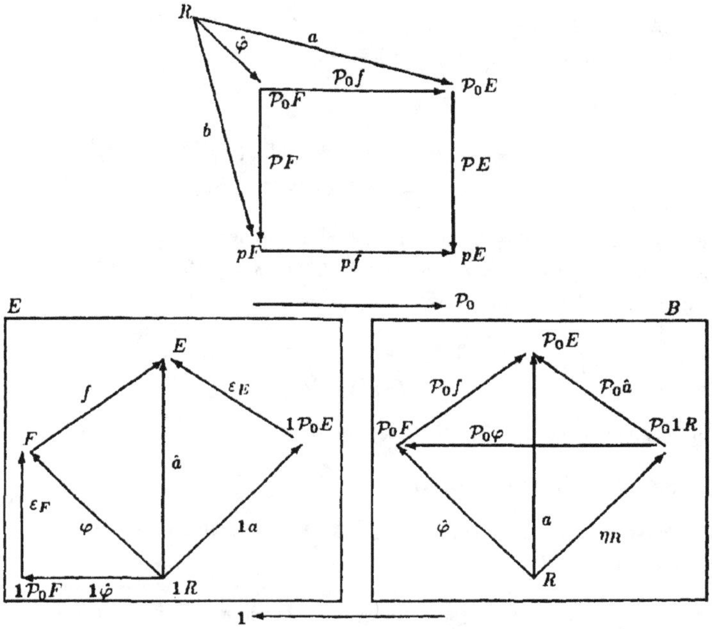

Figure 4-5

Proposition 4.2.8 *In the context of Definition 4.2.7, we have a comprehension category* $\mathcal{P} : \mathbf{E} \to \mathbf{B}^\to$ *given by* $\mathcal{P} : E \mapsto p(\varepsilon_E)$ *where* ε *is the co-unit of the adjunction.*

Proof: We have the situation depicted in Figure 4-5. We assume that we are given a cartesian map $f : E \to F$ in $\mathbf{E}$, and hence the problem is to show that the top square in Figure 4-5 is a pullback. We note first, that it commutes. This is easy to see, using the property of the terminal object functor that $p \circ \mathbf{1} = id_B$, it is nothing but the image under p of the morphism $\mathbf{1}\mathcal{P}_0(f) \to f$ in $\mathbf{E}^\to$, which commutes by the property of adjunctions. Now we have to establish its universality, consider an object R, given with morphisms $a : R \to \mathcal{P}_0 E$, and $b : R \to pF$ in $\mathbf{B}$, and such that $\mathcal{P}E \circ a = pf \circ b$. Transposing a across the adjunction we have $\hat{a} : \mathbf{1}R \to E$ in $\mathbf{E}$, and a commuting triangle $\hat{a} = \varepsilon_E \circ \mathbf{1}a$. Taking the image of this under p we have

$$p(\hat{a}) = p(\varepsilon_E) \circ p(\mathbf{1}a)$$

$$
\begin{aligned}
&= \mathcal{P}E \circ a \\
&= pf \circ b
\end{aligned}
$$

by hypothesis Hence, since $p(\hat{a})$ factorizes through pf, we have, as a consequence of the cartesian-ness of f, an unique map φ $1R \to F$ such that $p\varphi = b$ and $\hat{a} = f \circ \varphi$. Transposing φ across the adjunction, we have the morphism $\hat{\varphi}$ $R \to \mathcal{P}_0 F$ We claim that $\hat{\varphi}$ is the mediating morphism To see this note that $\varphi = \varepsilon_F \circ 1\hat{\varphi}$ through the adjunction Hence,

$$
\begin{aligned}
p(\varphi) &= p(\varepsilon_F) \circ p(1\hat{\varphi}) \\
&= \mathcal{P}F \circ \hat{\varphi}
\end{aligned}
$$

But $p(\varphi) = b$, hence we have that $b = \mathcal{P}F \circ \hat{\varphi}$ On the other hand, we have $a = \mathcal{P}_0(\hat{a}) \circ \eta_R$, but $\hat{a} = f \circ \varphi$, hence $\mathcal{P}_0(\hat{a}) = \mathcal{P}_0 f \circ \mathcal{P}_0 \varphi$ Thus we have that $a = \mathcal{P}_0 f \circ \mathcal{P}_0 \varphi \circ \eta_R$, but then $\mathcal{P}_0 \varphi \circ \eta_R = \hat{\varphi}$, hence we have that $a = \mathcal{P}_0 f \circ \hat{\varphi}$ Hence the proposition

The next result illustrates interesting properties of the fibered terminal object, for a comprehension category with unit notably that fibered global sections correspond to what we have called "sections" in the base, and that morphisms in the slices are preserved in the fibers via the domains of cartesian functors

Proposition 4.2.9 *([40, Lemma 4 1 10]) Let $\mathcal{P}$ $\mathbf{E} \to \mathbf{B}^{\to}$ be a comprehension category with unit, via 1 $\mathbf{B} \to \mathbf{E}$ Then*

1. *for $E \in \mathbf{E}_A$, $|E| \cong \mathbf{E}_A(1A, E)$,*

2. *for $E \in \mathbf{E}_A$, and u $A \to pE$, $\mathbf{B}/pE(u, \mathcal{P}E) \cong \mathbf{E}_A(1A, u^*(E))$*

Proof: Let us consider the first proposition We have, for every $s \in \mathbf{E}_A(1A, E)$, that its transpose $\hat{s}$ across the adjunction satisfies $s = \varepsilon_E \circ 1\hat{s}$ Hence

$$
\begin{aligned}
p(s) &= p(\varepsilon_E) \circ p(1\hat{s}) \\
&= p(\varepsilon_E) \circ \hat{s}
\end{aligned}
$$

since $p \circ 1 = \mathrm{Id}_{\mathbf{B}}$, but then $p(s) = \mathrm{id}_A$, hence we have that $p(\varepsilon_E) \circ \hat{s} = \mathrm{id}_A$, which implies that $\hat{s} \in |E|$ Conversely, starting out with any $r \in |E|$, we shall have an unique $\hat{r}$ $1A \to E$ in $\mathbf{E}_A$--its transpose Hence, for $E \in \mathbf{E}_A$, $|E| \cong \mathbf{E}_A(1A, E)$ As for the second proposition, by Lemma 4 2 4, for every u $A \to pE$ in $\mathbf{B}$, we have that $|u^*(E)| \cong \mathbf{B}/pE(u, \mathcal{P}E)$, but by the previous result, $|u^*(E)| \cong \mathbf{E}_A(1A, u^*(E))$

Fiberwise cartesian closure may be refined, in the context of Comprehension categories, into explicit structural conditions for "sums" and "products," the interpretation of these type-theoretic operations are defined through a translation of the corresponding notions in the context of hyperdoctrines ([76]), triposes ([37]), or *PL*-categories ([78]) that is sum and product types are defined through left and right adjunctions to relevant substitution functors and take the following form

Definition 4.2.10 (*[40, Definition 4 2 1]) Let $\mathcal{P}$ $\mathbf{E} \to \mathbf{B}^{\to}$ be a comprehension category, we say that $\mathcal{P}$ has* products *(respectively* sums*) if for any $E \in \mathbf{E}$ the weakening functor $\mathcal{P}E^*$ has a right adjoint Π_E (respectively, a left adjoint Σ_E), satisfying the Beck-Chevalley condition stated below*

- *For every cartesian morphism f $E \to E'$ in $\mathbf{E}$, the (canonical) natural transformation*

$$(pf)^*\Pi_{E'} \to \Pi_E(\mathcal{P}_0 f)^* \quad \textit{(respectively} \quad \Sigma_E(\mathcal{P}_0 f)^* \to (pf)^*\Sigma_{E'}\textit{)}$$

  is an isomorphism

The structure adumbrated in Definition 4 2 10 is that needed to model what are known as *weak sums* in Type theory (*cf* [40, Chapter 2 §2 4]) To interpret *strong sums*, we have a stronger condition, which we detail below

Definition 4.2.11 (*[40, Definition 4 2 10]) Consider a comprehension category $p \cdot \mathbf{E} \to \mathbf{B}$ having sums In any comprehension category, we have for any E, $D \in \mathbf{E}$ such that $pD = \mathcal{P}_0 E$, the map $comp_E(D) \equiv \overline{\mathcal{P}E} \circ \eta_D$ $D \to \mathcal{P}E^*(\Sigma_E D) \to \Sigma_E D$ We say that $\mathcal{P}$ has strong sums if the following condition obtains*

> *for every $comp_E(D)$ as above, and for every D' in $\mathbf{E}$, and $u, v \in \mathbf{B}$ forming a commutative square (see Figure 4-6), there is an unique $w \in \mathbf{B}$ satisfying $\mathcal{P}D' \circ w = v$ and $u = w \circ \mathcal{P}_0(comp_E(D))$*

It is known that the condition for strong sums is logically equivalent to the condition that the morphism $\mathcal{P}_0(\mathrm{comp}_E(D))$ be an isomorphism, this is the form in which we shall demonstrate this property in the sequel

Finally we have the following unit that gives us all we need to interpret a theory of dependent types (with strong sums)

Definition 4.2.12 *A* closed *comprehension category is a full comprehension category with unit, products and strong sums, and having a terminal object in the base*

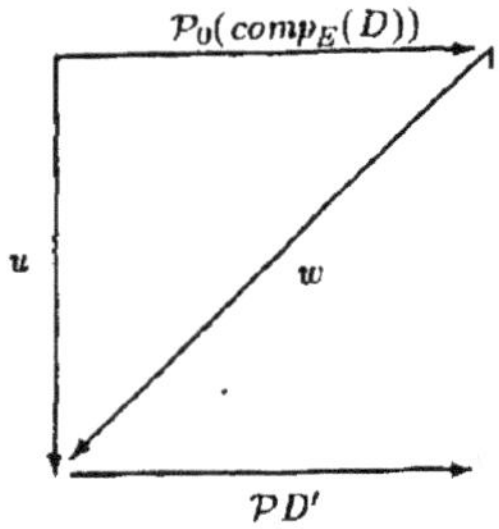

Figure 4-6 Condition for strong sums

This epitomizes all the properties of a locally small fibered cartesian closed category, as remarked earlier We state the following proposition for reference, and provide a suggestion of the proof.

Theorem 4.2.13 *([40, Lemma 4 3 9]) For a Closed Comprehension Category $\mathcal{P}$ $\mathbf{E} \to \mathbf{B}^{\to}$, the fibration $p = \text{cod} \circ \mathcal{P}$ is a fibered cartesian closed category*

Proof: As stated in the reference, strong sums are not needed for the proof For objects E and E' in the fiber $\mathbf{E}_{pE}$, the cartesian product $E \times E'$ is $\Sigma_E \mathcal{P}E^*(E')$. The second projection $\pi_{E'}$ $E \times E' \to E'$ may be seen to be the co-unit $\epsilon_{E'}$ of the adjunction $\Sigma_E \dashv \mathcal{P}E^*$ As for the first projection, we have the following construction we have the pullback square of $\mathcal{P}E$ along itself, yielding us the morphism $\mathcal{P}E^*(E)$, we also have the pullback of $\mathcal{P}E'$ along $\mathcal{P}E$ yielding us the morphism $\mathcal{P}E^*(E')$, this morphism gives us a cone over the appropriate diagram of the first pullback square There is thus a mediating morphism f $\mathcal{P}E^*(E') \to \mathcal{P}E^*(E)$ in the fiber $\mathbf{E}_{\mathcal{P}_0 E}$, and we may transpose it across the adjunction, obtaining a morphism f^* $\Sigma_E \mathcal{P}E^*(E') \to E$ This is the first projection π_E As for the exponent, it is fairly straightforward though tedious to verify that $E \Rightarrow E' = \Pi_E \mathcal{P}E^*(E')$

We turn now to the close relationship between comprehension categories and display map categories we have remarked earlier that they really "amount to the same thing," additionally, since closed comprehension categories can interpret a theory of dependent types (with strong sums), we would anticipate that relative cartesian closure of display map categories required for interpreting the same class of theories, would correspond to the closure of the corresponding comprehension category We give a brief idea of a proof, which is quite straightforward

Proposition 4.2.14 *Given a display map category* **B**, *the corresponding Comprehension category described in Lemma 4.2.2 has sums and products if and only if* **B** *is relatively cartesian closed. Conversely, for any comprehension category, the corresponding display map category is relatively cartesian closed exactly when the former has sums and products.*

Proof: If **B** is relatively cartesian closed, then for any display map F, the pullback functor F^* has left and right adjoints (satisfying the Beck-Chevalley condition). Since the objects of the total category of the comprehension category are exactly the display maps, the condition is exactly equivalent to requiring that the comprehension category has sums and products. The converse follows on the same consideration. Similarly for the second part.

This tells us, in particular, that the category $\mathfrak{I}$ of the previous chapter may be cast in the form of a closed comprehension category. We shall see details of this construction in Chapter 6.

Finally, we shall demonstrate that comprehension categories (with unit) correspond pretty exactly to the locally small fibered cartesian closed categories of the last section—which is in fact what we would expect, given our understanding of local smallness as that general fibrational property that is a basis for the interpretation of a theory of dependent Types. We have the following result.

Theorem 4.2.15 ([40, Proposition 4.5.5]) *Let* $p : \mathbf{E} \to \mathbf{B}$ *be a fibered cartesian closed category. Then*

> p *is locally small if and only if there is a comprehension category with unit,* $\mathcal{P} : \mathbf{E} \to \mathbf{B}^{\to}$ *such that* $p = cod \circ \mathcal{P}$.

Proof: Let $1 : \mathbf{E} \to \mathbf{B}$ denote the fibered terminal object.

⇒ From Definition 4.2.7, we have to prove the existence of a functor $\mathcal{P}_0 : \mathbf{E} \to \mathbf{B}$ right adjoint to 1. Consider $E \in \mathbf{E}_A$ for some $A \in \mathbf{B}$. Let us put $\mathcal{P}E = \pi : [1A, E] \to A$; now for any $B \in \mathbf{B}$ we have the following sequence of isomorphisms:

$$\begin{aligned}
\mathbf{E}(1B, E) &\cong \biguplus_{u : B \to A} \mathbf{E}_B(1B, u^*(E)) && \text{by property of cartesian maps}\\
&\cong \biguplus_{u : B \to A} \mathbf{E}_B(u^*(1A), u^*(E)) && \text{since } 1B \cong u^*(1A)\\
&\cong \biguplus_{u : B \to A} \mathbf{B}/A(u, \mathcal{P}E) && \text{by definition of } \mathcal{P}\text{, and local smallness}\\
&\cong \mathbf{B}(B, \mathcal{P}_0 E) && \text{putting } \mathcal{P}_0 = \mathrm{dom} \circ \mathcal{P}
\end{aligned}$$

The naturality of this isomorphism in E and B is straightforward. Hence we see that the functor $\mathcal{P}_0$ as defined is a right adjoint to 1.

$\Leftarrow$ We have to demonstrate the existence of a representing arrow $\pi : [E, E'] \to A$ in **B** for any $E, E' \in \mathbf{E}_A$, consider any $u : B \to A$ in **B** We have

$$\begin{aligned} \mathbf{E}_B(u^*(E), u^*(E')) &\cong \mathbf{E}_B(1B, u^*(E) \Rightarrow u^*(E')) && \text{fiberwise exponents} \\ &\cong \mathbf{E}_B(1B, u^*(E \Rightarrow E')) && \text{fibered exponents} \\ &\cong \mathbf{B}/A(u, \mathcal{P}(E \Rightarrow E')) && \text{from Proposition 4.2.9} \end{aligned}$$

Hence we may take $\mathcal{P}(E \Rightarrow E')$ as the appropriate representing arrow.

The final remark we have is regarding the generalization of the notion of products and sums to fibrations *relative* to comprehension categories. We have the following definition

Definition 4.2.16 *([40, Definition 1 2 1]) Let* $q : \mathbf{D} \to \mathbf{B}$ *be a fibration and* $\mathcal{P} : \mathbf{E} \to \mathbf{B}^{\to}$ *be a comprehension category We say that* q *has* $\mathcal{P}$*-products (respectively* $\mathcal{P}$*-sums) if for any* $E \in \mathbf{E}$ *the weakening functor* $\mathcal{P}E^* : \mathbf{D}_{pE} \to \mathbf{D}_{\mathcal{P}_0 E}$ *has a right adjoint* Π_E *(respectively, a left adjoint* Σ_E*), satisfying the Beck-Chevalley condition stated in Definition 4.2.10.*

The fibration **D** may arise from a comprehension category $\mathcal{D} : \mathbf{E} \to \mathbf{B}^{\to}$, in which case we say that $\mathcal{D}$ has $\mathcal{P}$-products (or $\mathcal{P}$-sums)

This completes our exposition of the basic structures involved in the interpretation of theories of dependent Types In the next chapter we continue the exposition towards the theme of impredicative theories

Chapter 5

Full Internal Sub-Categories

A theory of dependent types is a generalization of the typed λ-Calculus, in very much the same way that (First-order) predicate logic is a generalization of the propositional logic; their correspondence being along the Curry-Howard isomorphism. Semantically, this generalization does not add any level of complexity: as in the case of the semantics of the typed λ-Calculus, we may very well remain within (fibrations over) a (classical) universe of sets; we need only a local form of completeness, which essentially amounts to having products (and co-products) indexed by objects of the base category. A level of complexity however may be added when we consider generalizations to various impredicative calculi: the most straightforward generalization is of course to consider the polymorphic λ-Calculus; this is, as we know, the calculus of the proofs of second-order logic ([24, 27, 48, 78]). Universal quantification over all propositions is impredicative, and local forms of completeness no longer suffice, in other words, we may not remain any more within classical set theory ([65]). Historically, this problem was solved by constructing global limits within a non-classical universe of sets ([62]): specifically, through the construction of a *small complete category* within an intuitionistic universe ([34, 36]). Such an object is essentially an *internal* category within the ambient topos (which is the categorical form of an intuitionistic universe) and closed under all (internal) limits (suitably defined). The interaction between the two forms of completeness—or, in other words, the requirement that both dependent *and* impredicative forms of quantification be modeled within the same framework, adds a considerable degree of complexity to the problem. The appropriate level at which one has to work, then, is one at which the fibrational and the internal categorical framework may be seen as intrinsically related, and their structural effects be epitomized within a single general framework. Within such a framework, the small complete category is more appositely structured as an object known as a *full internal sub-category* ([34]). In fact, the original construction of a small complete category by Hyland, was facilitated by the requirement that the object constructed be a full internal sub-category of the ambient topos For such objects, the (internal) global sections functor is full and faithful, and the (internal) limit structure is "determined" by that of the ambient category The framework within which the fibrational and internal categorical structures may be synthesized, is obtained as the generalization of the Hyland-Pitts model of the Theory of Constructions (within a fibrational framework)—and is titled *CC-Category* by B Jacobs ([40]) In this chapter, we shall provide an account of this development, culminating in the description of a CC-Category, and of a full internal sub-category—the latter being the form in which, in the subsequent chapters, we shall embed our system of Types within the Realizability Topos

5.1 Internal Categories

In this section we provide a brief introduction to the notion of an internal category The matter will be mainly expository and for most of the advanced results and proofs, we shall refer the reader to the references In some sense, internal category theory complements the theoretical function of fibered category theory Both allow us a formulation of a theory of variable categories, and each has its particular elegance Fibrations is probably a more general framework, and offers a more intuitive notion of dependent objects Moreover, the framework permits a formulation of a class of related abstract objects—sheaves and fiber bundles to name two On the other hand, internal categories offer an intuitive notion of categories relative to an "universe" for instance, topological groups, and "synthetic" objects as manifolds or domains relative to a topos As we shall see, this allows a fine-grained and elegant treatment of matters like completeness In the last chapter, we shall explore the synthetic approach *vis-a-vis* domains—an investigation that assumes considerable theoretical importance in view of the fact that domains can now be thought of as *sets* and *with full function spaces*, in the spirit of Pitt's shibboleth, "Polymorphism is set-theoretic, constructively " There is of course, a correlation between the two frameworks, and we shall comment on that towards the end of this section

We shall work within a category **B** that is assumed to have pullbacks. The definition of an internal category is a simple generalization of the idea of an algebraic object within a category—for instance, a monoid object or a ring object (*cf* [49, Chapter 3 §6]) The logical axioms for a category belong to a certain class of logical theories, which may be modeled in any category with finite limits This class is named **Lim** theories by Hyland and Pitts ([38]), and *left-exact* theories by Barr and Wells ([7]) The relevant structures needed to model the axioms of this theory are described below (*cf* [4, Chapter 7], [42, Chapter 2]).

Definition 5.1.1 *An internal category* **E** *(relative to an ambient category* **B***) is a 6-tuple*

$$(E_0, E_1, \partial_0, \partial_1, \mathrm{id}_{\mathbf{E}}, \bullet_{\mathbf{E}})$$

where the types of each component are as follows

$$\begin{array}{rl} E_0, E_1 & \mathbf{B}^0 \\ \partial_0, \partial_1 & E_1 \to E_0 \\ \mathrm{id}_{\mathbf{E}} & E_0 \to E_1 \\ \bullet_{\mathbf{E}} & E_2 \to E_1 \end{array}$$

where the object E_2 (and other objects involved in the commutation conditions in the sequel) are as defined in the cluster of (four) pullback diagrams at the bottom of Figure 5-1, and the diagrams shown in the rest of the figure commute

The attentive reader would probably note that an isomorphism involved in the figure stating the associativity for composition has been elided The commuting diagrams are simply a categorical form of the corresponding axioms for a category object, as may be easily verified Thus, an internal category is simply a category object in an (ambient) category that has enough structure to satisfy the axioms in its definition In the definition above, the component E_0 is the object of objects of the internal category **E**, while E_1 is the object of morphisms, ∂_0 and ∂_1 are the domain and co-domain morphisms respectively, while $\mathrm{id}_{\mathbf{E}}$ and $\bullet_{\mathbf{E}}$ are the internal identity and internal composition respectively. A simple example of an internal category is the *discrete* category $|D|$ obtained from any object $D \in \mathbf{B}^0$: its object of objects and that of morphisms are both D, while the internal identity is simply the identity id_D, while the other components follow from these conditions immediately.

We may carry out many of the standard constructions in Category theory internally The definition of an internal functor is a case in point and we provide the definition below

Definition 5.1.2 *An internal functor F between internal categories* **E** *and* **E**$'$ *consists of a pair of morphisms $F_0 : E_0 \to E_0'$ and $F_1 : E_1 \to E_1'$, and such that the following commutation conditions are satisfied*

$$\begin{array}{rcl} F_0 \circ \partial_0 & = & \partial_0' \circ F_1 \\ F_0 \circ \partial_1 & = & \partial_1' \circ F_1 \\ F_1 \circ \mathrm{id}_{\mathbf{E}} & = & \mathrm{id}_{\mathbf{E}'} \circ F_0 \\ F_1 \circ \bullet_{\mathbf{E}} & = & \bullet_{\mathbf{E}'} \circ (F_1 \times F_1) \end{array}$$

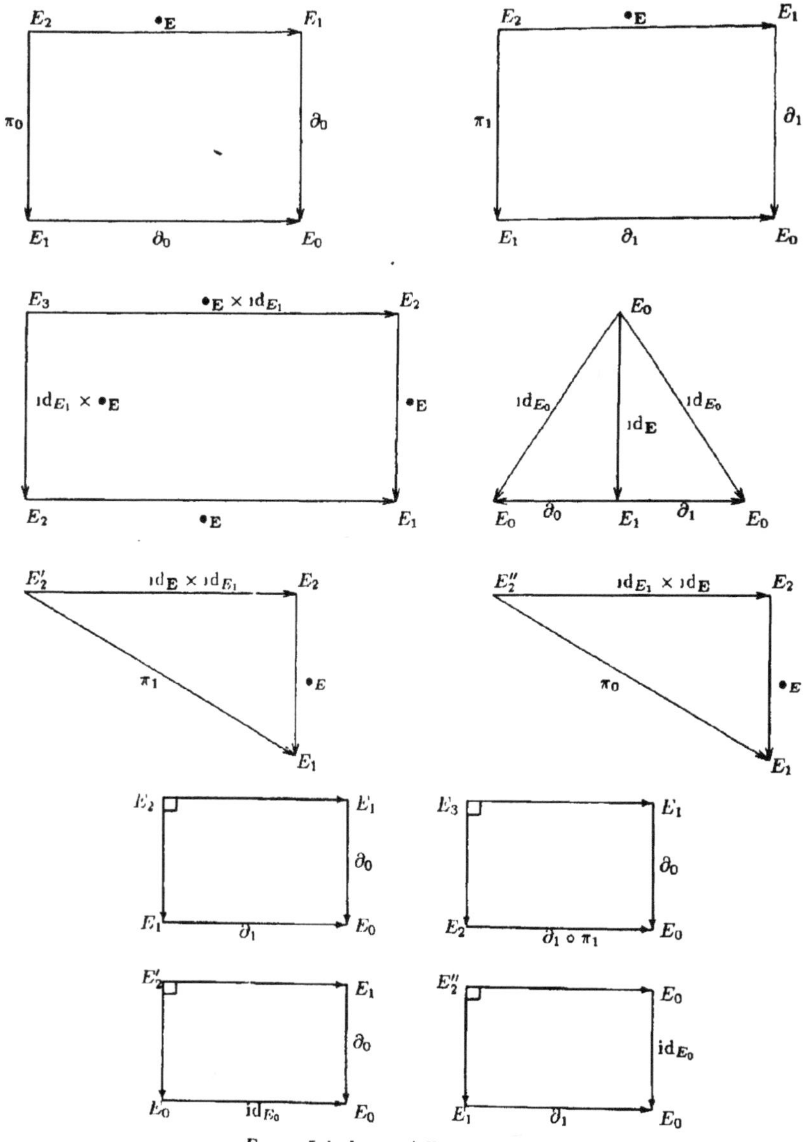

Figure 5-1 Internal Categories

Thus, we have the category of internal categories (of **B**), which we denote as Cat(**B**) In fact, as is well-known, we have a 2-Categorical structure on Cat(**B**) ([40, Chapter 1 §4])

Definition 5.1.3 *A natural transformation σ $F \to G$ (where $F, G \cdot \mathbf{E} \to \mathbf{E}'$ are internal functors) is given as a morphism $\sigma \cdot E_0 \to E_1'$ which makes the diagrams in Figure 5-2 commute*

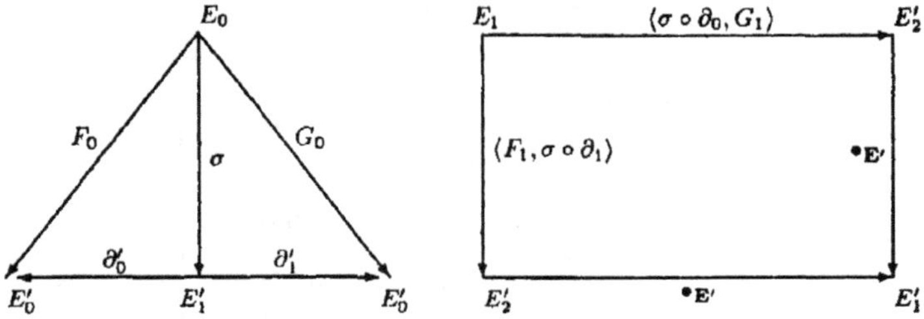

Figure 5-2 Internal Natural Transformations

The most significant benefit of being able to endow Cat(**B**) with a 2-categorical structure is that we may define internal adjunctions on its basis Actually there are two ways of going about this one may consider the (standard) definition of an adjunction as a triple consisting of two functors, and a bijection between certain hom-sets in the two categories however, this requires the notion of an indexed collection of isomorphisms between objects that can represent hom-sets This can be done through the notion of an *internal presheaf* on the objects in Cat(**B**); an excellent exposition of this method is in [4] The other way is to use an alternative definition of an adjunction for which we refer the reader to [49, Chapter 4, Theorem 2] The essential idea is that an adjunction can be defined in terms of two natural transformations, and certain composite transformations that evaluate to the identity natural transformation, we have the following definition

Definition 5.1.4 *Given internal categories* **C** *and* **D** *(in some ambient category), and internal functors F $\mathbf{C} \to \mathbf{D}$ and $G \cdot \mathbf{D} \to \mathbf{C}$, and natural transformations η . $\mathbf{id}_{\mathbf{C}} \to GF$ and ϵ $\mathbf{id}_{\mathbf{D}} \to FG$ (where $\mathbf{id}_{\mathbf{X}}$ denotes the identity functor on the internal category* **X***), we say that F is a left adjoint G, or G is a right adjoint to F, or that $\langle F, G\ \eta, \epsilon \rangle$ constitutes an adjunction between* **C** *and* **D** *if and only if the following commutations obtain*

$$G \xrightarrow{\eta G} GFG \xrightarrow{G\epsilon} G = \mathbf{id}_G$$
$$F \xrightarrow{F\eta} FGF \xrightarrow{\epsilon F} F = \mathbf{id}_F$$

where id_X, *for a internal functor* X *denotes the identity natural transformation on* X, *and the relevant composition of natural transformations is the vertical composition*

On this basis, we can proceed to define the significant notion of an internal cartesian closed category We provide a brief sketch of the process, referring the reader to [40, Chapter 1 §4] for the details

Construction 5.1.5 *An internal category* $\mathbf{E}$ *in* $\mathrm{Cat}(\mathbf{B})$ *is said to have an internal terminal object, if the unique internal functor* $1_{\mathbf{E}} \cdot \mathbf{E} \to |1|$ *(where* 1 *is the terminal object of* $\mathbf{B}$*), has an (internal) right adjoint* $\mathbf{E}$ *is said to have internal cartesian products if the (internal) diagonal functor* $\Delta \ \mathbf{E} \to \mathbf{E} \times \mathbf{E}$ *has an (internal) right adjoint* $(\times)$ *From the functor* $(\times)$, *and the inclusion functor* $\imath \ |E_0| \to \mathbf{E}$ *we may construct the functor* $\overline{(\times)} \ |E_0| \times \mathbf{E} \to |E_0| \times \mathbf{E}$—*and we say that* $\mathbf{E}$ *has internal exponents if* $\overline{(\times)}$ *has an (internal) right adjoint*

In this thesis, we shall not be using too many of these concepts we shall demonstrate a somewhat more complicated limit structure on the internal category we would construct in the next chapter, and an exposition of this structure within the current framework would be rather cumbersome On the other hand, if the internal category meets certain conditions—and thus admitting the structure of what is known as a full internal sub-category—then the limit structure of this category "agrees" with (in fact, is determined by) that of the ambient category Hence the corresponding properties are easier to state and prove, and we shall adopt this method

The notion which is essential for defining the conditions under which an internal category qualifies as a full internal sub-category, is that of *externalization* It is also the notion that illustrates the underlying correlation between the theory of internal categories, and that of fibrations ([4, Chapter 7, §4,5], [40, Chapter 1 §4]) We furnish the following definition

Definition 5.1 6 *For an internal category* $\mathbf{M}$ *in* $\mathrm{Cat}(\mathbf{B})$ *we define the* externalization *of* $\mathbf{M}$ *as the category* $\sum \mathbf{M}$ *having the following constituents*

Objects: *Objects are* $\langle A, f \ A \to M_0 \rangle$, *for* $A \in \mathbf{B}^0$

Morphisms: *A morphism* $\langle A, f \ A \to M_0 \rangle \to \langle B, g \ B \to M_0 \rangle$ *are pairs* $\langle u, h \rangle$ *such that* $u \ A \to B$ *and* $h \ A \to M_1$ *are morphisms in* $\mathbf{B}$, *and the following equations hold*

$$\partial_0 \circ h = f \qquad \partial_1 \circ h = g \circ u$$

We may define a functor $[\mathbf{M}] \ \sum \mathbf{M} \to \mathbf{B}$ as illustrated in Proposition 5 1.7 below, the interesting fact is that this is a fibration

Proposition 5.1.7 *The functor* $[\mathbf{M}] : \sum \mathbf{M} \to \mathbf{B}$ *defined so as to have the following action*

$$\langle A, f : A \to M_0 \rangle \mapsto A \qquad \langle u, h \rangle \mapsto u$$

is a fibration

Proof: Obtains easily on the following consideration: for an object $\langle A, f : A \to M_0 \rangle$ in $\sum \mathbf{M}$, and a morphism $g : X \to A = [\mathbf{M}](\langle A, f \rangle)$, the cartesian lifting of g at $\langle A, f \rangle$ can be seen to be the morphism $\langle g, k \rangle \cdot \langle B, f \circ g \rangle \to \langle A, f \rangle$ where $k \equiv \mathrm{id}_{\mathbf{M}} \circ (f \circ g) . B \to M_1$

This correspondence actually has a deeper structure: it may be extended so as to yield a 2-functor $\mathrm{Cat}(\mathbf{M}) \to \mathrm{Fib}(\mathbf{M})$. For details we refer the reader to [40, *ibid*]. A fibration would be said to be *small* if it is equivalent to a fibration obtained from the externalization of some internal category.

The complementarity between the two approaches towards a theory of variable categories (that is, internal category theory and fibered category theory) is partially exemplified by Proposition 5.1.7: every internal category yields a (split) fibration through its externalization. Moreover, we may note that this fibration is essentially a **B**-indexed category. Assuming **B** is locally small, the structure of the this indexed category is such as to be, essentially, an internal category in the presheaf category $\mathbf{Sets}^{\mathbf{B}^{op}}$. There is, in fact, the converse aspect to the complementarity: every (split) fibration yields an internal category in the presheaf category. We state the result below for completeness.

Proposition 5.1.8 *([40, Proposition 1.4.8]) Let* $p : \mathbf{E} \to \mathbf{B}$ *be a split fibration, such that* **B** *is locally small, and all fibrations are small: there exists an internal category* $\hat{p}$ *in the pre-sheaf category* $\hat{\mathbf{B}} = \mathbf{Sets}^{\mathbf{B}^{op}}$*, and a change-of-base condition shown in Figure 5-3, where* Y *is the Yoneda embedding*

Proof: We sketch the outlines of the proof, the details may be checked up in the cited reference. The object of objects of the internal category is $\hat{p}_0 : \mathbf{B}^{op} \to \mathbf{Sets} : A \mapsto \mathrm{Obj}(\mathbf{E}_A)$ while the object of morphisms is $\hat{p}_1 : \mathbf{B}^{op} \to \mathbf{Sets} : A \mapsto \mathrm{Mor}(\mathbf{E}_A)$. The rest of the internal category structure is fairly obvious. The functor $H : \mathbf{E} \to \sum(\hat{p})$ is given as $H . E \mapsto \langle Y(pE), \hat{E} \rangle$ where $\hat{E}$ is the natural transformation $Y(pE) \to \hat{p}_0$ given as $\hat{E}_x : (u : x \to pE) \mapsto u^*(E) \in \mathbf{E}_x$. The rest of the details are not difficult to fill in.

With this brief sketch of the theory of internal categories, we end this section. In the next to sections we shall look at two important aspects of this theory: the notions of completeness, for internal categories (and fibrations), and subsequently, the notion of a full internal subcategory.

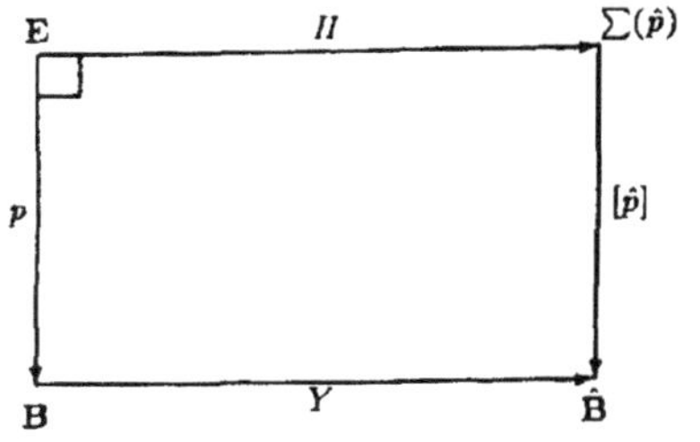

Figure 5-3: Internalization

5.2 Notions of Completeness

Much of the material in this section is far more general than what we would be requiring for the subsequent development of the thesis, we include it mainly for the sake of completeness. The translation of the standard notions of completeness from "naive" category theory to internal category theory is deeper than what one might expect Moreover, it is in this respect, that internal category theory is found to offer a more fine-grained notion of completeness (than fibered category theory) the notions may be translated in terms of fibrations, but, as we would see, they would not be very intuitive We start with notions of completeness for fibered categories The following definition is standard and is (I think) due to Bénabou

Definition 5.2 1 *A fibration is said to be* (strongly) complete *if it has*

- *fibered products — i e , for every morphism ϕ in the base, the re-indexing functor ϕ^* has a right adjoint Π_ϕ satisfying the Beck-Chevalley condition*
- *fiberwise finite limits*

This is the notion that we shall usually mean when we describe a fibration as complete. However, when we formulate the notion of completeness for internal categories, and specifically in the case of categories internal to a topos, we shall have two non-equivalent formulations—one being described as *weak* and the other as strong Thus, in the spirit of the complementarity between internal categories and fibered categories, we would require a corresponding notion of weak completeness for fibrations This notion is not very intuitive and an appreciation of the issues involved would require some idea of the semantics of intuitionistic logic (the Kripke-Joyal semantics) we shall not elaborate this[1] but merely record the definition for the

[1] The idea, very approximately, is this (familiarity with the internal language of a topos (*cf* Chapter 7) would help) the notion of completeness, when phrased in the internal language of a topos, requires a notion

sake of "completeness "

Definition 5.2.2 (*[61, Definition 3 8 39]) A fibration p* $\mathbf{E} \to \mathbf{B}$ *is said to be* weakly complete *if the following conditions hold*

- *Given any finite diagram D in any fiber* $\mathbf{E}_I$, *there is an epimorphism* $\alpha : K \to I$ *in* $\mathbf{B}$, *such that* $\alpha^*(D)$ *has a limit in* $\mathbf{E}_K$, *and re-indexing functors preserve finite limits.*

- *Given any map* $\phi : J \to I$, *there is an epimorphism* $\alpha : K \to I$ *such that if* $\psi : J \otimes_I K \to K$ *is the obvious map in the pullback (diagram) of* ϕ *along* α, *then* ψ^* *has a right adjoint* Π_ψ, *and all such right adjoints satisfy the Beck-Chevalley condition.*

We come now to the problem of framing corresponding notions of completeness for internal categories. The implicit assumption here is that we are in the context of categories internal to a topos The situation is more nuanced here, and we have a range of possible formulations that confront us The standard guideline in this field has been to formulate the property in such terms as to yield us models of the impredicative and dependent Type theories—in particular, the theory of Constructions The basic idea that the internal category should come equipped with the structure of a category with finite limits, is refined in two directions first, that we should consider not just single diagrams and their limiting cones, but a *family* of diagrams (possibly) of varying shapes (*cf* [61, pages 81–84], [66]), second, it is one thing to frame this condition in the internal language and require its validity, and quite another to require the actual existence of the structure that fulfills it (since the axiom of choice may fail) Taking these into considerations, we have the following formulations[2]

Definition 5.2.3 (*[61, Definition 3 8 34]) We say that an internal category* $\mathbf{C} \in \mathrm{Cat}(\mathbf{B})$ *is* weakly complete *if for all objects* $I \in \mathbf{B}$, *and for all internal categories* $\mathbf{D}$ *in the slice topos* $\mathbf{B}/I$, *the following validity holds*

$$\models \forall F . [\mathbf{D}, I^*(\mathbf{C})] \text{ “The category of cones over } F \text{ has a terminal object”}$$

where $[\mathbf{D}, I^*(\mathbf{C})]$ *denotes the category of internal functors from* $\mathbf{D}$ *to* $I^*(\mathbf{C})$ *both internal categories in* $\mathbf{B}/I$, *and the quoted statement is understood as an appropriate internal language statement*

---

of validity that is *local* Now local validity (or local truth, to use Grothendieck's usage) means "true on a cover," or in other words, true with respect to a covering object (*cf* [28, Chapter 14]) When we translate this in appropriate terms, we arrive at the formulation above A fuller exposition of this may be found in [61]

[2] We anticipate the exposition in Chapter 7, of the internal logic of a topos, the reader may like to refer to this for the relevant basic notions

The definition for strong completeness on the other hand actually asserts the existence of a limiting cone It has the following form

Definition 5.2.4 *We say that an internal category* $\mathbf{C} \in \mathrm{Cat}(\mathbf{B})$ *is* **strongly complete** *if for all objects* $I \in \mathbf{B}$, *and for all internal categories* $\mathbf{D}$ *in the slice topos* $\mathbf{B}/I$, *the diagonal functor* $\Delta \; I^{*}(\mathbf{C}) \to [\mathbf{D}, \mathbf{I}^{*}(\mathbf{C})]$ *has a right adjoint*

This definition thus asserts that for any I indexed family of diagrams (of possibly varying sizes) in $\mathbf{C}$, there exists a function that to each $i \in I$ assigns a limit cone in $\mathbf{C}$ over the corresponding diagram

Finally we have the result connecting the notions of completeness for fibrations and internal categories, which we record for reference (*cf* [36])

Theorem 5.2.5 (*[36, Proposition 4 4]) An internal category* $\mathbf{C}$ *in a topos* $\mathbf{B}$ *is strongly (respectively, weakly) complete, if and only if its externalization* $\sum(\mathbf{C})$ *is strongly (respectively, weakly) complete*

As we have mentioned at the beginning of this section, the definitions above are of greater generality than what we would be requiring for our purpose The fibrational model for the theory of Constructions needs, essentially, fibered products and sums (defined in the similar fashion as products— i e in terms of left adjoints to re-indexing functors) Moreover, the basic theory is developed in an ambient category that is not a topos (but one that is, as we shall see, a sub-category of a quasi-topos) hence the weak notions are not of much relevance to us Thus we would mainly be using the notion of strong completeness for fibered categories (comprehension categories, to be precise, and with the requirement of fibered sums instead of general fiberwise finite limits) The corresponding notion of completeness (let us name it *CC-completeness*) in terms of internal categories would be framed in the next section, once we have the notion of a full internal sub-category

5.3 Full Internal Sub-categories

The notion of an internal full sub category (or full internal sub-category) is an interesting and rich one it allows a compact and elegant description of many of the phenomena we are interested in - particularly the various limit structures required or available in either of the frameworks we have studied (fibered or internal) In fact, because of its peculiar constitution, it may be seen to stand at the junction of the two modes of description, and allows a passage between the internal mode of description and the fibered mode In particular instances of the ambient category, the limit structure of the internal category confirms to that of the ambient category, simplifying much of the burden of proof and in fact of definition, as we shall see. The essential idea behind this object is that it is an internal category, but one which is (isomorphic to) some full sub-category of the ambient category. The notion originated from the consideration, that for any morphism f in a topos it should be possible to construct the (internal) category corresponding to the full sub-category consisting of the fibers of f. We present a systematic description below.

Construction 5.3.1 *([34, Section 0.1]) We present the basic structures that would be invoked in the definition of a functor known as the (internal) global sections functor* $\coprod(\mathbf{M}) : \sum(\mathbf{M}) \to \mathbf{B}^{\to}$ *(for an internal category* $\mathbf{C} \in \mathrm{Cat}(\mathbf{B})$*) defined below. We consider an object* $f : A \to M_0$ *in the fiber of* $\sum(\mathbf{M})$ *over* A*. The internal category* $\mathbf{M}$ *is assumed to have an internal terminal object, defined according to the notion of strong completeness presented in the last section. Consider the sequence of pullbacks shown in Figure 5-4 (top, left). The map* $\langle \perp, \mathrm{id}_{M_0} \rangle : M_0 \to M_0 \times M_0$ *is constituted by the constant map* $\perp : M_0 \to M_0$ *that maps every object to the terminal object, and the identity map* id_{M_0} *on* M_0*. The pullbacks give us an object* $f^*(p)$ *that we shall take to be the image of the object* $f : A \to M_0$ *under the action of the functor. Consider now, the notion of a generic family of maps,* $s : P_0 \to P_1$*. The objects* P_0 *and* P_1 *are obtained through the second and third pullbacks shown (top, right and second row, left). Since the map* $\langle \perp, \mathrm{id}_{M_0} \rangle$ *is a monic, so is the map* k *in the first pullback hence* X *is a sub-object of* M_1*, which implies that* P_0 *is a sub-object of* M_2*—the object of composable morphisms (we ignore some trivial isomorphisms). Hence internal composition* $\bullet_{\mathbf{M}}$ *"restricts" to* P_0 *and we easily derive that* $p \circ \bullet_{\mathbf{M}} = \partial_1 \circ q$*. Thus we have a mediating morphism* $s : P_0 \to P_1$ *in the fourth diagram (second row, right), and this gives us the generic family of maps. Now we consider a map* $\langle A, f : A \to M_0 \rangle \to \langle A, g : A \to M_0 \rangle$ *in the fiber of the externalization over* A *which is essentially a morphism* $h : A \to M_1$*. We can pullback the generic family along* h *(as shown in the fifth figure, in the third row), and thus obtain a morphism* $h^*(s)$*. We also have that* $f = \partial_0 \circ h$ *and* $g = \partial_1 \circ h$ *and hence the last figure allows us to conclude that* $h^*(P_0) \cong R$ *(where* R *is the domain of* $f^*(p)$*) and* $h^*(P_0) \cong S$ *(where* S *is the domain of* $g^*(p)$*). Hence* $h^*(s)$ *can be construed as a map* $\coprod(\mathbf{M})(f) \to \coprod(\mathbf{M})(g)$*, and hence the image of the map* $\langle A, f : A \to M_0 \rangle \to \langle A, g : A \to M_0 \rangle$ *considered.*

Definition 5.3.2 *We describe the action of a functor known as the* (internal) global sections *functor,* $\coprod(\mathbf{M}) : \sum(\mathbf{M}) \to \mathbf{B}^{\to}$ *for an internal category* $\mathbf{C} \in \mathrm{Cat}(\mathbf{B})$*, and where we assume that* $\mathbf{B}$ *has all the structure needed to perform the construction. The action of* $\coprod(\mathbf{M})$ *is described as follows.*

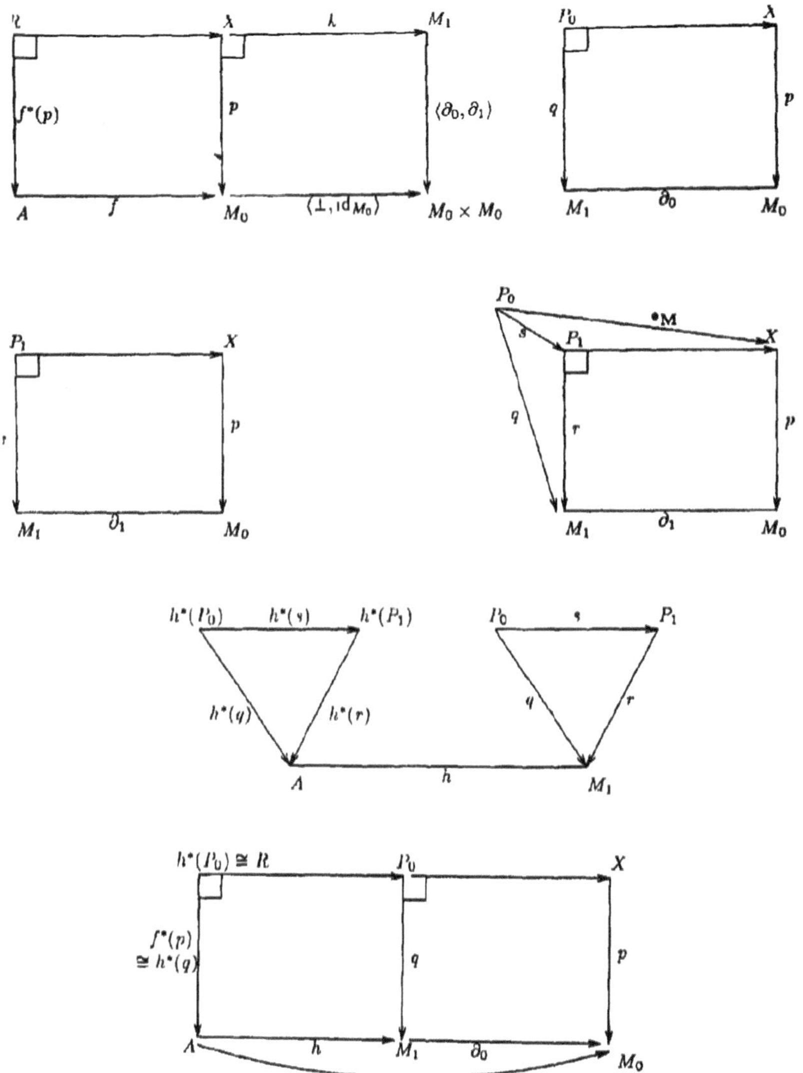

Figure 5.4 The internal global sections functor

On Objects: *For an object $f : A \to M_0$ in the fiber of $\sum(\mathbf{C})$ over A, the action is to map it to the object $f^*(p)$ shown in the Figure 5-4*

On Morphisms: *For a morphism $\langle A, f : A \to M_0\rangle \to \langle A, g : A \to M_0\rangle$ in the fiber over A, given as $\langle \mathrm{id}_A, h\rangle$ where $h : A \to M_1$, the action of $\coprod(\mathbf{M})$ is to map it to the morphism $h^*(s)$ indicated in the Figure 5-4*

The global sections functor thus intuitively corresponds to the notion of mapping an I-indexed collection of objects of an internal category onto an I-indexed collection of objects representing the (internal) global sections of the former On its basis we may define the notion of a full internal sub-category Recall that a full sub-category in the fibrational setting consists essentially of a collection of display maps notionally, the display maps represent families of objects of some (naive) sub-category of the ambient category, indexed by objects of the latter. In the case that the ambient category $\mathbf{B}$ is a topos (or at least locally cartesian closed), we may formulate this notion as a fibration $\mathbf{E}$ with a full and faithful cartesian functor to the codomain fibration $\mathbf{B}^{\to} \to \mathbf{B}$ In the general case we have the following definition

Definition 5.3.3 *An internal category $\mathbf{M} \in \mathrm{Cat}(\mathbf{B})$ is said to be a full internal sub-category if there is a full comprehension category of the form illustrated in Figure 5-5, which preserves fibered terminal objects if any*

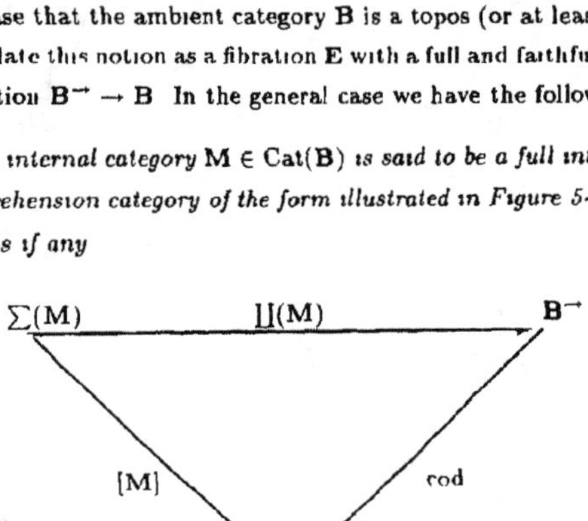

Figure 5-5 A full internal sub-category

Thus, a full internal sub category is one for which the (internal) global sections functor is a full comprehension category (and of course, with the commutation expressed in the figure) It may be interesting to contrast our definition with that given in [40, Definition 4 5 10]

The principal virtue of full internal sub-categories is that their limit structure agrees with that of the ambient category in an appropriate sense The sense in which this is so, can be conveyed through Theorem 5 3 4 below, which is part of the folklore of this subject We shall not prove it here, and a fuller account may be found in [34, Section 0.2]. The notion of a full internal sub-category was developed initially in connection with a topos, and the theorem is set in that context. As we have mentioned, in this setting, a full sub-category (in the fibrational sense) is given as fibration $\mathbf{E}$ with a full and faithful cartesian functor to the codomain fibration $\mathbf{B}^{\rightarrow} \rightarrow \mathbf{B}$. In terms of indexed categories, this may be represented as a full and faithful functor of indexed categories $\mathbf{E}(C) \rightarrow \mathbf{B}/C$. We have the following proposition.

Theorem 5.3.4 *Let $\mathbf{E}$ be a full sub-category of a locally cartesian closed category $\mathbf{B}$, with a terminal object, and so that the functor (of indexed categories) $\mathbf{E}(C) \rightarrow \mathbf{B}/C$ (where $\mathbf{E}(C) = \mathbf{E}_C$) preserves the terminal object, then, if $\mathbf{E}$ has finite limits, (i.e. fiberwise finite limits) and indexed products (i.e. fibered products), then these are preserved by the functor $\mathbf{E}(C) \rightarrow \mathbf{B}/C$.*

Since fibered limits and products are generally families of such indexed by the objects of $\mathbf{B}$, then when $\mathbf{E}$ is the externalization of an internal category, we may say that the limit structure of the internal category *agrees with* that of the ambient category. In the general case, when the ambient category is not locally cartesian closed, we may use the Theorem to formulate a *definition* of what it may mean for an internal category to be, for instance, *relatively cartesian closed*. Intuitively, it means, of course that the category is (internally) equipped with the structure of a relatively cartesian closed category. We may state this precisely as follows.

Definition 5.3.5 *A full internal sub-category is said to be a* full internal relatively cartesian closed sub-category *if the comprehension category in its definition (Definition 5.3.3) (i.e. the internal global sections functor) is a closed comprehension category.*

This definition, intuitively amounts to requiring that the sub-category internally represented by the internal category is relatively cartesian closed (actually, with strong sums). We shall see the utility of this definition in the succeeding chapters. In the sequel, we would encounter and be interested in full internal sub-categories that are internally relatively cartesian closed with respect to some sub-category of the ambient category. The precise definition of this is as follows.

Definition 5.3.6 *A full internal sub-category $\mathbf{M}$ of a category $\mathbf{E}$ is said to be a full internal relatively cartesian closed sub-category relative to a sub-category $\mathbf{B}$ of $\mathbf{E}$ if the functor $\coprod(\mathbf{M}) \circ \pi$ shown in Figure 5-6 is a closed comprehension category (which preserves fibered terminal objects if any), and such that the following conditions hold.*

1. *$\mathbf{M}$ is an internal category in $\mathbf{B}$ (and thus, in $\mathbf{E}$),*

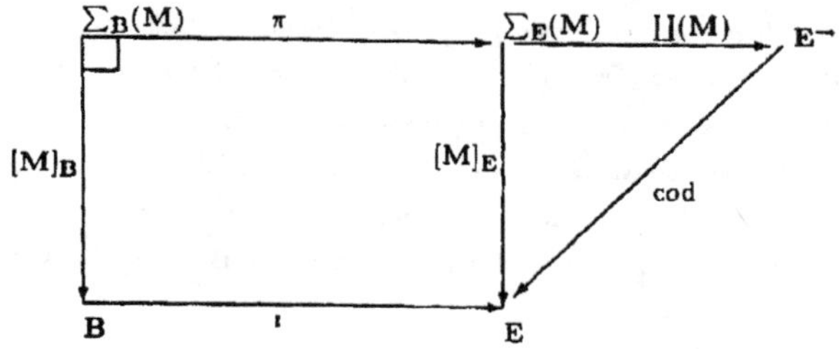

Figure 5-6 Relative closure.

2 The square indicated (where ι is the inclusion functor) is a change-of-base situation.

The externalizations have been subscripted with the names of the respective categories Note that according to the assumptions of the definition, $\coprod(\mathbf{M})$ is a full comprehension category, preserving terminal objects if any[3]

In the last part of this section we shall develop further the theme of the complementarity between the fibered and internal ways of looking at variable categories We shall see that if a fibration has a "small set of objects" relative to the base, (in the sense of having a *generic object*, as defined in the previous chapter) and furthermore, if it is *locally small*, then it is equivalent to the externalization of an internal category in the base We have the following important theorem, a version of which is proved as [40, Theorem 4 5 7], in our case, we assume only a display map structure in the base, rather than requiring all pullbacks.

Theorem 5.3.7 *Let p $\mathbf{E} \to \mathbf{B}$ be a locally small fibration, further, let $\mathbf{B}$ be a display map category, with the class of display maps closed under composition, and such that the representing arrows for the fiber-wise hom-sets are display maps, finally let the first projections from cartesian products also be display maps, then, every object $E \in \mathbf{E}$ determines an internal category (which we denote by ∇E), together with a full and faithful cartesian functor from the externalization $[E]$ $\sum(\nabla E) \to \mathbf{B}$ to p $\mathbf{E} \to \mathbf{B}$*

Proof: We shall refer to Figure 5-7 Let us see how we get our internal category first The object of objects, which we shall denote as Ω_0 is simply pE For the object of morphisms, we have the following construction consider the re-indexings of E along the cartesian projections π_0, π_1 $\Omega_0 \times \Omega_0 \to \Omega_0$, that is, $\pi_0^*(E)$ and $\pi_1^*(E)$ respectively

[3] We may also note that being a full internal sub-category of some full sub-category does *not* entail that it is one of the embedding category hence the condition has to be additionally imposed One simple reason for this is that the terminal objects of the latter and the former may not in general coincide, but even this is not a sufficient condition

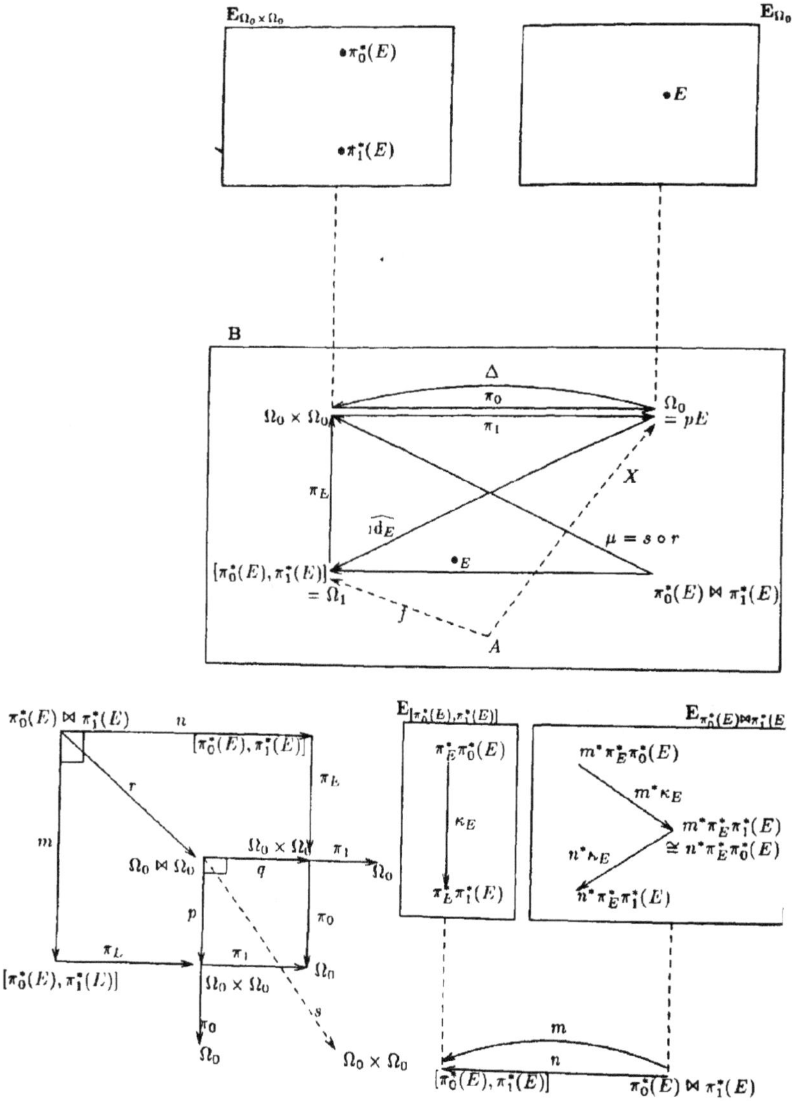

E_{Ω0×Ω0}
•π0*(E)
•π1*(E)
E_{Ω0}
•E
B
Δ
π0
π1
Ω0 × Ω0
Ω0
= pE
X
π_E
id_E
μ = s ∘ r
•_E
[π0*(E), π1*(E)]
= Ω1
f
A
π0*(E) ⋈ π1*(E)
π0*(E) ⋈ π1*(E)
n
[π0*(E), π1*(E)]
π_E
r
m
Ω0 ⋈ Ω0
Ω0 × Ω0
π1
Ω0
q
p
π0
π_E
π1
Ω0
[π0*(E), π1*(E)]
Ω0 × Ω0
π0
Ω0
s
Ω0 × Ω0
E_{[π0*(E), π1*(E)]}
π_E*π0*(E)
κ_E
π_E*π1*(E)
E_{π0*(E)⋈π1*(E)}
m*π_E*π0*(E)
m*κ_E
m*π_E*π1*(E)
≅ n*π_E*π0*(E)
n*κ_E
n*π_E*π1*(E)
m
n
[π0*(E), π1*(E)]
π0*(E) ⋈ π1*(E)

Figure 5-7

These objects are in the fiber $\mathbf{E}_{\Omega_0 \times \Omega_0}$, and we have the representing arrow (given by local smallness) π_E $[\pi_0^*(E), \pi_1^*(E)] \to \Omega_0 \times \Omega_0$ We shall claim that this is our object of morphisms Ω_1 To see this, let us construct the other components of the internal category

The internal domain and codomain morphisms are straightforward—namely· $\partial_0 = \pi_0 \circ \pi_E$ and $\partial_1 = \pi_1 \circ \pi_E$ respectively

Let us write Δ $\Omega_0 \to \Omega_0 \times \Omega_0$ for the diagonal arrow We note that $\pi_{0|1} \circ \Delta = \mathrm{id}_{\Omega_0}$ (where $\pi_{0|1}$ is either π_0 or π_1) Hence, $\Delta^* \circ \pi_{0|1}^* \cong (\pi_{0|1} \circ \Delta)^* \cong \mathrm{id}_{\Omega_0}^* \cong \mathrm{id}_{\mathbf{E}_{\Omega_0}}$ Hence $\mathrm{id}_E : E \to E$ can be thought of as isomorphic to an arrow (which we shall denote also as id_E) id_E $\Delta^*(\pi_0^*(E)) \to \Delta^*(\pi_1^*(E))$ Hence, by virtue of local smallness we have an (unique) arrow $\widehat{\mathrm{id}_E}$ $\Omega_0 \to [\pi_0^*(E), \pi_1^*(E)]$, such that $\widehat{\mathrm{id}_E}^*(\kappa_E) = \mathrm{id}_E$ (where κ_E is the generic map $\pi_E^*(\pi_0^*(E)) \to \pi_E^*(\pi_0^*(E))$ in the fiber over $[\pi_0^*(E), \pi_1^*(E)]$)—which gives us the internal identity

For the composition, we shall require the closure of display maps under arbitrary pullbacks We show the construction in the lower diagram of Figure 5-7. We denote by $\pi_0^*(E) \bowtie \pi_1^*(E)$, the pullback object of the pullback of $\pi_0 \circ \pi_E$. $[\pi_0^*(E), \pi_1^*(E)] \to \Omega_0$ over $\pi_1 \circ \pi_E$ · $[\pi_0^*(E), \pi_1^*(E)] \to \Omega_0$ By our assumptions, both π_E and π_0 are display maps, and so is their composition, hence the pullback exists and is a display map Now we also have the pullback of π_0 $\Omega_0 \times \Omega_0 \to \Omega_0$ over π_1 $\Omega_0 \times \Omega_0 \to \Omega_0$, we denote this pullback object as $\Omega_0 \bowtie \Omega_0$, and the (pullback) projections as p and q, as shown in the figure We have the obvious mediating morphism r $\pi_0^*(E) \bowtie \pi_1^*(E) \to \Omega_0 \bowtie \Omega_0$ We have the morphism $\pi_0 \circ p$ $\Omega_0 \bowtie \Omega_0 \to \Omega_0$ and $\pi_1 \circ q$ $\Omega_0 \bowtie \Omega_0 \to \Omega_0$, and hence the mediating morphism $s = \langle \pi_0 \circ p, \pi_1 \circ q \rangle$ $\Omega_0 \bowtie \Omega_0 \to \Omega_0 \times \Omega_0$ We write $\mu = s \circ r$, as indicated in the figure We have, through pullback, arrows m, n $\pi_0^*(E) \bowtie \pi_1^*(E) \to [\pi_0^*(E), \pi_1^*(E)]$ (and of course, corresponding compositions $\pi_E \circ m, \pi_E \circ n$ $\pi_0^*(E) \bowtie \pi_1^*(E) \to \Omega_0 \times \Omega_0$) The representing properties of $\pi_0^*(E) \bowtie \pi_1^*(E)$ give us maps $m^*(\kappa_E)$ $m^*\pi_E^*\pi_0^*(E) \to m^*\pi_E^*\pi_1^*(E)$, and $n^*(\kappa_E)$. $n^*\pi_E^*\pi_0^*(E) \to n^*\pi_E^*\pi_1^*(E)$, where κ_E is the generic map $\pi_E^*\pi_0^*(E) \to \pi_E^*\pi_1^*(E)$ in the fiber over $[\pi_0^*(E), \pi_1^*(E)]$ We have from our pullback, that $(\pi_1 \circ \pi_E \circ m) = (\pi_0 \circ \pi_E \circ n)$, hence we may say that $(m^* \circ \pi_E^* \circ \pi_1^*) \cong (n^* \circ \pi_E^* \circ \pi_0^*)$, hence we may compose and obtain a map $n^*(\kappa_E) \circ m^*(\kappa_E)$ $m^*\pi_E^*\pi_0^*(E) \to n^*\pi_E^*\pi_1^*(E)$. We may also note that $\pi_0 \circ \pi_E \circ m = \pi_0 \circ p \circ r = \pi_0 \circ s \circ r = \pi_0 \circ \mu$ (putting $\mu = s \circ r$ $\pi_0^*(E) \bowtie \pi_1^*(E) \to \Omega_0 \times \Omega_0$) and that $\pi_1 \circ \pi_E \circ n = \pi_1 \circ q \circ r = \pi_1 \circ s \circ r = \pi_1 \circ \mu$ Hence we have that our map $n^*(\kappa_E) \circ m^*(\kappa_E)$ is isomorphic to a map of $\mu^*(\pi_0^*(E)) \to \mu^*(\pi_1^*(E))$, and hence, by local smallness, we have an unique map $\bullet_E : \pi_0^*(E) \bowtie \pi_1^*(E) \to [\pi_0^*(E), \pi_1^*(E)]$, such that $\circ_E = \bullet_E^*(\kappa_E)$.

It is intuitively clear, rather tedious and not too illuminating to verify that the structure ∇E defined as the 6-tuple $(\Omega_0, \Omega_1, \partial_0, \partial_1, \widehat{id_E}, \bullet_E^*)$, in the base category $\mathbf{B}$, satisfies the axioms for an internal category. We shall now define a functor $\hat{E}$ from the externalization $\sum(\nabla E)$ to $\mathbf{E}$, its action on objects is as follows:

$$\hat{E} : [A \xrightarrow{X} \Omega_0] \longmapsto X^*(E)$$

Its action on arrows is given by the following construction. As we know, an arrow in $\sum(\nabla E)$, say from $X : A \to \Omega_0$ to $Y : B \to \Omega_0$ is of the form (u, f) where $u : A \to B$ in $\mathbf{B}$ and $f : A \to [\pi_0^*(E), \pi_1^*(E)]$ such that $\partial_0 \circ f = X$ and $\partial_1 \circ f = Y \circ u$. Now putting $v = \pi_E \circ f : A \to \Omega_0 \times \Omega_0$, we know that the representing property of $[\pi_0^*(E), \pi_1^*(E)]$ gives us an isomorphism $\varphi : \mathbf{B}/\Omega_0 \times \Omega_0(v, \pi_E) \to \mathbf{E}_A(v^*(\pi_0^*(E)), v^*(\pi_1^*(E)))$, of course $\varphi(f) = f^*(\kappa_E)$. Let us define $\bar{f} \equiv \varphi(f) : v^*(\pi_0^*(E)), v^*(\pi_1^*(E))$. Now we note the following: $X = \partial_0 \circ f = \pi_0 \circ \pi_E \circ f = \pi_0 \circ v$, hence $X^* \cong (v^* \circ \pi_0^*)$, again $Y \circ u = \partial_1 \circ f = \pi_1 \circ \pi_I \circ f = \pi_1 \circ v$, hence, $(u^* \circ Y^*) \cong (Y \circ u)^* \cong (v^* \circ \pi_1^*)$. Thus we may write (up to isomorphism of course) that $\bar{f} : X^*(E) \to u^* Y^*(E)$. Now we have the cartesian lifting of u, namely $\bar{u}(Y^*(E)) : u^* Y^*(E) \to Y^*(E)$; then we define the action of $\hat{E}$ on arrows as

$$[(u, f) : [A \xrightarrow{X} \Omega_0] \longrightarrow [B \xrightarrow{Y} \Omega_0]] \longmapsto [(\bar{u}(Y^*(E)) \circ \bar{f}) : X^*(E) \to Y^*(E)]$$

It is quite easy to prove (through the isomorphism φ, and the nature of this construction), that we have in $\hat{E}$, a full and faithful functor (see also [40, Theorem 4.5.7]).

Finally we note, that given a morphism $u : A \to B$ in $\mathbf{B}$, and an object $Y : B \to \Omega_0$ in the fiber of $[E]$ over B, we have that the re-indexing $u^*(Y) = Y \circ u$: the cartesian lifting of u at Y is $\bar{u}(Y) = (u, \widehat{id_E} \circ Y \circ u)$. Obviously, the domain of this lifting is the object $Y \circ u$ which is in the fiber over A. Let us see the image of this under the functor $\hat{E}$ as stated above, $\hat{E}(\bar{u}(Y)) = (\bar{u}(Y^*(E)) \circ \bar{f})$, where $f \equiv \widehat{id_E} \circ Y \circ u$[4]. Now $\bar{f}$ has been defined as $\varphi(f) = f^*(\kappa_E)$, hence we have that $\bar{f} = (\widehat{id_E} \circ Y \circ u)^*(\kappa_E) \cong u^*(Y^*(\widehat{id_E}^*(\kappa_E))) = u^*(Y^*(id_E)) = id_{(u^* \circ Y^*)(E)}$ (by functoriality). We have used the fact that $\widehat{id_E}^*(\kappa_E) = id_E$.[5] Hence we have that $\hat{E}(\bar{u}(Y)) = (\bar{u}(Y^*(E)) \circ \bar{f}) = \bar{u}(Y^*(E))$,

[4] The second occurrence of u refers to the cartesian lifting of u with respect to the fibration p, while the first is with respect to the fibration $[E]$.

[5] We may check that the domain and codomain of $\bar{f}$ are appropriate (i.e. both are $u^*(Y^*(E))$, up to isomorphism) since $f \equiv \widehat{id_E} \circ Y \circ u$, we have that the domain of $\bar{f}$ is $(\pi_E \circ f)^*(\pi_0^*(E)) \cong (\pi_0 \circ \pi_E \circ \widehat{id_E} \circ Y \circ u)^*$, but then $\pi_0 \circ \pi_I \circ \widehat{id_E} = id_E$, hence we have that $(\pi_I \circ f)^*(\pi_0^*(E)) \cong u^*(Y^*(E))$, again since $\pi_1 \circ \pi_E \circ \widehat{id_E} = id_E$, a similar argument yields that $(\pi_E \circ f)^*(\pi_1^*(E)) \cong u^*(Y^*(E))$.

which is obviously cartesian. Hence the proposition.

Theorem 5.3.8 *On the assumptions of Theorem 5.3.7, if the locally small fibration* $p: \mathbf{E} \to \mathbf{B}$ *has a generic object, then it is a small fibration.*

Proof: Let us denote the generic object as Λ, in the fiber over $p\Lambda \equiv \Omega_0$. We construct the internal category $\nabla\Lambda$ as in the proof of Theorem 5.3.7. The claim is that there is a categorical equivalence $\sum(\nabla\Lambda) \cong \mathbf{E}$. We have already seen the construction of the full, faithful and cartesian functor $\hat{\Lambda}: \sum(\nabla\Lambda) \to \mathbf{E}$, let us construct a functor $\check{\Lambda}: \mathbf{B} \to \sum(\nabla\Lambda)$. Since Λ is a generic object, for all $E \in \mathbf{E}$, we have a cartesian map $\vec{E}: E \to \Lambda$ (we assume that a choice of this map is implicit). Then the action of $\check{\Lambda}$ is as follows:

On objects $E \longmapsto p(\vec{E})$

On morphisms $E \xrightarrow{f} F \longmapsto (pf, [f])$

where $[f]$ is defined as follows. We have arrows $p\vec{F}, p\vec{E} \circ pf : pF \to \Omega_0$, hence an arrow $\langle p\vec{F}, p\vec{E} \circ pf\rangle : pF \to \Omega_0 \times \Omega_0$, obviously $\pi_0 \circ \langle p\vec{F}, p\vec{E} \circ pf\rangle = p\vec{F}$ and $\pi_1 \circ \langle p\vec{F}, p\vec{E} \circ pf\rangle = p\vec{E} \circ pf$. Hence, we have that $\langle p\vec{F}, p\vec{E} \circ pf\rangle^*(\pi_0^*(\Lambda)) \cong (p\vec{F})^*(\Lambda) = F$ and $\langle p\vec{F}, p\vec{E} \circ pf\rangle^*(\pi_1^*(\Lambda)) \cong (pf)^*((p\vec{E})^*(\Lambda)) = (pf)^*(E)$. Now by the cartesian property of the arrow $\overline{pf}(E) : (pf)^*(E) \to E$, we have an arrow $f' : F \to (pf)^*(E)$ such that $f = \overline{pf}(E) \circ f'$. As we have seen, we may write, up to isomorphism, that $f' : \langle p\vec{F}, p\vec{E} \circ pf\rangle^*(\pi_0^*(\Lambda)) \to \langle p\vec{F}, p\vec{E} \circ pf\rangle^*(\pi_1^*(\Lambda))$, hence this gives us, by local smallness, an arrow $[f] : pf \to [\pi_0^*(\Lambda), \pi_1^*(\Lambda)]$.

It is straightforward to verify that the pair $(\hat{\Lambda}, \check{\Lambda})$ forms an equivalence, and hence the proposition.

We have, on the other hand, that small fibrations are locally small and have a generic object. The proof is easy and we sketch it below.

Theorem 5.3.9 *Every small fibration is locally small and with a generic object.*

Proof: We refer to Figure 5-8. Consider the externalization $[\mathbf{C}]: \sum(\mathbf{C}) \to \mathbf{B}$ of an internal category $\mathbf{C}$ in $\mathbf{B}$. For arbitrary objects $X, X' : A \to C_0$ in the fiber over A, the representing object for the fiber-wise hom-set functor (or the generic family of maps $X \to X'$) is given as the object $[X, X']$ shown in the pullback square in the figure, along with the projection $\pi_0 : [X, X'] \to A$. The generic object for the fibration is simply the identity id_{C_0} in the fiber over C_0.

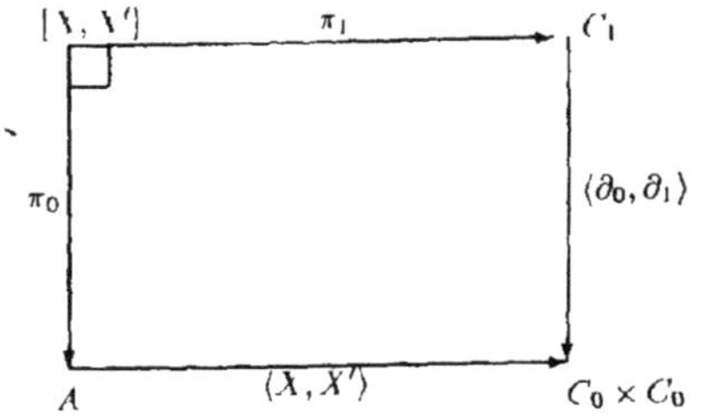

Figure 5-8 Small fibrations are locally small

A particularly simple instance of Theorem 5.3.7 is the construction of the following full internal sub-category— where in the context of the theorem, p is the codomain fibration $p = \text{cod}: \mathbf{B}^{\to} \to \mathbf{B}$ and with $\mathbf{B}$ being locally cartesian closed.

Construction 5.3.10 *Starting with any arrow $G: A \to C$ in* **B**, *a locally cartesian closed category, we may obtain an internal category* Full(G) *(that is actually a full internal sub-category) as follows. The object of objects is C, the object of morphisms is the domain of the local exponential $\pi_0^*(G) \Rightarrow \pi_1^*(G)$, where $\pi_0, \pi_1: C \times C \to C$ are the cartesian projections. The domain map $\partial_0 = \pi_0 \circ (\pi_0^*(G) \Rightarrow \pi_1^*(G))$ and the codomain map $\partial_1 = \pi_1 \circ (\pi_0^*(G) \Rightarrow \pi_1^*(G))$. The other components are straightforward.*

5.4 The CC-Categorical Framework

In this last section, we shall present the full Theory of Constructions, along with a general categorical model for it, developed by B. Jacobs ([40, Chapter 5]), reformulating within the framework of comprehension categories, an earlier construction of Hyland and Pitts ([38, Section 2.1.3]). We shall work within the general context of (Intuitionistic) Type theories, given in Section 3.1. We have the following two forms of judgements (each having three kinds of instances), made in contexts endowed with the structure of a poset

Structural Judgements	K,	$S \in K$,	$s \in A$
Equality Judgements	$K = L$,	$S = T \in K$,	$s = t \in A$

For the significance of the meta variables used in this presentation, we refer the reader to the conventions stated subsequently. We also have the general principle of substitution stated in Definition 3.1.2, along with the usual rules of equality at all levels. The expressions in the theory are stratified into two levels: Orders and Types. Terms at the first level are known

E-1	$\dfrac{s \in A \quad A = B \in \text{Type}}{s \in B}$	$\dfrac{S \in K \quad K = L}{S \in L}$
E-2	$\dfrac{s = t \in A \quad A = B \in \text{Type}}{s = t \in B}$	$\dfrac{S = T \in K \quad K = L}{S = T \in L}$
S-1	$\dfrac{p \in P\,[\Gamma] \quad q \in Q\,[\Gamma', \xi \in P > \Gamma]}{q(p/\xi) \in Q(p/\xi)\,[\Gamma'(p/\xi) > \Gamma]}$	$\dfrac{p = p' \in P\,[\Gamma] \quad q = q' \in Q\,[\Gamma', \xi \in P > \Gamma]}{q(p/\xi) = q'(p'/\xi) \in Q(p/\xi)\,[\Gamma'(p/\xi) > \Gamma]}$
S-2	$\dfrac{p \in P\,[\Gamma] \quad K\,[\Gamma', \xi \in P > \Gamma]}{K(p/\xi)\,[\Gamma'(p/\xi) > \Gamma]}$	$\dfrac{p = p' \in P\,[\Gamma] \quad K = K'\,[\Gamma', \xi \in P > \Gamma]}{K(p/\xi) = K'(p'/\xi)\,[\Gamma'(p/\xi) > \Gamma]}$
A	$\dfrac{A \in \text{Type}\,[\Gamma]}{x \in A\,[x \in A > \Gamma]}$	$\dfrac{K\,[\Gamma]}{X \in K\,[X \in K > \Gamma]}$
W	$\dfrac{A \in \text{Type}\,[\Gamma] \quad J\,[\Gamma' > \Gamma]}{J\,[\Gamma', x \in A > \Gamma]}$	$\dfrac{K\,[\Gamma] \quad J\,[\Gamma' > \Gamma]}{J\,[\Gamma', X \in K > \Gamma]}$

Table 5 1 Basic Clauses

as *Operators* while those at the second, simply as *Terms* Types are Operators of the Order *Type* of all Types We shall use the following variable conventions metavariables $K, L, M,$ would be used for Orders, $S, T, U,$ for Operators, $A, B, C,$ for Types, and $s, t, u,$ for Terms We shall use generic variables $P, Q, R,$ to denote expressions that are either Types or Orders, and $p, q, r,$ for those that are either Operators or Terms Operator variables will be generally taken from the set $X, Y, Z,$, while Term variables from $x, y, z,$ The free variable set of an expression χ will be denoted as $FV(\chi)$ For general variables, we shall use the symbols $\xi, \eta, \zeta,$ The account of the theory is taken from [38] Table 5 3 gives the clauses for the closure of Orders indexed over Types, Table 5 2 for the closure of Orders indexed over Orders, Table 5 4 for the closure of Types indexed over Types, and Table 5 5 for the closure of Types indexed over Orders We shall label the rules using the following convention a typical label for a clause shall be of the form A/B,X-Y-N where A and B will be from the set $\{O, I\}$ and interpreted as Order or Type respectively, the / symbol denotes "indexed over" (the A being indexed over B in this context), X will be a symbol from the set $\{1, \sum, \prod, C\}$ and interpreted respectively as Unit, Sum Product and Constant, Y shall be from the set $\{F, I, E, =\}$ and interpreted respectively as Formation, Introduction, Elimination and Equality, the number N would be optional and label multiple versions of a clause The general clauses for equality, substitution, assumption and weakening (labeled as E, S, A, W respectively) are collected together in Table 5 1 We would drop the A/B part of a label, in the tables below, since the caption on the table would contain that information

1-F	$\overline{1_O}$	
1-I	$\star_O \in 1_O$	
1 =	$\dfrac{T \in 1_T}{T = \star_O \in 1_O}$	
Σ-F	$\dfrac{L\,[X \in K, \Gamma]}{\Sigma X \in K\; L\,[\Gamma]}$	$\dfrac{K = K'[\Gamma] \quad L = L'\,[X \in K, \Gamma]}{\Sigma X \in K\; L = \Sigma X \in K'\; L'\,[\Gamma]}$
Σ-I	$\dfrac{S \in K \quad T \in L(S/X)}{\langle S, T\rangle \in \Sigma X \in K\; L}$	$\dfrac{S = S' \in K \quad T = T' \in L(S/X)}{\langle S, T\rangle = \langle S', T'\rangle \in \Sigma X \in K\; L}$
Σ-E-1	$\dfrac{U \in \Sigma X \in K\; L}{Fst(U) \in K}$	$\dfrac{U = U' \in \Sigma X \in K\; L}{Fst(U) = Fst(U') \in K}$
Σ-E-2	$\dfrac{U \in \Sigma X \in K\; L}{Snd(U) \in L(Fst(U)/X)}$	$\dfrac{U = U' \in \Sigma X \in K.L}{Snd(U) = Snd(U') \in L(Fst(U)/X)}$
Σ-=-1	$\dfrac{S \in K \quad T \in L(S/X)}{Fst(\langle S, T\rangle) = S \in K}$	$\dfrac{S \in K \quad T \in L(S/X)}{Snd(\langle S, T\rangle) = T \in L(S/X)}$
Σ-=-2	$\dfrac{U \in \Sigma X \in K\; L}{\langle Fst(U), Snd(U)\rangle = U \in \Sigma X \in K\; L}$	
Π-F	$\dfrac{L\,[X \in K, \Gamma]}{\Pi X \in K\; L\,[\Gamma]}$	$\dfrac{K = K'[\Gamma] \quad L = L'\,[X \in K, \Gamma]}{\Pi X \in K\; L = \Pi X \in K'\; L'\,[\Gamma]}$
Π-I	$\dfrac{T \in L\,[X \in K, \Gamma]}{\lambda X \in K\; T \in \Pi X \in K\; L\,[\Gamma]}$	$\dfrac{K = K'\,[\Gamma] \quad T = T' \in L\,[X \in K, \Gamma]}{\lambda X \in K\; T = \lambda X \in K'.T' \in \Pi X \in K\; L\,[\Gamma]}$
Π-E	$\dfrac{U \in \Pi X \in K\; L \quad S \in K}{US \in L(S/X)}$	$\dfrac{U = U' \in \Pi X \in K\; L \quad S = S' \in K}{US = U'S' \in L(S/X)}$
Π =	$\dfrac{S \in K\,[\Gamma] \quad T \in L\,[X \in K, \Gamma]}{(\lambda X \in K\; T)S = T(S/X) \in L(S/X)\,[\Gamma]}$	$\dfrac{U \in \Pi X \in K\; L}{\lambda X\; UX = U \in \Pi X \in K\; L}$
C-I-1	$Type$	$\overline{L(\xi_1, \ldots, \xi_n)\,[\Gamma]}$
C-I-2	$\dfrac{K\,[\Gamma]}{T(\xi_1, \ldots, \xi_n) \in K\,[\Gamma]}$	

Table 5.2 Orders indexed over Orders

Σ-F	$\frac{K\ [x \in A, \Gamma]}{\Sigma x \in A.K\ [\Gamma]}$	$\frac{A = A' \in Type\ [\Gamma] \quad K = K'\ [x \in A, \Gamma]}{\Sigma x \in A.K = \Sigma x \in A'.K'\ [\Gamma]}$
Σ-I	$\frac{s \in A \quad S \in K(s/x)}{\langle s, S\rangle \in \Sigma x \in A.K}$	$\frac{s = s' \in A \quad S = S' \in K(s/x)}{\langle s, S\rangle = \langle s', S'\rangle \in \Sigma x \in A.K}$
Σ-E-1	$\frac{T \in \Sigma x \in A.K}{fst(T) \in A}$	$\frac{T = T' \in \Sigma x \in A.K}{fst(T) = fst(T') \in A}$
Σ-E-2	$\frac{T \in \Sigma x \in A.K}{Snd(T) \in K(fst(T)/x)}$	$\frac{T = T' \in \Sigma x \in A.K}{Snd(T) = Snd(T') \in K(fst(T)/x)}$
Σ-=-1	$\frac{s \in A \quad S \in K(s/x)}{fst(\langle s, S\rangle) = s \in A}$	$\frac{s \in A \quad S \in K(s/x)}{Snd(\langle s, S\rangle) = S \in K(s/x)}$
Σ-=-2	$\frac{T \in \Sigma x \in A.K}{\langle fst(T), Snd(T)\rangle = T \in \Sigma x \in A.K}$	
Π-F	$\frac{K\ [x \in A, \Gamma]}{\Pi x \in A.K\ [\Gamma]}$	$\frac{A = A' \in Type\ [\Gamma] \quad K = K'\ [x \in A, \Gamma]}{\Pi x \in A.K = \Pi x \in A'.K'\ [\Gamma]}$
Π-I	$\frac{S \in K\ [x \in A, \Gamma]}{\lambda x \in A.S \in \Pi x \in A.K\ [\Gamma]}$	$\frac{A = A' \in Type\ [\Gamma] \quad S = S' \in K\ [x \in A, \Gamma]}{\lambda x \in A.S = \lambda x \in A'.S' \in \Pi x \in A.K\ [\Gamma]}$
Π-E	$\frac{T \in \Pi x \in A.K \quad s \in A}{Ts \in K(s/x)}$	$\frac{T = T' \in \Pi x \in A.K \quad s = s' \in A}{Ts = T's' \in K(s/x)}$
Π-=	$\frac{s \in A\ [\Gamma] \quad S \in K\ [x \in A, \Gamma]}{(\lambda x \in A.S)s = S(s/x) \in K(s/x)\ [\Gamma]}$	$\frac{T \in \Pi x \in A.K}{\lambda x.Tx = T \in \Pi x \in A.K}$

Table 5.3: Orders indexed over Types.

1-F
$$1_T \in Type$$

1-I
$$\star_T \in 1_T$$

$\bullet\,-$
$$t \in 1_T$$
$$t = \star_T \in 1_T$$

Σ-F
$$\frac{B \in Type\ [x \in A, \Gamma]}{\Sigma x \in A\ B \in Type\ [\Gamma]} \qquad \frac{A = A' \in Type[\Gamma] \quad B = B' \in Type\ [x \in A, \Gamma]}{\Sigma x \in A.B = \Sigma x \in A'.B' \in Type\ [\Gamma]}$$

Σ-I
$$\frac{s \in A \quad t \in B(s/x)}{\langle s, t \rangle \in \Sigma x \in A.B} \qquad \frac{s = s' \in A \quad t = t' \in B(s/x)}{\langle s, t \rangle = \langle s', t' \rangle \in \Sigma x \in A.B}$$

Σ-E-1
$$\frac{u \in \Sigma x \in A\ B}{fst(u) \in A} \qquad \frac{u = u' \in \Sigma x \in A\ B}{fst(u) = fst(u') \in A}$$

Σ-E-2
$$\frac{u \in \Sigma x \in A\ B}{snd(u) \in B(fst(u)/x)} \qquad \frac{u = u' \in \Sigma x \in A\ B}{snd(u) = snd(u') \in B(fst(u)/x)}$$

Σ-=-1
$$\frac{s \in A \quad t \in B(s/x)}{fst(\langle s, t \rangle) = s \in A} \qquad \frac{s \in A \quad t \in B(s/x)}{snd(\langle s, t \rangle) = t \in B(s/x)}$$

Σ-=-2
$$\frac{u \in \Sigma x \in A.B}{\langle fst(u), snd(u) \rangle = u \in \Sigma x \in A\ B}$$

Π-F
$$\frac{B \in Type\ [x \in A, \Gamma]}{\Pi x \in A\ B \in Type\ [\Gamma]} \qquad \frac{A = A' \in Type[\Gamma] \quad B = B' \in Type\ [x \in A, \Gamma]}{\Pi x \in A\ B = \Pi x \in A'\ B' \in Type\ [\Gamma]}$$

Π-I
$$\frac{t \in B\ [x \in A, \Gamma]}{\lambda x \in A\ t \in \Pi x \in A.B\ [\Gamma]} \qquad \frac{A = A' \in Type\ [\Gamma] \quad t = t' \in B\ [x \in A, \Gamma]}{\lambda x \in A\ t = \lambda x \in A'\ t' \in \Pi x \in A.B\ [\Gamma]}$$

Π-E
$$\frac{u \in \Pi x \in A\ B \quad s \in A}{us \in B(s/x)} \qquad \frac{u = u' \in \Pi x \in A\ B \quad s = s' \in A}{us = u's' \in B(s/x)}$$

Π-=
$$\frac{s \in A\ [\Gamma] \quad t \in B\ [x \in A, \Gamma]}{(\lambda x \in A\ t)s = t(s/x) \in B(s/x)\ [\Gamma]} \qquad \frac{u \in \Pi x \in A\ B}{\lambda x\ ux = u \in \Pi x \in A\ B}$$

C-I
$$\frac{A\ [\Gamma]}{f(x_1, \quad , x_n) \in A\ [\Gamma]}$$

Table 5.4 Types indexed over Types

Σ-F
$$\frac{A \in Type\,[X \in K, \Gamma]}{\Sigma X \in K\, A \in Type\,[\Gamma]} \qquad \frac{K = K'[\Gamma] \quad A = A' \in Type\,[X \in K, \Gamma]}{\Sigma X \in K.A = \Sigma X \in K'\, A' \in Type\,[\Gamma]}$$

Σ-I
$$\frac{S \in K \quad s \in A(S/X)}{\langle S, s\rangle \in \Sigma X \in K.A} \qquad \frac{S = S' \in K \quad s = s' \in A(S/X)}{\langle S, s\rangle = \langle S', s'\rangle \in \Sigma X \in K.A}$$

Σ-E-1
$$\frac{s \in \Sigma X \in K\, A\,[\Gamma] \quad t \in B(\langle X, x\rangle/z)\,[x \in A, X \in K, \Gamma]}{E(s, (X, x)\, t) \in B(s/z)\,[\Gamma]}$$

Σ-E-2
$$\frac{s = s' \in \Sigma X \in K.A\,[\Gamma] \quad t = t' \in B(\langle X, x\rangle/z)\,[x \in A, X \in K, \Gamma]}{E(s, (X, x)\, t) = E(s', (X, x).t') \in B(s/z)\,[\Gamma]}$$

Σ-=-1
$$\frac{S \in K\,[\Gamma] \quad s \in A(S/X)\,[\Gamma] \quad t \in B(\langle X, x\rangle/z)\,[x \in A, X \in K, \Gamma]}{E(\langle S, s\rangle, (X, x)\, t) = t(S/X, s/x) \in B(\langle S, s\rangle/z)\,[\Gamma]}$$

Σ-=-2
$$\frac{s \in \Sigma X \in K\, A\,[\Gamma] \quad t \in B[z \in \Sigma X \in K\, A, \Gamma]}{E(s, (X, x)\, t(\langle X, x\rangle/z)) = t(s/z) \in B(s/z)\,[\Gamma]}$$

Π-F
$$\frac{A \in Type\,[X \in K, \Gamma]}{\Pi X \in K\, A \in Type\,[\Gamma]} \qquad \frac{K = K'[\Gamma] \quad A = A' \in Type\,[X \in K, \Gamma]}{\Pi X \in K\, A = \Pi X \in K'\, A' \in Type\,[\Gamma]}$$

Π-I
$$\frac{s \in A\,[X \in K, \Gamma]}{\lambda X \in K.s \in \Pi X \in K\, A\,[\Gamma]} \qquad \frac{K = K'\,[\Gamma] \quad s = s' \in A\,[X \in K, \Gamma]}{\lambda X \in K\, s = \lambda X \in K'\, s' \in \Pi X \in K\, A\,[\Gamma]}$$

Π-E
$$\frac{t \in \Pi X \in K\, A \quad S \in K}{tS \in A(S/X)} \qquad \frac{t = t' \in \Pi X \in K\, A \quad S = S' \in K}{tS = t'S' \in A(S/X)}$$

Π-=
$$\frac{S \in K\,[\Gamma] \quad s \in A\,[X \in K, \Gamma]}{(\lambda X \in K.s)S = s(S/X) \in A(S/X)\,[\Gamma]} \qquad \frac{t \in \Pi X \in K\, A}{\lambda X\, tX = t \in \Pi X \in K.A}$$

Table 5 5 Types indexed over Orders.

The assumption and weakening clauses have the restriction that x and X do not appear in Γ or in Γ' As we can see, the elimination clauses for the sums of Types over Orders are formulated in the Martin-Lof style, using the elimination constant E This is due to a syntactic constraint which does not allow the projection constant Fst to be defined. The basic categorical model for this theory was given by Hyland and Pitts in [38] The model, and its underlying logic was presented partially in Chapter 3, the system considered at that time was simply the system of Types indexed over themselves (corresponding to the clauses in Table 5 4) The categorical model for the complete system is a generalization of the earlier structure, which was a relatively cartesian closed category In this generalization, we need *two* classes of display maps—representing the (dependent) Types and Orders The indexing of Orders over Types allows, for any Type A, the formation of the Order $\Sigma x \cdot A\ 1_O$· hence, we may model this by requiring that the display maps for Types be contained in that for Orders Since Display map categories are more elegantly formulated as Comprehension Categories (as we have described in Chapter 4), we shall model the theory in a system of Comprehension Categories There are essentially two other significant points we have to take care of First, the fact that we have an Order *Type* whose Operators are all Types, requires that we model the free Type variable (i e $X \in Type$), this is done by requiring the fibration (corresponding to the Comprehension category for Types) have a *generic object* Second, the rules for the sum of Types indexed over Orders needs some care they are quite strong (in a technical sense too) and inadequate care in modeling them would lead us to a version Girard's Paradox, specifically, in categorical models modeling strong sums, sums are usually given by *composition* (with the morphism underlying the substitution functor), in this case, while sums would still be given as left adjoints to the substitution functor, the incapacity to define the projection constant Fst, does not permit us to model the situation through composition any more, yet, the sums remain strong of course the problem is handled then, by requiring that the inclusion of the (fibration of) Types into the (fibration of) Orders, have a (fibered) *left adjoint*, this, along with the requirement that we have strong sums in Types, give us a model for the strong sums of Orders indexed over Types The resulting categorical structure is described in [40]—where it is called a *CC-Category*—and we reproduce it in Definition 5 4 1 below

Definition 5.4.1 *A CC Category is the structure shown in Figure 5-9, and with the following conditions on the constituents*

1 *$\mathcal{Q}$ is a closed comprehension category*

2 *$\mathcal{I}$ is a full and faithful functor, and $\mathcal{P} = \mathcal{Q} \circ \mathcal{I}$ is a closed comprehension category,*

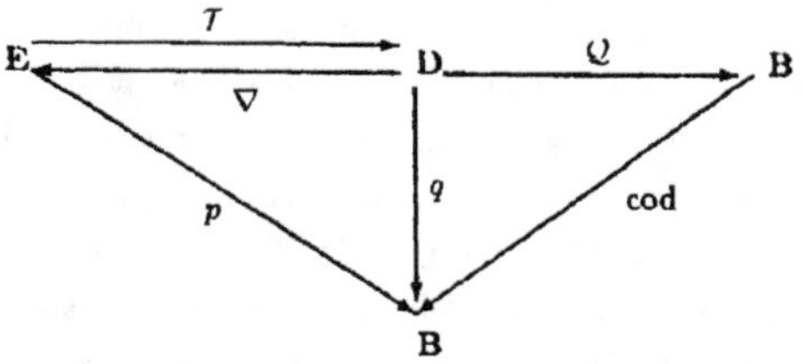

Figure 5-9 The CC-Category

moreover, $\mathcal{I}$ is a morphism from the fibration $p = \text{cod} \circ \mathcal{P}$ to $q = \text{cod} \circ \mathcal{Q}$, hence, it is a full, faithful and cartesian functor

3. *$\mathcal{I}$ has a fibered left adjoint ∇*

4. *There is an object $\Omega \in \mathbf{D}$ such that $q\Omega$ is terminal, and p has a generic object above $\mathcal{Q}_0\Omega$*

It is fairly straightforward to verify that this structure is indeed a model for the theory of Constructions. We may remark that the left adjoint ∇ endows $\mathcal{P}$ with $\mathcal{Q}$-sums (and products), on the other hand, $\mathcal{Q}$ has $\mathcal{P}$ sums (and products) through $\mathcal{I}$. Both classes of sums are strong, and we can see that all the clauses in the theory are appropriately modeled. In particular, Theorem 4.2.15 entails, in this context, that p is a locally small fibration, and thus (from Theorem 5.3.8) that it is a small fibration (see below for precise statements), this allows us to model the Order *Type*, and the rest of the structure gives us impredicative products over Types. We may summarize the relevant entailments of Definition 5.4.1

Proposition 5.4.2 *([40, Proposition 5.2.7]) In the context of Definition 5.4.1, we have the following propositions*

1. *The fibration p is a fibered cartesian closed category*

2. *The fibration p is a small fibration*

3. *If the functor $\mathcal{P} = \mathcal{Q}\mathcal{I}$ is the (internal) global sections functor for the internal category given on the basis of Item 2 above, then the latter is a full internal relatively cartesian closed sub-category (in $\mathbf{B}$)*

Proof. Item 1 follows from Theorem 4.2.13. From Theorem 4.2.15 (and the previous item) we have that p is locally small; we also know (from Proposition 4.2.6) that $\mathbf{B}$ is a display map category, and we can verify that the various pullbacks needed in the proofs of Theorems 5 3 7 and 5 3 8 exist in **B**—which entails Item 2 Finally, Item 3 follows from Definition 5 3.5

Remark 5.4.3 *We should remark that, in close analogy to Theorem 3 1.5 of Chapter 3, which asserted the (bi-) categorical equivalence between the category of Martin-Löf Type theories and that of relatively cartesian closed categories, we may demonstrate one between the category of CC-categories (appropriately defined) and that of the theories of constructions (again, with an appropriate notion of morphisms) The arguments are a straightforward generalization of those for the earlier theorem and we do not labour the details. The interested reader may consult the reference ([38, §2 13]) where the argument is indicated, though in terms of the display map formulation rather than in those of a CC-Category, the adaptation to to the latter requires minor and systematic alterations which can be easily carried out on the basis of Propositions 4 2 2 and 4 2 6 of Chapter 4*

We shall invoke this result implicitly in the next chapter, where we would induce a theory of constructions on the basis of a concrete instance of a CC-Category, the latter is essentially the relatively cartesian closed structure $\mathfrak{Y}$ in Chapter 3, extended into an impredicative theory, and cast in the current framework of Comprehension categories.

Chapter 6

The Theory of Constructions

In Section 3 2 we have seen the construction of the category $\Im$, which was a model for a calculus of dependent Types In this section, we shall see if we can extend our framework so as to capture impredicative features, and thus model the whole of the Theory of Constructions. The fundamental difficulty is to model an *Order* of all Types in the system syntactically, this amounts to modeling a free Type variable. The basic strategy is to take advantage of the fact that in our construction of $\Im$, every Type was presented through an expression of the language Λ_0· hence, we may form an object consisting of all these terms (appropriately quotiented), which then becomes an object of the *names* of all the Types in the system Of course, this is not a Type itself, hence, we have to have a level of Orders besides the Types, and then see if this level is closed under the usual forms of quantification As was the case for $\Im$, every Type and Order in the system, is presented through (the equivalence class of) a certain syntactic expression—of a language that extends the language Λ_0 of Chapter 3 The constructions are carried out within the framework developed in the last two chapters—namely fibered category theory, and specifically, Comprehension categories. The resulting structure would be seen to be what has been described in the last chapter as a *CC-Category*. In this structure, the category of Types could be conceptualized as a full internal sub-category within the base category of the CC-Category, and admitting the kind of completeness needed to model the theory of Constructions (CC-Completeness, as we have informally termed it) Thus, the first part of our program for a "Constructive semantics of the λ-Calculus"—in which we induce (under the rules of dependency and quantification) a full constructive Type theory on the basis of the Types (of proof-objects) of the pure terms—is substantiated

6.1 The Syntax

We initiate the constructions by defining a calculus of terms and operators, which can be seen to extend the language Λ of Chapter 3. We shall re-use some of the symbols from that chapter, since they would be interpreted only in the current context. We should note that the next few definitions are not to be considered as independent of each other, but as sub-definitions of a single definition of the class (names) of Types and Orders, which we shall denote as Θ^0, the definition being inductive, should be interpreted as the smallest set of expressions satisfying it. We define below, a language that would consist of all the expressions that make up the names of the Types and Orders.

Definition 6.1.1 *Let us fix a set of variables $\mho$, and a suitably large set of (constant)* typed *function symbols χ. each function symbol F has a type consisting of a pair of expressions in Θ^0, the first component of which would be denoted as* dom(F) *and the second as* cod(F) *(a more precise qualification of the size of the set χ would be made subsequently). Thus, a typical element of χ would be denoted as F : $(\mathrm{dom}(F), \mathrm{cod}(F))$, though we would suppress the type of F whenever this information is unnecessary. The symbol λ would denote the class of λ-terms generated from $\mho$. The substitution operator would be denoted as $\cdot(\ /\ )$, and the pairing operator as $\langle\ ,\ \rangle$. The language Λ' is defined inductively by the following rules*

1 $\lambda \subset \Lambda'$

2 $1_O, \Gamma \in \Lambda'$

3 $\Sigma x : \alpha\ \beta \in \Lambda'$, *for* $\alpha, \beta \in \Lambda'$, $x \in \mho$

4 $\Pi x : \alpha\ \beta \in \Lambda'$, *for* $\alpha, \beta \in \Lambda'$, $x \in \mho$

5 $\alpha(F(\beta)/x) \in \Lambda'$, *for* $F \in \chi$, $\alpha, \beta \in \Lambda'$, x free *in* α *(see below)*

6 $\langle \alpha, \beta \rangle \in \Lambda'$, *for* $\alpha, \beta \in \Lambda'$

7 $\langle F, n \rangle$, *for* $F \in \chi$, $n \in \lambda$

8 $\nabla(T) \in \Lambda'$, *for* $T \in \Lambda'$

We shall use the following convention with respect to Item 6. when both α and β are λ-terms, the pairing operator would be identified with the pairing combinator of the λ-Calculus, hence, it would be purely a notational device (unless otherwise indicated). We have in this language, in addition to the standard (unary) binding operator λx, (binary) binding operators $\Sigma x : \alpha$.

and $\Pi x.\alpha$, the rules for bound variables are given as in Definition 3.2.3. We shall denote by Λ'^0 the class of *closed* Λ'-terms.

We shall define on the set of Λ'-terms, an equivalence relation $\simeq$, similar to the relation defined in Definition 3.2.4 and signified by the same symbol.

Definition 6.1.2 *For arbitrary Λ'-terms A, a, we define by $A(a/x)$ the result of substituting the* free *occurrences of x in A, by a. The equivalence relation $\simeq$ on the class of Λ'-terms is defined to smallest relation satisfying the following set of inductive rules*

1. *$\simeq$ on the sub-class $\lambda \subset \Lambda'$ is the relation $\simeq$ as defined in Definition 3.2.1,*

2. *for Λ-terms A, B, we have that $A \simeq B$ if and only if there exists a Λ'-term C with variables $x_1, \ldots, x_n$ free, such that $A = C(a_1/x_1, \ldots, a_n/x_n)$ and $B = C(b_1/x_1, \ldots, b_n/x_n)$, for Λ'-terms $a_1, \ldots, a_n$ and $b_1, \ldots, b_n$, with $a_i \simeq b_i$ for $1 \leq i \leq n$*

Thus $\simeq$ is the (syntactic) congruence generated by the relation restricted to the subset of λ-terms. The equivalence classes with respect to the relation $\simeq$ would be denoted by the [ ] notation as before.

The Orders and Types that constitute our system, would be presented on the basis of $\simeq$-equivalence classes of a sub class of (closed) Λ'-expressions: the corresponding objects in the category of Types and Orders would be the *denotations* of these expressions: the link between a Λ'^0 expression naming a Type (or an Order) and its denotation would be established through an operation $\oint$ as in Chapter 3. The classes of expressions constituting the names of the Types and Orders would be defined in two stages: first, we shall over-generate the classes, and present, on the basis of the inductive syntax of Definition 6.1.3 below, a system of expressions that is a proper superset of the actual system of (the names of) the Types and Orders, in the next stage, we shall prune the system to yield us the valid classes of expressions, on the basis of the well-definedness of the denotational operation defined subsequently. The system of expressions is defined below: they are stratified into sub-classes corresponding to the Types and Orders fibered over (dependent on) themselves and each other.

Definition 6.1.3 *The strata are given through the following set of simultaneous inductive definitions*

Types *The set of Type expressions is denoted by the symbol Λ, and is composed of the classes Λ_0 and Λ_1 defined below*

Basic Types *The set of Basic Type expressions, Λ_0, is the smallest set satisfying the following conditions*

$$[x] \in \Lambda_0 \quad \textit{where} \quad x \in \lambda$$
$$[\Sigma x \quad \alpha\, \beta] \in \Lambda_0 \quad \textit{where} \quad [\alpha], [\beta] \in \Lambda_0$$
$$[\Pi x \quad \alpha\, \beta] \in \Lambda_0 \quad \textit{where} \quad [\alpha], [\beta] \in \Lambda_0$$
$$[\nabla(T)] \in \Lambda_0 \quad \textit{where} \quad [T] \in \Phi$$

Complex Types *The set of Complex Type expressions, Λ_1, is given by the following conditions*

$$[\Sigma x \quad \phi\, \alpha] \in \Lambda_1 \quad \textit{where} \quad [\phi] \in \Lambda_1 \bigcup \Phi, [\alpha] \in \Lambda_0$$
$$[\Pi x \quad \phi\, \alpha] \in \Lambda_1 \quad \textit{where} \quad [\phi] \in \Lambda_1 \bigcup \Phi, [\alpha] \in \Lambda_0$$

Orders *The set of Order expressions Φ is the smallest set satisfying the following conditions.*

$$[1_O], [\Gamma] \in \Phi$$
$$[\Sigma x \quad \phi\, R] \in \Phi \quad \textit{where} \quad [\phi] \in \Phi \bigcup \Lambda, [R] \in \Phi$$
$$[\Pi x \quad \phi\, R] \in \Phi \quad \textit{where} \quad [\phi] \in \Phi \bigcup \Lambda, [R] \in \Phi$$

We have, in addition to the rules above, the following set of substitution and transformation rules, each is applicable to either of the strata Λ_1 or Φ, for which we use the generic symbol Δ

$$[\Sigma y \quad A\, B(F(y)/x)] \in \Delta \quad \textit{where} \quad [\Sigma x \quad C\, B] \in \Delta, F \quad \langle [A], [C] \rangle$$
$$[\Sigma x \quad A\, \Sigma y \quad B\, C(\langle x, y\rangle / y)] \in \Delta \quad \textit{where} \quad [\Sigma y \quad (\Sigma x \quad A\, B)\, C] \in \Delta$$
$$[\Sigma x \quad A.\Pi y \quad B\, C(\langle x, y\rangle / y)] \in \Delta \quad \textit{where} \quad [\Sigma y \quad (\Sigma x\, .\, A.B).C] \in \Delta$$

In the statement of these rules, we use the pairing operator explicitly *(cf. remark following Definition 6 1 1) We shall denote the union $\Lambda \cup \Phi$ as Θ The restriction of the classes of the expressions defined above to (equivalence classes of) closed Λ'-terms would be denoted by $\Lambda_0^0, \Lambda_1^0, \Phi^0$ respectively, and Λ^0, and Θ^0*

From the term syntax of Λ', we have the notion of an *occurrence* (of a sub-term) in any term x such that $[x] \in \Theta_0$, we shall denote by $\mathrm{occ}(x)$ the set of occurrences in x, which is but the domain of x (when x is considered as a tree) The replacement of the sub-term at $\gamma \in \mathrm{occ}(x)$ by some term y would be denoted as $x[y]_\gamma$, and thus, the obvious generalization for a set of replacements at a set of occurrences The sub-term of x at $\gamma \in \text{occ}(x)$ would be denoted as $x|_\gamma$

The (partial) operation $\oint$ which gives the *denotations* of the classes of expression in Θ^0 defined above, and which are the objects in the category of Orders and Types, is defined below We have seen, in Chapter 3, that the denotations of the Types are essentially sets of equivalence classes of λ-terms with respect to the relation $\simeq$ That would remain to be the case for the basic Types; for the other classes, they would be sets of equivalence classes of (a sub-class of) Λ'-terms, with respect to the $\simeq$. We shall embed these sets within a class of objects that are known in the literature as ω-Sets These are essentially sets, but with a set of *realizers* (λ-terms) attached to each element We furnish a (slightly modified, *cf* Remark 6 2 27) definition below, though the salient properties of the category ω-**Set** would be explored in the next chapter

Definition 6.1.4 *The category* ω-**Set** *has the following constituents*

Objects: *Objects are pairs* $\langle X, \vdash \rangle$ *where* X *is a set and* $\vdash$ *is a relation in* $\lambda \times X$, *and such that* $\forall x \in X\ \exists n \in \lambda\ n \vdash x$. *We say that* n realizes x *We would annotate the relation as* $\vdash_X$ *whenever necessary*

Morphisms: *A morphism* f $\langle X, \vdash_X \rangle \to \langle Y, \vdash_Y \rangle$ *is a map* $f \cdot X \to Y$ *satisfying the following condition*

$$\exists n \in \lambda\ \forall x \in X\ \forall p \in \lambda\ (p \vdash_X x \Rightarrow (n\ \ p) \vdash_Y f(a))$$

we say that n tracks f *(denoted by* $n \vdash f$*), for any morphism* f, *we shall denote a code which tracks it, generically, as* $\hat{f}$

The operation $\oint$ acts on Θ^0 terms to yield objects of the category ω-**Set** it is defined relative to an (partial) *interpretation* $\langle\ \rangle$ (given in advance) of the set χ of function symbols as morphisms of the category For F $\langle A, B \rangle$, we shall stipulate that $\langle F \rangle$ $\oint A \to \oint B$, whenever defined Obviously, not every symbol in the set χ need have a well-defined interpretation—for instance, either of the denotations of domain and co-domain may not be defined, we would be concerned, in what follows, only with that subset of χ that has a valid interpretation—we would call it the *valid* subset, and use the symbol $\bar{\chi}$ for it As mentioned earlier, we shall qualify the size of the set χ as being large enough for every morphism f $\oint[A] \to \oint[B]$ ($A, B \in \Theta^0$) in ω-**Set** to have some symbol $F \in \chi$ such that $\langle F \rangle = f$

The rules for the evaluation of the operation $\oint$ requires that we should consider it as defined over a class of expressions which is a superset of Θ^0 this larger class would be denoted by the symbol as Θ^0_+, and is defined below

Definition 6.1.5 *The class of expressions known denoted as Θ^0_+ are obtained according to the following rules*

$$\Theta^0 \subset \Theta^0_+$$

$$[\Sigma x \quad A\ B] \in \Theta_0 \bigwedge [a] \in \oint[A] \quad \Rightarrow \quad [B(a/x)] \in \Theta^0_+$$

The main clauses in the definition of $\oint$ below, are supplemented by the following substitution rule for the evaluation of the operation on Θ^0_+ expressions containing occurrences of function symbols from (the valid subset of) χ

- *for x containing a sequence $\gamma \equiv \{\gamma_1, \cdot \quad , \gamma_n\} \subset \mathrm{occ}(x)$ of occurrences such that $\forall 1 \leq i \leq n \ x|_{\gamma_i} = F_i(p_i)$ with $F_i \in \bar{\chi}$, we have that*

$$\oint[x] = \oint[y] \text{ where } \exists q_1 \quad q_n \ \forall 1 \leq i \leq n \ [q_i] = \langle F_i\rangle([p_i]) \bigwedge y \equiv x[q_1]_{\gamma_1} \quad [q_n]_{\gamma_n}$$

The main clauses in the definition of $\oint$ on Θ^0 expressions are set out below.

Definition 6 1 6 *The operation $\oint$ yields objects in the category ω-**Set**, with the underlying sets consisting of certain $\simeq$-equivalence classes of terms of a sub-class of Λ' expressions The definition uses an auxiliary operation operation $\bar{\nabla}(\ )$ which is defined subsequently*

$$\oint[x] \quad = \quad \{[b(\Omega/\bot)] \mid \exists y \in \lambda \ y \simeq x \bigwedge b \in \int y\} \ \text{for } x \in \lambda$$

$$\oint[\Sigma x \quad \alpha\ \beta] \quad = \quad \{[\langle a, b\rangle] \mid [a] \in \oint[\alpha], [b] \in \oint[\beta(a/x)]\}$$

we denote the first projection $\pi_0 \quad \oint[\Sigma x \quad \alpha\ \beta] \to \oint[\alpha]$ as π^β_α

$$\oint[\Pi x \quad \alpha\ \beta] \quad = \quad \begin{cases} \{[f] \mid \forall [a] \in \oint[\alpha]\ \exists [b] \in \oint[\beta(a/x)]\ \forall n \in \lambda \ n \vdash [a] \Rightarrow fn \vdash [b]\} \\ \quad \text{for } [\alpha], [\beta] \in \Lambda^0_0 \\ \{[\langle F, f\rangle] \mid (F \quad \langle [\alpha], [\Sigma x \quad \alpha\ \beta]\rangle) \in \bar{\chi} \bigwedge \pi^\beta_\alpha \circ F = \mathrm{id} \bigwedge f \vdash F\} \\ \quad \text{otherwise} \end{cases} \tag{6 1}$$

$$\oint[1_O] \quad = \quad \{[\Omega]\}$$

$$\oint[\Gamma] \quad = \quad \{[x^*] \mid [x] \in \Lambda^0_0 \bigwedge \oint[x] \text{ is defined}\} \tag{6 2}$$

$$\oint[\nabla(T)] \quad = \quad \{[\nabla(x)] \mid [x] \in \oint[T]\} \tag{6.3}$$

The operation $(\ )^*$ in Clause 6 2 is defined as follows

$$x^* = \begin{cases} \Sigma y \quad x\ \Omega & \text{if } x \in \lambda \\ x & \text{otherwise} \end{cases}$$

As we can see, the sets in the range of the operation $\oint$ would in general consist of (equivalence classes of) terms from a sub-class Λ'. We define the operation $\bar{\nabla}(\ )$ on such terms through the following clauses

1. *for $x \in \lambda$, we have $\bar{\nabla}(x) = x$*

2. *for $\langle x, y\rangle$, we have $\bar{\nabla}(\langle x, y\rangle) = \langle\bar{\nabla}(x), \bar{\nabla}(y)\rangle$*

3. *for all other elements not covered by the clauses above, we have $\bar{\nabla}(x) = \Omega$*

It may be easily verified that this definition covers the relevant class of expressions. Finally we define the realizability relation $\vdash$, presenting sets in the range of $\oint$ as ω-sets, through the following clauses

1. *for $x \in \lambda$ we have $n \vdash [x] \Leftrightarrow n \in [x]$*

2. *$n \vdash [\langle x, y\rangle] \Leftrightarrow \pi_0(n) \vdash [x] \bigwedge \pi_1(n) \vdash [y]$, unless $\langle x, y\rangle \in \lambda$ in which case the previous clause applies*

3. *for all other equivalence classes of terms, not covered by the clauses above, we have $n \vdash [X] \Leftrightarrow n \simeq \Omega$*

The operator $\bar{\nabla}$ invoked on the right hand side of Equation 6.3 can be seen to have the action of replacing every sub-term of its argument that is not a λ-term, by the λ-term Ω. It leaves the rest of the term unchanged. As we can see, the operation $\oint$ is partial on its domain, and as we have mentioned earlier, we shall prune each of the classes we have defined in Definition 6.1.3—symbolized by the symbols $\Lambda^0_0, \Lambda^0_1, \Phi^0$ and Λ^0 and Θ^0—to admit only such expressions for which the operation $\oint$ is defined. Such classes would be characterized as *valid* and in the sequel, we shall use the symbols above, as well as the names Basic Types, Complex Types, and so on, for only the valid classes of expressions defined and stratified according to Definition 6.1.3.

We have a couple of simple propositions that follow easily from the definition above.

Proposition 6.1.7 *For an Order $[\phi] \in \Phi^0$, the map $\eta_\phi : \oint[\phi] \rightarrow \oint[\nabla(\phi)] : [x] \mapsto [\bar{\nabla}(x)]$ is tracked by the identity λ-term I.*

Proof: We shall consider the various classes of expressions that may make up the level of Orders. The proposition is trivially true for the classes $[1_O]$ and $[\Gamma]$: the operator ∇ yields the Basic Type $[\Omega]$, and the map η_ϕ is tracked by the λ-term I. Now consider an Order of the form $[\Sigma x : \phi . R]$: by an easy structural induction, any $[x] \in \oint[\Sigma x : \phi . R]$

can be seen to have the following property: x is constructed by induction on items 6 and 7 of Definition 6.1.1, and there exists a set π of occurrences of sub-terms in x that exhausts all sub-terms of x not in the set λ, moreover, the definition of the operator $\bar{\nabla}$ tells us that $\bar{\nabla}(x)$ is obtained precisely by replacing all such occurrences of sub-terms in the set π by the λ-term Ω, now consider the map η_ϕ $[x] \mapsto [\bar{\nabla}(x)]$ $(\phi \equiv \Sigma x \,.\, T.R)$. from the way that the operation $\vdash$ is defined, we can see that $[x]$ is realized by λ-terms n such that all the nodes corresponding to the occurrences in the set π are nodes in n too, and are (labeled by) terms in $[\Omega]$; this condition holds precisely for any realizer for $[\bar{\nabla}(x)]$ too, since exactly those occurrences have been replaced by Ω. $\bar{\nabla}(x)$ agrees with x at all other occurrences. Hence exactly the same set of λ-terms realize both $[x]$ and $[\nabla(x)]$ and the map η_ϕ in this case can be seen to be tracked by I. A similar argument works for an Order of the form $[\Pi x \,.\, \phi.R]$ any object in its denotation is of the form $\langle F, f\rangle$, and the operator ∇ acts on it to yield $\langle\Omega, f\rangle$, both $\langle F, f\rangle$ and $\langle\Omega, f\rangle$ are tracked by the same set of terms (namely $[\langle\Omega, f\rangle]$) and thus the map η_ϕ is tracked by the identity

Corollary 6.1.8 *For any term x such that $[x] \in Y \equiv \oint[y]$, $y \in \Theta^0$, we have that the set of realizers $\{n \mid n \vdash_Y [x]\} = [\nabla(x)]$*

Proof: We use exactly the same argument, now extended to all classes of expressions in Θ^0

6.2 The Structure

We shall use the syntax of Θ^0, and the definition of $\oint$ to construct the fibrations that instance the relevant CC-Category. As before, we shall work in the framework of Comprehension Categories

Definition 6.2.1 *We define the category* **B** *to be the following sub-category of the category* ω-**Set**

Objects: *Objects are sets of the form $\oint[\phi]$ for $[\phi] \in \Theta^0$*

Morphisms: *All morphisms in the category are* ω-**Set** *morphisms, they are of two types*

s-morphism: *s-morphisms may be defined on the basis of the following clauses:*

1. *The identity map on any object, tracked by the λ-term $\lambda x.x \equiv I$, is a s-morphism,*

2 *An s-morphisms* F $\oint[\Sigma x \ \alpha\ \beta] \rightarrow \oint[\Sigma y\ \ \gamma\ \delta]$ *is a* ω-**Set** *morphism such that for some s-morphism* G $\oint[\alpha] \rightarrow \oint[\gamma]$ *the diagram shown in Figure 6-1 commutes*

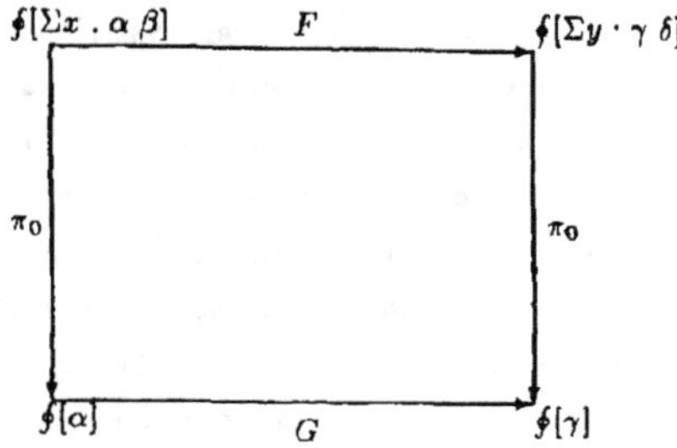

Figure 6-1 s-morphisms

F-morphism: *A F-morphism is defined to be a map isomorphic to the projection map* π_0 $\oint[\Sigma x \ \ \alpha\ \beta] \rightarrow \oint[\alpha]$ $[\langle a, b\rangle] \mapsto [a]$.

We have constructed the objects of **B** so as to be ω-Sets, and we can easily verify that **B** is a (non-full) sub-category of the latter, through an embedding we shall denote in the sequel as $\imath$, we record the fact below.

Proposition 6.2.2 **B** *is a sub-category of* ω-**Sets**

There are, of course, ω-**Set** morphisms which are not present as **B** morphisms—specifically morphisms between objects of the form $\Sigma x \ \ \phi\ \psi$, for which the commutation conditions in the definition of s-morphism fail The embedding is thus not full We may see from this fact that we have been generous in stipulating the size of the set χ in the sequel, we shall require only those morphisms in ω-**Set** that are in the image of the embedding $\imath$, to have a name in the valid fragment of χ.

The category **B** would be the base of our fibrations

Definition 6.2 3 *The Category* $\bar{\Phi}$ *is composed of the following classes of entities*

Objects· *Objects are families* $T \equiv \{T_x\}_{x\in\phi}$ *such that there exists a valid* Φ^0*-expression* $[\Sigma y\ \ \phi'.\hat{T}]$ *such that* $\phi = \oint[\phi'] \in$ **B** *and for each* $x \equiv [a] \in \phi$, $T_x \equiv \oint[\hat{T}(a/y)]$

Morphisms. *A morphism* f' $\{T_x\}_{x\in\phi} \rightarrow \{R_y\}_{y\in\psi}$ *consists of a s-morphism* u $\phi \rightarrow \psi$ *in* **B**, *along with a family of maps* $f \equiv \{f_x\ \ T_x \rightarrow R_{u(x)}\}_{x\in\phi}$, *such that there exists a*

λ-term $\bar{f}$ (called the realizer for the family) such that any member f_x of the family f is tracked by the λ-term $\bar{f}a$, for any $a \vdash x$

It may be guessed that the category $\tilde{\Phi}$ would represent the fibration for Orders The corresponding construct for the Types is as follows

Definition 6.2.4 *The Category $\tilde{\Lambda}$ is composed of the following classes of entities*

Objects: *Objects are families $\alpha \equiv \{\alpha_x\}_{x\in\phi}$ such that there exists a valid Λ^0-expression $[\Sigma y \quad \phi' \, \tilde{\alpha}]$ such that $\phi = \oint[\phi'] \in \mathbf{B}$ and for each $x \equiv [a] \in \phi$, $\alpha_x \equiv \oint[\hat{\alpha}(a/y)]$*

Morphisms: *A morphism $f' \quad \{\alpha_x\}_{x\in\phi} \to \{\beta_y\}_{y\in\psi}$ consists of a s-morphism $u \cdot \phi \to \psi$ in $\mathbf{B}$, along with a family of maps $f \equiv \{f_x \cdot \alpha_x \to \beta_{u(x)}\}_{x\in\phi}$, such that there exists a λ-term $\bar{f}$ (called the realizer of the family) such that any f_x is tracked by the term $\bar{f}a$, for any $a \vdash x$*

We can see that according to the definitions above, any object of $\tilde{\Phi}$—say the family $T \equiv \{T_x\}_{x\in\oint[\phi]}$ in Definition 6 2 3, corresponds to an object $\bar{T}$ of the form $\oint[\Sigma x \quad \phi \, \hat{T}] \in \mathbf{B}$, conversely, any object in $\mathbf{B}$ of the form $\oint[\Sigma x \quad \phi \, R]$ with $[\Sigma x \quad \phi \, R]$ an Order expression, corresponds to an object $\{R_{[y]}\}_{[y]\in\oint[\phi]}$ of $\tilde{\Phi}$, with

$$R_{[y]} \equiv \oint[R(y/x)]$$

We would refer to this object as $\underline{\Sigma x \quad \phi \, R}$, as we can see, *every* object of $\tilde{\Phi}$ can be thought of as given by $\underline{\Sigma x \quad \phi \, R}$ for some $[\Sigma x \quad \phi \, R] \in \Phi^0$ In the sequel, we would be a bit loose, and refer to any object of $\tilde{\Phi}$ as an object (of the form) $\Sigma x \cdot \phi.T$ (for suitable T) Similar remarks apply to objects of $\tilde{\Lambda}$

We may define now, the functors that would constitute our Comprehension Category

Definition 6.2 5 *The functor $Q \quad \tilde{\Phi} \to \mathbf{B}^{\to}$ is defined to have the following action.*

On Objects: *The object $T \equiv \{T_x\}_{x\in\oint[\phi]}$ is mapped by Q to the F-morphism $\pi_0 \quad \bar{T} \to \phi$ in $\mathbf{B}^{\to}$*

On Morphisms· *The morphism $T \equiv \{T_x\}_{x\in\oint[\phi]} \to R \equiv \{R_y\}_{y\in\oint[\psi]}$ consisting of a s-morphism $u \quad \oint[\phi] \to \oint[\psi]$ in $\mathbf{B}$, along with a family of maps $f \equiv \{f_x \cdot T_x \to R_{u(x)}\}_{x\in\oint[\phi]}$, is mappped by Q to the commuting square in $\mathbf{B}$, shown in Figure 6-2. where the action of the $\mathbf{B}$-morphism $\bar{f}$ is as follows*

$$\bar{f} \quad [\langle a, t\rangle] \mapsto [\langle u(a), f_a(t)\rangle]$$

where $[a] \in \oint[\phi]$ and $[t] \in T_{[a]}$

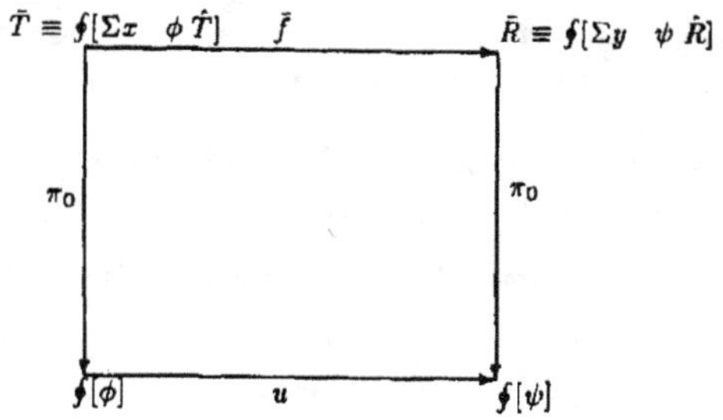

Figure 6-2 Functor Q on morphisms

To validate this definition we must show that $\bar{f}$ is a valid **B**-morphism—i e it has a realizer

Proposition 6.2.6 *The morphism $\bar{f}$, as defined above, is a valid* **B***-morphism*

Proof: We may verify that $\bar{f}$ is tracked by the λ-term corresponding to

$$\lambda x \; \langle (u' \circ \pi_0)(x), (\hat{f}(\pi_0(x)))(\pi_1(x)) \rangle$$

where u' tracks u and $\hat{f}$ is the realizer for the family f

As is usual in higher-order Type theory, there is an embedding of Types into Orders, categorically, this corresponds to a full and faithful cartesian functor from the fibration of Types into that of Orders This functor would be denoted as $\mathcal{I}$ in our system

Definition 6.2.7 *The functor $\mathcal{I}$ $\tilde{\Lambda} \rightarrow \tilde{\Phi}$ is defined to have the following action on objects and arrows*

On Objects: *Consider an object $\underline{\Sigma x \;\; \phi \, \alpha}$, the action of $\mathcal{I}$ may be defined as follows*

$$\mathcal{I} \cdot \underline{\Sigma x \;\; \phi . \alpha} \mapsto \underline{\Sigma x \;\; \phi \, \Sigma y \;\; \alpha \, 1_O}$$

On Morphisms: *Consider a morphism $\{\alpha_x\}_{x \in \phi} \rightarrow \{\beta_y\}_{y \in \psi}$ in $\tilde{\Lambda}$, given by a s-morphism $u \;\; \phi \rightarrow \psi$ in* **B***, along with a family of maps $f \equiv \{f_x \;\; \alpha_x \rightarrow \beta_{u(x)}\}_{x \in \phi}$ Its image under $\mathcal{I}$ is the $\tilde{\Phi}$ morphism consisting of the s-morphism u along with the family $f' \equiv \{f'_x\}_{x \in \phi}$, where the effect of any f'_x may be represented as $\langle (f_x \circ \pi_0), \Omega \rangle$*

The realizer for the family f' is easily seen to be the λ-term corresponding to the combinator $\lambda x \; \langle (\hat{f} x) \circ \pi_0, \Omega \rangle$ (where $\hat{f}$ is the realizer for the family f) Functorial properties may be easily verified and we shall not labour the point, cartesian-ness is also easy, and we shall prove that after the Comprehension Category structures have been verified

As we had mentioned earlier, an important consideration in (the interpretation of) the closure of Types under existential quantification over Orders, is the reflection of the fibration of Orders into that of Types This requires the existence of a (fibered) left adjoint to the "inclusion" functor $\mathcal{I}$

Definition 6.2.8 *The functor $\nabla : \bar{\Phi} \to \bar{\Lambda}$ is defined to have the following action on objects and arrows*

On Objects: *Consider an object $\underline{\Sigma x . \phi\, T}$, the action of ∇ on this is*

$$\underline{\Sigma x . \phi\, \alpha} \mapsto \underline{\Sigma x . \phi\, \nabla(T)}$$

On Morphisms: *The morphism $T \equiv \{T_x\}_{x\in\phi} \to R \equiv \{R_y\}_{y\in\psi}$ consisting of a s-morphism $u : \phi \to \psi$ in $\mathbf{B}$, along with a family of maps $f \equiv \{f_x : T_x \to R_{u(x)}\}_{x\in\phi}$, is mappped by ∇ to the $\bar{\Lambda}$ morphism consisting of the s-morphism $u . \phi \to \psi$, and the family of maps $\nabla(f) \equiv \{\nabla(f_x) : \nabla(T_x) \to \nabla(R_{u(x)}) . [\bar{\nabla}(a)] \mapsto [\bar{\nabla}(b)]\}_{x\in\phi}$, where $[a] \in T_x$, $[b] \in R_{u(x)}$, and $f_x : [a] \mapsto [b]$*

We have to verify that this definition is valid

Proposition 6.2.9 *The functor ∇ as defined above is a valid functor.*

Proof: Since T_x and $R_{u(x)}$ are both valid (basic) Orders, for any $x \in \phi$, we shall argue for general $[T], [R] \in \bar{\Phi}^0$ and a $\bar{\Phi}$-morphism $F : \oint[T] \to \oint[R]$ (i e F and its domain and co-domain are in the fiber over the terminal object $\oint[1_O]$, no generality is lost in this move) As we have seen, the action of ∇ on F is the $\bar{\Lambda}$-morphism $\nabla(F) : \oint[\nabla(T)] \to \oint[\nabla(R)] : [\bar{\nabla}(x)] \mapsto [\bar{\nabla}(y)]$ where $F : [x] \mapsto [y]$ We claim that this is well-defined, i e for any $[\bar{\nabla}(x)] \in \oint[\nabla(T)]$ there is an unique $[\bar{\nabla}(y)]$ in $\oint[\nabla(R)]$ satisfying the condition that $F : [x] \mapsto [y]$ Note that this obtains immediately if $\oint[T] \cong \oint[\nabla(T)]$—for then for any $[\bar{\nabla}(x)]$ we have an unique $[x]$ such that $\eta_T : [x] \mapsto [\bar{\nabla}(x)]$ (*cf* Proposition 6.1 7), and hence we shall have an unique $[\bar{\nabla}(y)]$ such that $F : [x] \mapsto [y]$ Now suppose this is not so i e we have distinct $[x], [x'] \in \oint[T]$ such that $[\bar{\nabla}(x)] = [\bar{\nabla}(x')]$ Suppose $F([x]) = [y]$ and $F([x']) = [y']$ From Corollary 6 1 8 we have that $\{n \mid n \vdash [x]\} = [\bar{\nabla}(x)]$, hence $\{n \mid n \vdash [x]\} = \{n \mid n \vdash [x']\}$ But the set $\{m \mid m \vdash [y]\} = [fn]$ where f tracks F, and $n \in [\bar{\nabla}(x)]$ Hence $\{m \mid m \vdash [y]\} = \{m \mid m \vdash [y']\}$ both being $[fn]$ for some $n \in [\bar{\nabla}(x)]$, but $\{m \mid m \vdash [y]\} = [\bar{\nabla}(y)]$ (by Corollary 6 1 8); hence $[\nabla(y)] = [\nabla(y')]$ Hence we have an unique $[\bar{\nabla}(y)]$ satisfying our condition even in this case. The only other condition we have to check is that the family $\nabla(f)$ in the context of our definition, has a realizer. This follows easily from the consideration that both $[x]$ and $[\bar{\nabla}(x)]$ are tracked by the same class of λ-terms and thus each $\nabla(f_x)$ is tracked by the same λ-term that tracks f_x. Hence the realizer for $\nabla(f)$ is the same as that for f.

We may now establish the basic facts about the structures that we have defined.

Lemma 6.2.10 *Let $\mathcal{P} \equiv \mathcal{Q} \circ \mathcal{I}$ · then $p \equiv$ cod $\circ\, \mathcal{P}$ is a fibration.*

Proof: Consider an object $\alpha' \equiv \underline{\Sigma x \cdot \phi\, \alpha}$ in $\tilde{\Lambda}$, and any morphism $u : \psi \rightarrow \phi$ in **B**. The cartesian lifting of u at α' may be constructed thus: consider the pullback of $\pi_0 : \oint[\Sigma x \cdot \phi\, \alpha] \rightarrow \oint[\phi]$ along u shown in Figure 6-3 where y does not occur free in

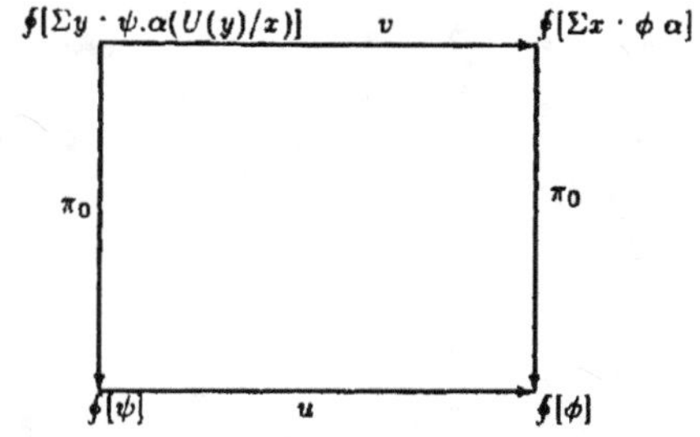

Figure 6-3 Cartesian lifting of u.

α. Let U be the symbol in the set of valid function symbols $\tilde{\chi}$ such that $\langle U \rangle = u$. The term $\Sigma y \cdot \psi\, \alpha(U(y)/x)$ is a valid Type expression and the corresponding family $\underline{\Sigma y \cdot \psi\, \alpha(U(y)/x)}$, an object of $\tilde{\Lambda}$. Moreover, reasoning as in the category of Sets shows us that this square is indeed a pullback cone. The morphism v is essentially the identity Q-definable map I, and the corresponding morphism in $\tilde{\Lambda}$ consists of the s-morphism u along with the constant family $\{I_x\}_{x \in \phi}$, realized by the term $\lambda \nu\, I$ (I being the standard identity combinator), universal properties of the pullback cone yields that this is a cartesian map—and hence, the cartesian lifting of u at α'.

In the sequel, we shall confuse (the name of) a **B** morphism with the symbol in the set χ which is assigned the former by the interpretation function $\langle\,\rangle$. This convention shall extend to combinations of B-morphisms built up by composition (indicated by the symbol $\circ$), and other categorical operations (on morphisms)—such as pairing, for which we shall use the symbol $\langle\ ,\ \rangle$ We shall freely mix the functional notation with a combinatory notation—for instance, the composition combinator would also be denoted as $\circ$ the meaning would be clear form the context. We shall also use the symbols π_0 and π_1 generically for cartesian projections, projections constituting a pullback cone, and also for the projection combinator in the λ-Calculus It should be remarked that such overloading of symbols is motivated in all such cases, the λ-term tracking the corresponding morphism would be constituted (as a combinator) exactly as the expression for the morphism built up as indicated above—a standard aspect of the correspondence between cartesian closed categories and the typed λ-calculi ([44, 14])

Lemma 6 2.11 *We have the following implication*

$$f \text{ cartesian in } \bar{\Lambda} \Longrightarrow \mathcal{P}(f) \text{ is a pullback in } \mathbf{B}$$

Proof: Consider objects $\underline{\alpha} \equiv \underline{\Sigma x\ \ \phi\,\alpha}$ and $\underline{\beta} \equiv \underline{\Sigma y\ \ \psi\,\beta}$ in $\bar{\Lambda}$, and a cartesian morphism $f\ \ \underline{\alpha} \to \underline{\beta}$, consisting of a s-morphism $u\ \ \oint[\phi] \to \oint[\psi]$, and a family $\{f_x\ \ \alpha_x \to \beta_{u(x)}\}_{x\in\oint[\phi]}$ As stated in Definition 6 2 5, the image of f under $\mathcal{P}$ is (isomorphic to) the commuting square in $\mathbf{B}$, shown in Figure 6-4 Now the assumption that f is

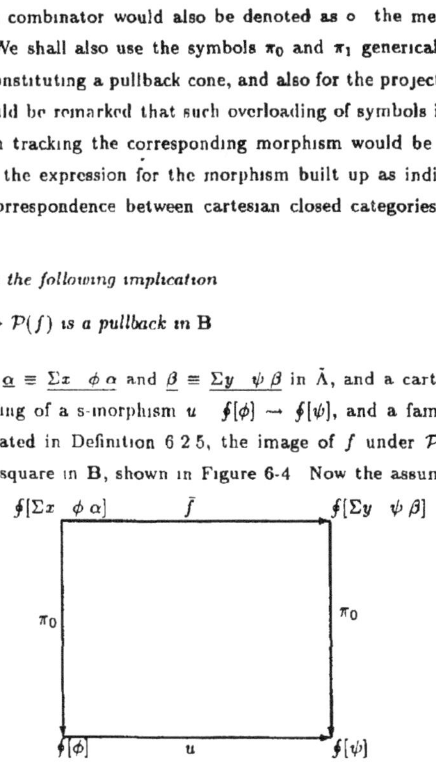

Figure 6-4 $\mathcal{P}f$ is a pullback in $\mathbf{B}$

cartesian, entails that any other morphism $g\ \ \underline{\Sigma x\ \ \phi\,\gamma} \to \underline{\beta}$ "over u," factors through f through an unique morphism g/f over the identity id_ϕ Then $(\,\mathrm{dom} \circ \mathcal{P})(g/f)$ is the mediating morphism, and we have the universal property of the square

The last two results tell us that $\mathcal{P}$ is a Comprehension Category

Theorem 6.2.12 *$\mathcal{P}$ is a full comprehension category with unit*

Proof: From Lemma 6 2 10 and Lemma 6.2 11 we have that $\mathcal{P}$ is a Comprehension Category It is easily seen to be full for objects $\underline{\alpha} \equiv \underline{\Sigma x\ \ \phi\,\alpha}$ and $\underline{\beta} \equiv \underline{\Sigma y\ \ \psi\,\beta}$ in $\bar{\Lambda}$, any morphism f $\mathcal{P}(\underline{\alpha}) \to \mathcal{P}(\underline{\beta})$ in $\mathbf{B}^{\to}$ would be a commuting square of the form shown in Figure 6-4, where f, u are now arbitrary $\mathbf{B}$ morphisms There exists a morphism $\hat{f}$ in $\tilde{\Lambda}$ corresponding to $(\bar{f}, u)$, that consists of the s-morphism u, and the family $\{f_x\}_{x \in \oint[\phi]}$, such that any f_x in the family is tracked by the λ-term corresponding to $\lambda\nu\, \pi_1 \circ (\bar{f}\langle\bar{\nabla}(a), \nu\rangle)$, where $\bar{f}$ tracks $\bar{f}$, and $x \equiv [a]$ The defining property of s-morphisms (cf Definition 6.2 1) tells us that this is a valid $\tilde{\Lambda}$ morphism· the realizer for the family can be seen to be $\lambda\mu\nu\, \pi_1 \circ (\bar{f}\langle\mu, \nu\rangle)$

The fibration $p \equiv$ cod $\circ\, \mathcal{P}$ has a fibered terminal object for any object $\oint[\phi] \in \mathbf{B}$, the terminal object in the fiber over $\oint[\phi]$ can be seen to be the object $\underline{\Sigma x : \phi\, \Omega}$ Note that when $\phi \in \Lambda_0$, we have the object $\underline{\Sigma x \;\; \phi\, x} \equiv \underline{\Sigma x \;\; \phi\, \Omega}$, which may also be taken to be the terminal object The terminal object functor 1_p $\mathbf{B} \to \tilde{\Lambda}$ $\oint[\phi] \mapsto \underline{\Sigma x \;\; \phi\, \Omega}$ and can be verified to be a right adjoint to $\mathcal{P}_0 \equiv$ dom $\circ\, \mathcal{P}$ Hence the proposition

The proofs of the Lemma 6 2 10 through Theorem 6 2 12 can be seen to be generalizable to the category $\tilde{\Phi}$. Hence we may assert the following

Theorem 6 2 13 *The functor* $\mathcal{Q}$ $\tilde{\Phi} \to \mathbf{B}^{\to}$ *is a full comprehension category with unit*

Proof: We simply replace, in the proofs of the Lemma 6 2 10 through Theorem 6 2 12, $\tilde{\Lambda}$ by $\tilde{\Phi}$ All the arguments may be seen to be valid for the latter.

We explore next, the relevant quantificational structure of the Comprehension categories

Proposition 6.2.14 *The Comprehension Category* $\mathcal{Q}$ *has* $\mathcal{Q}$*-sums*

Proof: This proposition states that for any object $T \equiv \underline{\Sigma x \;\; \phi\, T} \in \tilde{\Phi}$, the re-indexing functor $(\mathcal{P}T)^*$ has a left adjoint Σ_T satisfying the Beck-Chevalley condition As we have seen in the proof of Lemma 6 2 10, the re-indexing functor takes an object $\underline{\Sigma x \;\; \phi\, R}$ to the object $\underline{\Sigma y \;\; (\Sigma x \;\; \phi\, T)\, R(\pi_0(y)/x)}$ (using π_0 as the name of the morphism $\mathcal{P}T$). We claim that the left adjoint to $(\mathcal{P}T)^*$ has the following action

$$\underline{\Sigma y \;\; (\Sigma x \;\; \phi\, T)\, R} \longmapsto \underline{\Sigma x \;\; \phi\, \Sigma y \;\; T\, R(\langle x, y\rangle/y)}$$

economizing on variables in the substitution as before Let us see how this comes about Consider a $\tilde{\Phi}$ object given as $\underline{\Sigma z \;\; \phi\, S}$, and a $\tilde{\Phi}$ morphism

$$U \;\; \underline{\Sigma y \;\; (\Sigma x \;\; \phi\, T)\, R} \to \underline{\Sigma y \;\; (\Sigma x \cdot \phi\, T)\, S(\pi_0(y)/z)}$$

over the identity of course, U is actually a family $\{U_y\}_{y \in \oint[\Sigma x \;\; \phi\, T]}$ We assume that the family is realized by a term u Now for any $[a] \in \oint[\phi]$, the member of the family

$\underline{\Sigma y\ (\Sigma x\ \ \phi\, T)\ R(\pi_0(y)/x)}$ indexed by $[a]$ is $\oint[\Sigma y \cdot T(a/x)\ R(\langle a, y\rangle/y)]$: a typical element of this is $[\langle b, c\rangle]$ with $[b] \in \oint[T(a/x)]$ and $[c] \in \oint[R(\langle a,b\rangle/y)]$. On the other hand, a typical element of the member of the family $\underline{\Sigma y\ (\Sigma x\ \ \phi\, T)\ R}$ corresponding to an index $[\langle a, b\rangle] \in \oint[\Sigma x\ \ \phi\, T]$ is $[c] \in \oint[R(\langle a,b\rangle/y)]$ (for the same a, b, c as in the previous sentence) Now suppose $U_{[\langle a, b\rangle]} : [c] \mapsto [s]$ for $[s] \in \oint[S(a/z)]$: we shall define an (unique) $\tilde{\Lambda}$ morphism $U^* \cdot \underline{\Sigma x\ .\ \phi.\Sigma y\ .\ T.R(\langle x, y\rangle/y)} \to \underline{\Sigma z\ \ \phi.S}$, having the following action $U^*_{[a]}\ \ [\langle b, c\rangle] \mapsto [s]$ Suppose the realizer for U was the term u: since $[\langle a, b\rangle]$ is realized by the set $[\bar\nabla(\langle a, b\rangle)] = [\langle \bar\nabla(a), \bar\nabla(b)\rangle]$, we can say that $U_{[\langle a, b\rangle]}$ is tracked by the term $u\langle\bar\nabla(a), \bar\nabla(b)\rangle \equiv n$ (say) Then we can see that $U^*_{[a]}$ is tracked by the λ-term corresponding to $n \circ \pi_1$, and thus the realizer for the family (U^*) is the term corresponding to $\lambda y \lambda x\ (u\langle y, \pi_0(x)\rangle)(\pi_1(x))$. We check the factorization condition through the unit. Consider the object obtained by re-indexing the object $\underline{\Sigma x\ \ \phi\ \Sigma y \cdot T\ R(\langle x, y\rangle/y)}$ along $\mathcal{P}T$. we shall denote it as X—the precise Φ^0 expression for it is not very important; we have a $\tilde\Phi$ morphism $\eta\ \ \underline{\Sigma y\ \ (\Sigma x\ \ \phi\, T).R} \to X$, and we may say, of any member of it, indexed by $[\langle a, b\rangle] \in \oint[\Sigma x\ \ \phi\, T]$, that $\eta_{[\langle a, b\rangle]}\ \ [c] \mapsto [\langle b, c\rangle]$ where all symbols are interpreted as in the context of their earlier use, the family may be seen to be realized by the term corresponding to $\lambda xy.\langle \pi_1(x), y\rangle$ We also have the morphism U' obtained by re-indexing U^* and we can see that its member indexed by $[\langle a, b\rangle]$ has the following action $U'_{[\langle a, b\rangle]}\ \ [\langle b, c\rangle] \mapsto [s]$ (where, as we had stated earlier $U_{[\langle a, b\rangle]}\ \ [c] \mapsto [s]$) This family is realized by the term corresponding to $\lambda yx\ (u\langle \pi_0(y), \pi_0(x)\rangle)(\pi_1(x))$ As we can easily see, for any $[\langle a, b\rangle] \in \oint[\Sigma x\ \ \phi\, T]$, we have that if $U_{[\langle a, b\rangle]} \cdot [c] \mapsto [s]$, then we would have that $U'_{[\langle a, b\rangle]} \circ \eta_{[\langle a, b\rangle]}\ \ [c] \mapsto [\langle b, c\rangle] \mapsto [s]$ and hence the proposition

We would expect the Beck-Chevalley condition to be satisfied since the operation is essentially one of composition We make the reasoning explicit Consider a cartesian morphism $f \cdot \underline{\Sigma x \cdot \phi\ R(u(x)/y)} \to \underline{\Sigma y\ \ \psi\ R}$, as we have seen (cf. Lemma 6.2.11), this may be taken to be the general form of any cartesian morphism. We shall denote the domain by E and the codomain as E'. we have seen that this may be taken to be the general form of any cartesian morphism. The image of f under $\mathcal{P}$ is the pullback square (in **B**) shown in Figure 6-5 We consider an object $P \equiv \underline{\Sigma z \cdot (\Sigma y \cdot \psi\ R)\ S}$ We have to show that the canonical natural transformation $\Sigma_E(\mathcal{P}_0 f)^* \to (pf)^*\Sigma_{E'}$ is an isomorphism. Referring to the figure, the action of $(\mathcal{P}_0 f)^*$ on P is the $\tilde\Phi$ object

$$\underline{\Sigma a\ \ (\Sigma x \cdot \phi\ R(u(x)/y))\ S(\langle (u \circ \pi_0)(a), \pi_1(a)\rangle/z)}$$

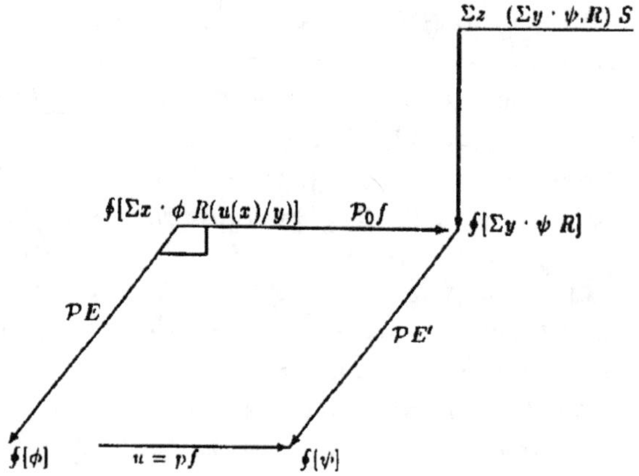

Figure 6-5 The Beck-Chevalley Condition

with the usual conventions[1]. The action of Σ_E on this object can be seen to be

$$\begin{aligned} & \underline{\Sigma x \cdot \phi\, \Sigma a \quad R(u(x)/y)\; S(\langle (u \circ \pi_0)(a), \pi_1(a)\rangle/z)(\langle x, a\rangle/a)} \\ = \; & \underline{\Sigma x \,.\, \phi\, \Sigma a \quad R(u(x)/y)\; S(\langle u(x), a\rangle/z)} \end{aligned} \tag{6.4}$$

upon simplifying the substitutions. On the other hand, the action of $\Sigma_{E'}$ on P is the object

$$\underline{\Sigma y \quad \psi\, \Sigma z \quad R\; S(\langle y, z\rangle/z)}$$

The action of $(pf)^* = u^*$ on this is the object

$$\begin{aligned} & \underline{\Sigma x \quad \phi\, (\Sigma z \quad R\; S(\langle y, z\rangle/z))(u(x)/y)} \\ = \; & \underline{\Sigma x \,.\, \phi\, \Sigma z \quad R(u(x)/y)\; S(\langle u(x), z\rangle/z)} \end{aligned} \tag{6.5}$$

upon simplifying the substitutions Comparing Equation 6 4 and Equation 6 5, the proposition follows easily

The proposition that $\mathcal{Q}$ has $\mathcal{Q}$-products is entirely analogous We make the details explicit.

Proposition 6.2.15 *The Comprehension Category $\mathcal{Q}$ has $\mathcal{Q}$-products*

[1] cf Remark after Lemma 6 2 10

Proof: This proposition states that for any object $T' \equiv \underline{\Sigma x \ \phi\, T} \in \bar{\Phi}$, the re-indexing functor $(\mathcal{P}T)^*$ has a right adjoint Π_T satisfying the Beck-Chevalley condition As we have seen in the proof of Lemma 6 2 10, the re-indexing functor has the following action on objects

$$\underline{\Sigma x \ \phi\, R} \longmapsto \underline{\Sigma y \ (\Sigma x \ \phi\, T)\ R(\pi_0(y)/x)}$$

We claim that the right adjoint to this has the following action

$$\underline{\Sigma y \ (\Sigma x \ \phi\, T)\ R} \longmapsto \underline{\Sigma x \ \phi\, \Pi y \ T\ R(\langle x, y\rangle/y)}$$

Let us see how this comes about Consider a $\bar{\Phi}$ object given as $\underline{\Sigma z \cdot \phi\, S}$, and a $\bar{\Phi}$ morphism

$$U \ \underline{\Sigma y \ (\Sigma x \ \phi\, T)\ S(\pi_0(y)/z)} \to \underline{\Sigma y \ (\Sigma x : \phi.T).R}$$

over the identity of course, U is actually a family $\{U_y\}_{y \in \oint[\Sigma x \ \phi\, T]}$. We assume that the family is realized by a term u Now for any $[a] \in \oint[\phi]$, the member of the family $\underline{\Pi y \ (\Sigma x \ \phi\, T)\ R(\pi_0(y)/x)}$ indexed by $[a]$ is $\oint[\Pi y \ T(a/x)\ R(\langle a, y\rangle/y)]$ Now consider a typical element of the family $\underline{\Sigma z\,.\,\phi.S}$ indexed by $[a] \in \oint[\phi]$—say $[d] \in \oint[S(a/z)]$ Consider the **B**-morphism $F \ \oint[T(a/x)] \to \oint[\Sigma y \ T(a/x)\ R(\langle a, y\rangle/y)]$, which has the following action.

$$F \cdot [b] \ \mapsto \ [\langle\langle a, b\rangle, c\rangle] \qquad (6\ 6)$$

$$\text{where } [c] \ = \ U_{[\langle a, b\rangle]}([d]) \qquad (6\ 7)$$

This may be seen to be tracked by the code $f \equiv \lambda x\ \langle\langle\bar{\nabla}(a), x\rangle, (u\langle\bar{\nabla}(a), x\rangle)(\bar{\nabla}(d))\rangle$ It can easily be seen that $[\langle F, f\rangle] \in \oint[\Pi y : T(a/x)\ R(\langle a, y\rangle/y)]$ We define a (unique) morphism

$$U^* \ \underline{\Sigma z \ \phi\, S} \to \underline{\Sigma x \ \phi\, \Pi y \ T\ R(\langle x, y\rangle/y)}$$

the member of which indexed by $[a] \in \oint[\phi]$ has the following action.

$$U^*_{[a]} \ [d] \mapsto [\langle F, f\rangle]$$

the family may be seen to be realized by the λ-term corresponding to

$$\lambda z y\ \langle \Omega, \lambda x\ \langle\langle z, x\rangle, (u\langle z, x\rangle)y\rangle\rangle$$

We have to verify the factorization condition through the co-unit Consider the object obtained by re-indexing the object $\underline{\Sigma x \ \phi\, \Pi y : T\ R(\langle x, y\rangle/y)}$ along $\mathcal{P}T$ we shall denote it as X—the precise Φ^0 expression for it is not very important, we have a $\bar{\Phi}$ morphism $\epsilon \ X \to \underline{\Sigma y \ (\Sigma x \ \phi\, T)\ R}$ and we assert of any member of it, indexed by $[\langle a, b\rangle] \in$

$\oint[\Sigma x\ \ \phi\, T]$, that $\epsilon_{[\langle a,b\rangle]}$ $[\langle F,f\rangle] \mapsto [c]$ where $[c]$ is as given by Equation 6 7 (for general $[\langle F,f\rangle]$ in its domain) The family can be seen to be realized by the term corresponding to $\lambda yx.\pi_1((\pi_1(x))(\pi_1(y)))$ We also have the morphism U' obtained by re-indexing U^* and we can see that its member indexed by $[\langle a,b\rangle]$ has the following action $U'_{[\langle a,b\rangle]}$ $[d] \mapsto [\langle F,f\rangle]$ and the family can be seen to tracked by the term corresponding to

$$\lambda zy\ \langle \Omega, \lambda x\ \langle\langle \pi_0(z), x\rangle, (u\langle \pi_0(z), x\rangle)y\rangle\rangle$$

Composing, we have $\epsilon_{[\langle a,b\rangle]} \circ U'_{[\langle a,b\rangle]} \cdot [d] \mapsto [c]$ where, in this case, by Equation 6 6, we have $[c] = U_{[\langle a,b\rangle]}([d])$ In other words, we have, for every $[\langle a,b\rangle]$

$$\epsilon_{[\langle a,b\rangle]} \circ U'_{[\langle a,b\rangle]}\ \ [d] \mapsto U_{[\langle a,b\rangle]}([d])$$

and hence we can say that $U = \epsilon \circ U'$

The Beck-Chevalley condition has to be verified Consider a cartesian morphism

$$f\ \ \underline{\Sigma x\ \ \phi\ R(u(x)/y)} \to \underline{\Sigma y\ \ \psi\ R}$$

for which we denote the domain by E and the codomain as E' The image of f under $\mathcal{P}$ is the pullback square (in **B**) shown in Figure 6-5 We consider an object $P \equiv \underline{\Sigma z\ \ (\Sigma y\ \ \psi\ R)\ S}$ We have to show that the canonical natural transformation $(pf)^*\Pi_{E'} \to \Pi_E(\mathcal{P}_0 f)^*$ is an isomorphism Referring to the figure, the action of $\Pi_{E'}$ on P is the object

$$\underline{\Sigma y \cdot \psi\ \Pi z\ \ R\ S(\langle y,z\rangle/z)}$$

The action of $(pf)^* = u^*$ on this is the object

$$\begin{aligned} &\underline{\Sigma x : \phi\ (\Pi z\ \ R\ S(\langle y,z\rangle/z))(u(x)/y)} \\ =\ &\underline{\Sigma x\ \ \phi\ \Pi z\ \ R(u(x)/y)\ S(\langle u(x),z\rangle/z)} \end{aligned} \tag{6 8}$$

upon simplifying the substitutions On the other hand, the action of $(\mathcal{P}_0 f)^*$ on P is the $\bar{\Phi}$ object

$$\underline{\Sigma a\ \ (\Sigma x\ \ \phi.R(u(x)/y))\ S(\langle (u \circ \pi_0)(a), \pi_1(a)\rangle/z)}$$

The action of Π_E on this object can be seen to be

$$\begin{aligned} &\underline{\Sigma x\ \ \phi\ \Pi a : R(u(x)/y).S(\langle (u \circ \pi_0)(a), \pi_1(a)\rangle/z)(\langle x,a\rangle/a)} \\ =\ &\underline{\Sigma x\ \ \phi\ \Pi a\ \ R(u(x)/y)\ S(\langle u(x),a\rangle/z)} \end{aligned} \tag{6 9}$$

upon simplifying the substitutions Comparing Equation 6 8 and Equation 6 9, the proposition follows easily

Since the left adjoint established in Theorem 6 2 14 is obtained essentially through composition (in **B**), we would expect that the the sums thus yielded are strong

Theorem 6.2.16 *The Comprehension Category $\mathcal{Q}$ has strong $\mathcal{Q}$-sums*

Proof: Let us assume the same context as in the proof of Theorem 6 2.14 We have an object $X \equiv \underline{\Sigma y : (\Sigma x : \phi.T)\ R}$, we have the action of the left adjoint Σ_T (to the re-indexing functor $(\mathcal{P}T)^*$) on X given as the object $\underline{\Sigma x\ \ \phi\, \Sigma y\ \ T\ R(\langle x, y\rangle/y)}$ Re-indexing this, we have the object $(\mathcal{P}T)^*\Sigma_T(X)$, and a (cartesian) morphism $\kappa_X\ \ (\mathcal{P}T)^*\Sigma_T(X) \to \Sigma_T(X)$; we have the unit of the adjunction $\eta_X\ \ X \to (\mathcal{P}T)^*\Sigma_T(X)$ and we claim that the image, under $\mathcal{Q}_0$ of the composite $\rho \equiv \kappa_X \circ \eta_X$ is an isomorphism The family $\rho \equiv \{\rho_{[\langle a,b\rangle]}\ \ X_{[\langle a,b\rangle]} \to (\Sigma_T(X))_{[a]}\}_{[\langle a,b\rangle]\in \oint[\Sigma x\ \ \phi\, T]}$ can be seen to have the following action $\rho_{[\langle a,b\rangle]}\ \ [c] \mapsto [\langle b, c\rangle]$, where as usual, $[c] \in \oint[R(\langle a,b\rangle/y)]$, $[b] \in \oint[T(a/x)]$ and $[a] \in \oint[\phi]$ The family ρ is realized by the term corresponding to $\lambda yx\ \langle \pi_1(y), x\rangle$ The image of this under $\mathcal{Q}_0$ is given as $\mathcal{Q}_0(\rho)\ \ \oint[\Sigma y\ \ (\Sigma x\ \ \phi\, T)\ R] \to \oint[\Sigma x\ \ \phi\, \Sigma y\ \ T\ R(\langle x,y\rangle/y)]$, and has the following action $\mathcal{Q}_0(\rho)\ \ [\langle\langle a,b\rangle, c\rangle] \mapsto [\langle a, \langle b, c\rangle\rangle]$ It can be seen to be tracked by the term corresponding to $\langle \pi_0 \circ \pi_0, \langle \pi_1 \circ \pi_0, \pi_1\rangle\rangle$, and is easily seen to be an isomorphism Thus, on the basis of the remark following Definition 4 2 11, the proposition follows

We can see now that $\mathcal{Q}$ is a closed comprehension category

Theorem 6.2 17 *$\mathcal{Q}$ is a Closed Comprehension Category*

Proof: We know that **B** has a terminal object—namely $\int(\Omega) = \int(1_O) = \{\perp\}$ The sequence of results Theorem 6 2 13, Theorem 6 2 14, Theorem 6 2 15 and Theorem 6 2 16 then tells us that $\mathcal{Q}$ is a Closed Comprehension Category

We may note that the sequence of results that lead up to Theorem 6 2 17, may be easily generalized to the Comprehension Category $\mathcal{P}$ the reader may verify, that the relevant proofs may be carried out relative to $\bar{\Lambda}$ and the Comprehension Category $\mathcal{P}$, by simply using Type expressions in the place of Order Expressions Hence we may assert the following theorem

Theorem 6.2.18 *$\mathcal{P}$ is a Closed Comprehension Category*

Proof: Straightforward translation of the arguments in the proofs of Theorem 6 2 13, Theorem 6 2 14, Theorem 6 2 15 and Theorem 6 2 16 in the context of the Comprehension Category $\mathcal{P}$ The only modification occurs in the proof of Theorem 6 2 15, in the case that $[\Sigma x \cdot \phi\ T]$ happens to be a Basic Type In that case, we have

$$\oint[\Pi y\ \ T(a/x)\ R(\langle a,y\rangle/y)] =$$
$$\{[f] \mid \forall[b] \in \oint[T(a/x)]\ \exists[c] \in \oint[R(\langle a,b\rangle/y)]\ \forall n \in \lambda\ \ n \vdash [b] \Rightarrow [fn] \vdash [c]\}$$

Since this representation differs from the one assumed in the earlier proof, we reformulate it as follows. Consider a typical element of the family $\underline{\Sigma z\ \ \phi\ S}$ indexed by $[a] \in \oint[\phi]$—say $[d] \in \oint[S(a/z)]$ Consider the λ-term $f \equiv \lambda x\ (u\langle\bar{\nabla}(a), x\rangle)(\bar{\nabla}(d))$ it can be verified that $[f] \in \oint[\Pi y : T(a/x)\ R(\langle a,y\rangle/y)]$ We define a (unique) morphism

$$U^*\ \ \underline{\Sigma z\ \ \phi\ S} \rightarrow \underline{\Sigma x\ \ \phi\ \Pi y\ \ T\ R(\langle x,y\rangle/y)}$$

the member of which indexed by $[a] \in \oint[\phi]$ has the following action

$$U^*_{[a]} \cdot [d] \mapsto [\lambda x\ (u\langle\nabla(a), x\rangle)(\bar{\nabla}(d))]$$

the family may be seen to be realized by the λ-term corresponding to $\lambda zyx\ (u\langle z, x\rangle)y$ We have to verify the factorization condition through the co-unit Consider the object obtained by re-indexing the object $\underline{\Sigma x\ \ \phi\ \Pi y\ \ T\ R(\langle x,y\rangle/y)}$ along $\mathcal{P}T$ we shall denote it as X—the precise Φ^0 expression for it is not very important; we have a $\bar{\Phi}$ morphism $\epsilon\ .\ X \rightarrow \underline{\Sigma y\ \ (\Sigma x\ \ \phi\ T)\ R}$ and we may say, of any member of it, indexed by $[\langle a,b\rangle] \in \oint[\Sigma x\ \ \phi\ T]$, that $\epsilon_{[\langle a,b\rangle]}\ \ [f] \mapsto [c]$ where $[f] \in \oint[\Pi y \cdot T(a/x)\ R(\langle a,y\rangle/y)]$ and $f\bar{\nabla}(b) \vdash [c] \in \oint[R(\langle a,b\rangle/y)]$, this may be verified to be well-defined The family is realized by the term corresponding to $\lambda yx\ x(\pi_1(y))$ We also have the morphism U' obtained by re-indexing U^* and we can see that its member indexed by $[\langle a,b\rangle]$ has the following action $U'_{[\langle a,b\rangle]}\ \ [d] \mapsto [\lambda x\ (u\langle\bar{\nabla}(a), x\rangle)(\nabla(d))]$, and the family can be seen to tracked by the term corresponding to $\lambda zyx\ (u\langle\pi_0(z), x\rangle)y$ Composing, we have $\epsilon_{[\langle a,b\rangle]} \circ U'_{[\langle a,b\rangle]}$ $[d] \mapsto [c]$ where $(\lambda x\ (u\langle\bar{\nabla}(a), x\rangle)(\bar{\nabla}(d)))(\bar{\nabla}(b)) \vdash [c]$ or $(u\langle\bar{\nabla}(a), \bar{\nabla}(b)\rangle)(\bar{\nabla}(d)) \vdash [c]$; but $(u\langle\bar{\nabla}(a), \bar{\nabla}(b)\rangle)$ tracks $U_{[a]}$ hence $(u\langle\nabla(a), \nabla(b)\rangle)(\nabla(d)) \vdash U_{[a]}([d])$ or $[d] \mapsto U_{[a]}([d])$ and hence we can say that $U = \epsilon \circ U'$ Hence the proposition

We claim now that the fibration p has a generic object

Theorem 6.2.19 *There is an object* $\{\oint[\Gamma]\}_{x \in \oint[1_O]}$ *in* $\bar{\Phi}$ *such that* $q(\{\oint[\Gamma]\}_{x \in \oint[1_O]}) = \oint[1_O]$ *terminal in* $\mathbf{B}$, $\mathcal{Q}_0(\{\oint[\Gamma]\}_{x \in \oint[1_O]}) \cong \oint[\Gamma]$, *and such that the object* $\{\oint[x]\}_{x \in \oint[\Gamma]} \in \tilde{\Lambda}$ *is generic for the fibration* p

Proof· Consider any object $A \equiv \underline{\Sigma x\ \ \phi\ \alpha}$ in $\tilde{\Lambda}$, in the fiber over ϕ, and consider the map $\bar{A}\ \ \oint[\phi] \rightarrow \oint[\Gamma]$ given as follows·

$$\bar{A}\ \ [a] \mapsto [\alpha^*(a/x)]$$

where α^* is as defined in Definition 6 1 6, and $[a] \in \oint[\phi]$ This map is tracked by the term $\lambda x\,\Omega$ The cartesian lifting of $\bar{A}$ is $\bar{A}\ \ A \to \{\oint[x]\}_{x \in \oint[\Gamma]}$ given by the s-morphism $\bar{A}$, and the family $\bar{A}_{[a]}\ \ \oint[\alpha(a/x)] \to \oint[\alpha^*(a/x)]$, which maps $[b] \in \oint[\alpha(a/x)]$ either to $[b]$ or to $[\langle b, \Omega\rangle]$ in its co-domain depending on which of the clauses in the definition of α^* applies The realizer for the family is similarly I or $\langle I, \Omega\rangle$ respectively (I being the Identity combinator)

This is an all-important result and gives us the means to represent an Order of all Types—or equivalently, model the free Type variable If in addition we may prove that the Comprehension Category $\mathcal{P}$ has $\mathcal{Q}$-sums and $\mathcal{Q}$ products, then we have the closure of Types under impredicative forms of quantification over Orders We shall do this by establishing that the functor ∇ is a fibered left adjoint to the functor $\mathcal{I}$ Then, the construction of the relevant $\mathcal{Q}$-sums and products may simply be done by embedding the Types into the Orders, taking the sums or products in the latter, and then reflecting them back into the former through ∇ Let us establish the facts about ∇

Proposition 6.2.20 *The functor ∇ is cartesian*

Proof. Consider a cartesian morphism f in $\bar{\Phi}$ as we have seen in the proof of Lemma 6 2 11, f may be taken to be given as $f\ \ \underline{\Sigma x\ \ \phi\ R(u(x)/y)} \to \underline{\Sigma y\ \ \psi\ R}$, for suitable $\Sigma y \cdot \psi\ R$, ϕ and $u\ \ \oint[\phi] \to \oint[\psi]$ The image of f under ∇ is $\nabla(f)\ \ \underline{\Sigma x\ \ \phi\ \nabla(R(u(x)/y))} \to \underline{\Sigma y\ \ \psi.\nabla(R)}$ and we can easily see that this is cartesian in $\bar{\Lambda}$, from the following simple fact

$$\Sigma x \cdot \phi\ \nabla(R(u(x)/y)) = \Sigma x\ \ \phi\ (\nabla(R))(u(x)/y)$$

the left hand side representing the re-indexing of $\underline{\Sigma y\ \ \psi\ \nabla(R)}$ along u

Proposition 6 2.21 *The functor $\mathcal{I}$ is cartesian*

Proof The result is straightforward the action of $\mathcal{I}$ on any object essentially is to "pair" every element with the symbol Ω The result is isomorphic to the original object. Hence, pullback properties of the image of cartesian maps, are conserved We do not labour the details, which are quite straightforward

We have the main result

Theorem 6 2.22 *The functor ∇ is the fibered left adjoint to the functor $\mathcal{I}$*

Proof: We consider the following data, sketched in Figure 6-6 an object $\underline{\Sigma x\ \ \phi\ T} \in \bar{\Phi}$,

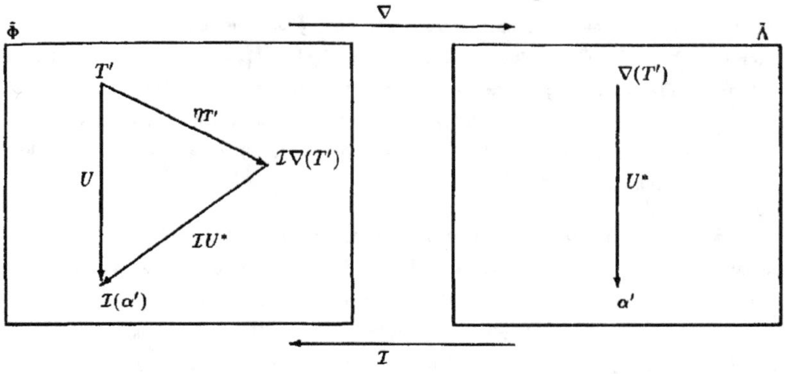

Figure 6-6 The Adjunction

an object $\underline{\Sigma y}\ \ \psi\, \alpha \in \bar{\Lambda}$ (we shall denote the former as T', and the latter as α'), and a morphism $U\ \ T' \rightarrow \mathcal{I}(\alpha')$, consisting of the s-morphism $v\ \ \phi \rightarrow \psi$, and a family of morphisms $f \equiv \{f_x\}_{x \in \oint[\phi]}$ Consider any $[a] \in \oint[\phi]$, and a typical element $[x]$ in the member of the family T' indexed by $[a]$ (*i e* $[x] \in \oint[T(a/x)]$) Suppose we have that $U_{[a]}\ \ [x] \rightarrow [\langle y, \Omega\rangle]$ where $[y] \in \oint[\alpha(b/y)]$ and $v([a]) = [b]$ We define a $\bar{\Lambda}$ morphism U^*, consisting of the s-morphism v, and a family $\{U^*_{[a]}\}_{[a] \in \oint[\phi]}$, the member indexed by $[a]$ has the following action $U^*_{[a]}\ \ [\nabla(x)] \rightarrow [y]$ where, as assumed before $U_{[a]}\ \ [x] \rightarrow [\langle y, \Omega\rangle]$ The argument sketched in the proof of Proposition 6.2.9, along with the fact that $y = \bar{\nabla}(y)$ (since α' is in $\bar{\Lambda}$), tells us that this map is well-defined and unique We can see that the family U^* is realized by the term corresponding to $\pi_0 \circ u$ where u realizes U We check the factorization through the unit $\eta_{T'}$ consider any member of the family $\eta_{T'}$—say indexed by $[a]$; we have that $(\eta_{T'})_{[a]}\ \ [x] \mapsto [\langle\bar{\nabla}(x), \Omega\rangle]$, while for the corresponding member of the family $\mathcal{I}U^*$ we have that $(\mathcal{I}U^*)_{[a]} \cdot [\langle\bar{\nabla}(x), \Omega\rangle] \mapsto [\langle y, \Omega\rangle]$; hence $(\mathcal{I}U^* \circ \eta_T)_{[a]}\ \ [x] \mapsto [\langle y, \Omega\rangle]$ and we have that $U = \mathcal{I}U^* \circ \eta_T$

We may thus assert the main result of this chapter

Theorem 6.2.23 *The structure set up in the Definitions 6 2 1-6 2 8 is a CC-Category*

Proof: This follows from the sequence of results Theorem 6 2 17, Lemma 6 2 10, Theorem 6 2 22 and Theorem 6 2 19, and the Theorem 6 2 18

Remark 6 2 24 *As we have stated in Proposition 5 4 2, this fact yield several important entailments We have from Item 1 (of Proposition 5 4 2) that p represents a fibered cartesian* *closed category, also that it is locally small. Item 2 tells us that it is small, and from the constructions, that it is (isomorphic to) the externalization of an internal category (in* **B***) whose object of objects is* $\oint[\Gamma]$. *We shall signify this internal category as* $\underline{\Lambda}$. *We may check, as concrete instances of the assumptions of Theorems 5.3.7 and 5.3.8, that representing arrows for the fiber-wise hom-sets are given as (images of, under the appropriate comprehension category) local exponentials, and these are display maps, so are the first projections. We may conclude, on the basis of Item 3, that that* $\underline{\Lambda}$ *is a full internal sub-category of* **B**—provided, of course, that $\mathcal{P}$ is the (internal) global sections functor. *This is not difficult to verify, and we do that below.*

Proposition 6.2.25 *The functor* $\mathcal{P}$ *is the internal global sections functor for the internal category* $\underline{\Lambda}$, *thus it is a full internal sub-category of* **B**.

Proof: Using the equivalence between $\bar{\Lambda}$ and the externalization $\sum(\underline{\Lambda})$, we can see that the image under $\mathcal{P}$ of any object $A \equiv \underline{\Sigma x \cdot \phi . \alpha}$ in $\bar{\Lambda}$ (which corresponds to the morphism $\bar{A} : \oint[\phi] \to \oint[\Gamma]$, using the notation of the proof of Theorem 6.2.19—and thus, to an object of the externalization $\sum(\underline{\Lambda})$ in the fiber over $\oint[\phi]$), is the object $\pi_0 : \oint[\Sigma x \cdot \phi . \alpha] \to \oint[\phi]$ in $\mathbf{B}^{\to}$, and this can be seen to be the pullback of the generic morphism $\pi_0 : \oint[\Sigma x \cdot \Gamma x] \to \oint[\Gamma]$ along the map $\bar{A}$. This is exactly the action of the internal global sections functor on objects. On the other hand, a morphism in the fiber over $\oint[\phi]$—say $f : \underline{\Sigma x \cdot \phi . \alpha} \to \underline{\Sigma x \cdot \phi . \beta}$—consists (essentially) of a family $\{f_x\}_{x \in \oint[\phi]}$ as we have seen. The action of $\mathcal{P}$ on this is the commutative square in **B** as described in Definition 6.2.5 (with u as the identity). Each morphism f_x in the family, is a morphism between (denotations of) objects in $\oint[\Gamma]$ and hence corresponds to [the re-indexing of the generic family of morphisms in the fiber above the object of maps Δ_1 of the internal category $\underline{\Lambda}$ along] a morphism $f' : \oint[\phi] \to \Delta_1$; this morphism can be seen to be tracked by the λ-term $\lambda x.nx$, where n is the realizer of the family f. It may also be verified that the generic morphism s (in the context of Figure 5-4) is simply the image of the generic family of maps (given by local smallness) in the fiber over Δ_1 (cf. Figure 5-7) under the action of $\mathcal{P}_0$. It is quite straightforward to verify that $\bar{f}$—in the commuting triangle which is the image of f under $\mathcal{P}$—is (isomorphic to) the pullback of the generic morphism s along f'. This is again precisely the action of the internal global sections functor on morphisms, and hence the proposition.

Finally, we can see from the arguments above, that $\underline{\Lambda}$ is a full internal relatively cartesian closed sub-category of **B**.

Theorem 6 2.26 *The internal category $\underline{\Delta}$ is a full internal relatively cartesian closed subcategory of* **B**.

Proof: We know that the functor $\mathcal{P}$ is a closed comprehension category Hence, from Proposition 6.2.25 above and the definition, the result is immediate

Remark 6.2.27 *Before ending this chapter, we should clarify a point regarding the definition of the category ω-***Set** *given earlier Normally, the realizers are elements of a combinatory algebra, usually the (closed) term model of the λ-Calculus In this case, we have taken them to be λ-terms themselves, which is strictly speaking incorrect However, in the case of our category* **B**, *the set of realizers of any element is a ≃-equivalence class of terms, and ≃* extends *the β-equivalence Hence the slight incorrectness does not make a difference to any of the arguments In the next chapter, we shall use the correct definition*

This brings the first part of our study to a close In this part, we have systematically developed the idea of a Heyting-semantics of λ-expressions, in close analogy to that for propositions The epitome of this development is the categorical structure that interprets—and thus instantiates (*cf* Remark 5 4 3)—a full Theory of Constructions In the next part of our study, we explore the relationship between this kind of semantics, and the traditional denotational semantics of the Tarski-Scott persuasion The guiding idea would still be the strict analogy with the corresponding situation for propositions Predictably, this would entail a move towards Toposes, and intuitionistic logic Remarkably, we shall see that the nature of our constructions permit a fairly smooth transition into denotational semantics—*internal to the Topos* currently a rich theoretical field of study

Chapter 7

The Realizability Topos

In the earlier chapters, we have traced the induction, on the basis of the λ-Types, of a structure admitting an interpretation of a (impredicative) theory of dependent Types This structure was seen to be an instance of a CC-Category, which means that it carries an interpretation of, and thus instantiates, a Theory of Constructions This development marks the completion of one of the major aims of this thesis it realizes the program of a Heyting semantics for programs (λ-terms) around the general axis of the Curry-Howard isomorphism As we have mentioned in the Introduction, a Heyting semantics is a two-step process: it is completed by giving a "standard" logical interpretation of the category of Types as an adequately complete internal category in some non-standard universe of (intuitionistic) sets Such interpretations are by now well-known the small complete category of Modest sets within the Moggi Hyland Realizability Topos ([33, 34, 36, 61]; we shall describe it in this chapter), the classifying topos of pre-sheaves over the hyperdoctrine model of the polymorphic λ-Calculus ([62]), the algebraic and the algebraic-localic toposes ([38])—to name a few In this dissertation we shall not labour this second step of the process, instead, we shall turn to the question of the relationship between the constructive semantics developed thus far and the traditional Tarskian (denotational) semantics (of the terms) , *within the general framework of a non-standard intuitionistic universe* More specifically, we shall display the process of the construction of (in a sense, canonical) denotations of the terms—as the directed completions of the Type of their proof objects—within the Realizability Topos in which the latter is embedded as a full internal sub-category The resultant class of objects would be seen (in the next chapter) to be a small category of *internal* directed-complete partial orders (dcpos), and having a structure generalizing that of the corresponding object in the case of propositions From a logical point of view, this has rich implications the denotational domains can be formally regarded as (non-standard) sets with *standard* function spaces—and hence we may reason freely about them in the internal logic Thus, in a sense we have in them a rudimentary abstract logic of programs[1]

This relationship would be composed and explored within a framework that has gained considerable significance ever since the endeavor of Scott to conceptualize the domains of denotations of Programs as (non-standard) *Sets* with ***full function spaces*** ([74])—something clearly impossible in the classical universe The idea developed, from Scott, through Pitts and Hyland ([37, 62, 34, 35]), and to Rosolini ([68]), Phoa ([58]) and a number of other researchers, that denotations of the Types in programming languages could be formally regarded as Sets, if only the constructions were carried out *internally* within (a categorical model) of an intuitionistic universe Such an universe had been known since Lawvere, as an ***elementary topos*** (through an elegant reformulation of the existing notion of a Grothendieck Topos, constructed for entirely different purposes) A significant turn in this history, towards recursion theory and Computer Science, was Hyland's construction of the ***effective topos*** ([33])—in some sense, the categorical model of the world of constructive mathematics; and to a great extent, a generalization of the idea of the interpretation of intuitionistic logic in terms of the category of sheaves on a locale ([37], as re-formulated by Fourman and Scott as the notion of an Ω-Set ([20]) It was thus, a matter of great significance, when Hyland and his collaborators announced the discovery of a complete internal category within the effective topos ([34, 36]) complete in a way as to admit the interpretation of the polymorphic lambda calculus This category has since been come to be known as the category of ***modest sets***—a name suggested by Dana Scott originally In this chapter, we shall present some of the background required to appreciate this history, and embed our earlier constructions in a suitable way within its framework In the next chapter, we would take up formally the theme of denotational semantics internal to the Topos

7.1 Partial Equivalence Relations

In this section, we shall be presenting some of the material that is well-known in the semantics of impredicative Calculi (for example, System F, and its various extensions), and which shall serve as a background *and* motivation for the constructions in which this chapter would culminate We shall not pretend to be comprehensive or very rigorous the interested reader may consult any of the list of references on this subject that we shall provide in the bibliography The basic material is drawn, with a few alterations, from the excellent discussion by

[1] We are reminded of a similar attempt by Abramsky to develop a logic of programs as dual structure of their denotational domains ([2], also [88])

W. Phoa in [61]

The Partial Equivalence Relations have been known, in their present form, as a "sufficiently" complete category of objects within the Effective Topos, since the late eighties; the basic framework had been known earlier, from the works of Kreisel, Girard, Troelstra and Scott. After the demonstration by Reynolds, that the Polymorphic Lambda Calculus could not have any Set-theoretic models, it was left to Hyland, Moggi and later, Pitts, to show that the salient constructions of a Set-theoretic interpretation *could* be carried out in a formal universe of sets, provided the logic was intuitionistic and not classical. In other words, the kind of completeness required for interpreting impredicative quantification, could be obtained in a suitable *internal category* within a Topos-theoretic model of IZF Set Theory An instance of such an internal category turns out to be the (image of the) category of partial equivalence relations (abbreviated hereafter as PER) But before the arguments are cast in the logic of the relevant Topos, it is instructive to see how the requisite forms of completeness obtains in the category of PERs itself This is the subject of this section

We shall work on basis of the combinatory algebra λ, composed of the *closed* term model of the λ-Calculus Hence mention of λ-terms in the sequel would generally mean the equivalence class thereof with respect to the β-equivalence We would generally term such a class, as a *code*, and confuse terms with their equivalence classes

Definition 7.1.1 *A* Partial Equivalence Relation *on* $\bar{\lambda}$ *is a symmetric and transitive relation on* $\bar{\lambda}$ *The* domain *of such a relation* R, *is defined as the set*

$$dom(R) \equiv \{x \in \bar{\lambda} \mid xRx\}$$

For any $x \in dom(R)$, *we shall write* $[x]_R$ *to denote the equivalence class of* x *with respect to the relation* R *The set of such equivalence classes would be denoted as* Ξ_R *and is defined formally as stated below*

$$\Xi_R \equiv \{[x]_R \mid x \in dom(R)\}$$

The subscripts R may be dropped from the notations if the relation is clear from the context We may construct a category from the class of PERs provided we have a notion of the morphisms

Definition 7.1.2 *The category* **PER** *has the following constituents*

Objects: *The objects are Partial Equivalence Relations over* $\bar{\lambda}$

Morphisms: *For* R, S *objects of* **PER**, *a morphism* $f \quad R \to S$ *is a map* $f \quad \Xi_R \to \Xi_S$ *satisfying*

$$\exists s \in \bar{\lambda}\ \forall x \in \bar{\lambda}\ (x \in \mathrm{dom}(R) \Rightarrow f([x]_R) = [s \quad x]_S) \qquad (7\ 1)$$

An element $s \in \bar{\lambda}$ that instances the condition in Equation 7.1, is said to be a code that tracks the morphism f. We may also define a morphism in **PER** *as the equivalence class of codes that track the corresponding map, with the equivalence relation (denoted as S^R) given by*

$$s(S^R)s' \longleftrightarrow \forall x \in \bar{\lambda}\ (x \in \mathrm{dom}(R) \Rightarrow s\ \ x(S)s'\ \ x)$$

and indicate this by $[s] : R \to S$

The category **PER** turns out to have strong completeness properties, we record the following fact for reference

Theorem 7.1.3 *The category* **PER** *is locally cartesian closed*

Proof: We shall merely sketch the proof let us first see how **PER** is cartesian closed The product of PERs R and S, is the PER $R \times S$ defined below

$$s(R \times S)t \Leftrightarrow \pi_0(s)R\pi_0(t) \bigwedge \pi_1(s)R\pi_1(t)$$

where π_0 and π_1 are the standard λ-definable projections The projection maps $R \leftarrow R \times S \rightarrow S$ are tracked by π_0 and π_1 respectively The terminal object in **PER** may be seen to be the PER **1** defined by: $\forall s, t \in \bar{\lambda}\ s\mathbf{1}t$

We can define binary exponents as follows for objects $R, S \in$ **PER**, we have the PER S^R defined by

$$\mathrm{dom}(S^R) = \{s \in \bar{\lambda} \mid s \text{ tracks an arrow } R \to S\}$$

with the equivalence relation defined as stated earlier

$$s(S^R)s' \longleftrightarrow \forall x \in \bar{\lambda}\ (x \in \mathrm{dom}(R) \Rightarrow s\ \ x(S)s'\ \ x)$$

The evaluation morphism $ev : S^R \times R \to S$ is tracked by $[\lambda x\ \pi_0(x)(\pi_1(x))]$

As for cartesian closure in the slices, consider the slice **PER**$/S$ the terminal object can be seen to be the identity map id_S. Consider now maps $[r] . R \to S$ and $[t] \cdot T \to S$. their binary product is the obvious map $R \times T \to S$ Finally, for exponents we shall see that the construction parallels the construction of a representing object for the maps over a fiber (in the context of local smallness). For any $x \in \mathrm{dom}(S)$ we define the ***fiber** over x* as the following PER R_x (or T_x as the case may be)

$$\mathrm{dom}(R_x) = \{y \in \mathrm{dom}R \mid [r](y) = x\} \qquad yR_xz \Leftrightarrow yRz$$

We define the PER Q as follows

$$\begin{aligned} \mathrm{dom}(Q) &= \{(x,n) \mid x \in \mathrm{dom}S,\ n \text{ tracks an arrow } R_x \to T_x\} \\ (x,n)T(x',n') &= xSx' \bigwedge n(T_x)^{R_x}n' \end{aligned}$$

The first projection $Q \to S$ turns out to be the exponential $[t]^{[r]}$ in the slice

It is also easy to see that **PER** has equalizers Consider arrows $[n],[m]$ $R \to S$ We define the domain of the equalizer as follows.

$$\begin{aligned} \mathrm{dom}(X) &\equiv \{r \in \mathrm{dom}(R) \mid (n\ \ x)S(m\ \ x)\} \\ \forall x,y \in \mathrm{dom}(X)\ x(X)y &\Leftrightarrow x(R)y \end{aligned}$$

and this tells us that **PER** has finite limits

We can now turn to the question of how **PER** may provide a model of the polymorphic lambda calculus (or System F) There are two ways in which this might be seen: first, by establishing the closure of **PER** under products indexed by its own set of objects, and second by establishing a suitable fibration p **PER** $\to$ **S** equipped with a generic object We provide a brief sketch of the first, the second is postponed to the next section

The basic problem in interpreting System F is to be able to model the impredicative Types of the form $\Pi X\ F(X)$ (where X is a Type variable, and $F(X)$ is a Type expression) and polymorphic abstraction terms of the form $\Lambda X\ \lambda x\ \ X\ x$, related through the following introduction and elimination rules

$$\frac{t\ \ F(X)\,[x\ \ A, X \cdot Type]}{\Lambda X\, t\ \ \Pi X\ F(X)\,[x\ \ A]} \qquad \frac{f\ \ \Pi X\ F(X)\,[x\ \ A] \qquad B\ \ Type}{f B\ \ F(B)\,[x\ \ A]}$$

As we have seen in an earlier chapter, we could interpret judgements of the form t $F(X)$ $[x$ A, X $Type]$ as a $Type$-indexed class of morphisms $\{f_p\ \ A \to F(p)\}_{p \in Type}$—with the additional condition perhaps, that the indexing was *uniform* (in some manner to be explicated) on $Type$ The problem upon refinement reduces to the following: suppose we interpret our Types as objects of some category **P**, and variable Types of the form $F(X)$ $[X$ $Type]$ were to be interpreted in the functor category $\mathbf{P}^{\mathbf{P}}$, then given an arbitrary functor $F(\_)$ $\mathbf{P} \to \mathbf{P}$, we require an object $\Pi(F) \in \mathbf{P}$, such that there is a bijective correspondence between the set of **P**-indexed set of morphism $\{f_p\ \ A \to F(p)\}_{p \in \mathbf{P}}$ and the set of **P**-morphisms $\mathrm{hom}(A, \Pi(F))$—for any object $A \in \mathbf{P}$ In other words, we require a right adjoint to the diagonal functor Δ $\mathbf{P} \to \mathbf{P}^{\mathbf{P}}$ (equivalently, the existence of limits of diagrams of type **P**) Now while these general limits might not exist (in the naive or external sense) they *do* exist (more precisely, an object with the property of $\Pi(F)$ described above) for a category like **PER**, provided the family $\{f_p\ \ A \to F(p)\}_{p \in \mathbf{P}}$ satisfies a particular condition namely, that every member is tracked by the same code We may describe such families as *uniform* We shall describe how such "limits" can be constructed below the key to their existence being that PERs are closed under arbitrary intersections the point to note however, is that such limits *do* exist (in the general sense as the right adjoint to the diagonal functor) when **PER** is regarded as an internal category (in some suitable ambient category), and the notions of adjunctions and etc. are appropriately internalized. We shall remark on this briefly in the sequel, and for an excellent discussion on this, refer the reader to [34, 36, 48].

Theorem 7.1.4 *The category* **PER** *has the property, that any diagram F of type* **PER** *has a u-limit $\Pi(F)$ in* **PER**, *by which we mean, that there exists a right adjoint to the diagonal functor Δ: **PER** $\to$ **PER**$^{\mathbf{PER}}$—the latter category being the category of functors **PER** $\to$ **PER** with uniform natural transformations (see below) as morphisms.*

Proof: We note that given an arbitrary collection of PERs $\{R_i\}_{i\in I}$, we may define their intersection as follows

$$s(\bigcap_{i\in I} A_i)t \Leftrightarrow \forall i \in I.\, sA_i t$$

Then given a functor F: **PER** $\to$ **PER**, we define

$$\Pi(F) \equiv \bigcap_{R\in\mathbf{PER}} F(R)$$

which is guaranteed to exist, as we have just seen. Now consider any object $A \in$ **PER** and an uniform natural transformation t: $\Delta(A) \to F$; this means we have a single code s tracking every morphism in the **PER**-indexed collection of morphism $\{t_R : A \to F(R)\}_{R\in\mathbf{PER}}$. This implies that for any $x \in \mathrm{dom}(A)$, the element $s \cdot x \in \mathrm{dom}(F(R))$ for every $R \in$ **PER**, and this gives us a morphism $t^*: A \to \Pi(F)$: $[x]_A \mapsto [s \cdot x]_{\Pi(F)}$. The other part of the bijection is easier: any $t^*: A \to \Pi(F)$ tracked by the code s, gives us the uniform family of maps $\{t_R : A \to F(R) : [x]_R \mapsto [s \cdot x]_{F(R)}\}_{R\in\mathbf{PER}}$, i.e. a (uniform) natural transformation $\Delta(A) \to F$. By the definition of $\Pi(F)$ as the intersection, the element $s \cdot x \in \mathrm{dom}(F(R))$ for every $R \in$ **PER** and hence this morphism in **PER**$^{\mathbf{PER}}$ is well-defined.

The details of the interpretation of polymorphic Types would appear considerably more perspicuous when set out in terms of (suitably) complete fibrations. However, the idea that polymorphic Types were interpreted in terms of right adjoints to something akin to a substitution (or re-indexing) functor, and that such right adjoints are available in **PER** through *intersections*, would still be basic to the treatment.

This interpretation of System F encounters a irremediable difficulty when sought to be extended to the interpretation of dependent Types. The straightforward intuition would be that since **PER** is locally cartesian closed, we could model dependent Types through the fibration cod: **PER**$^{\to}$ $\to$ **PER**: this is guaranteed to be locally small, and hence adequate for the interpretation However, we immediately encounter the difficulty that this fibration does not have a generic object. Such a generic object would be something like the set of all PERs, and while such a set exists, it is not a PER itself This deficiency rules out the interpretation of free Type variables, and thus of course, of polymorphic Types We could try to circumvent this difficulty through a fibration over a larger category—say **SET**, which would interpret the Orders· however, while the standard form of this fibration—namely, as families of PERs indexed by sets—has a generic object, *and* is suitably complete, it is *not* locally small—thus ruling out the possibility of modeling dependent Types. We would then try to look for an even larger base category, which would have both the properties of local smallness and the existence of a generic object It turns out that such a category is available, and this is the subject of the next section

7.2 ω-Sets

The development of this chapter parallels to some extent that of the preceding part of the thesis there, we had initially set up a relatively cartesian closed category which could model dependent Types, the problem was that this fibration did not possess a generic object In syntactic terms, this was taken to mean that we could not have a Type of all Types, and thus we had to move to a larger category which did have something like an Order of all Types We have a similar intuition here we shall preserve the fact that **PER** (fibered over itself) can support dependent Types, and look for a larger category which would have an object corresponding to the object of all PERs This has been known in the literature for some time as the category of ω-sets, and contains both **PER** and **SET** as full sub-categories We have already introduced this category in the previous chapter, and we reiterate the definition below

Definition 7.2.1 *The category* ω-Set *has the following constituents*

Objects: *Objects are pairs* $\langle X, \vdash \rangle$ *where* X *is a set and* $\vdash$ *is a relation in* $\bar{\lambda} \times X$, *and such that* $\forall x \in X \; \exists n \in \bar{\lambda} \; n \vdash x$, *we say that* n realizes x *We would annotate the relation as* $\vdash_X$ *whenever necessary*

Morphisms: *A morphism* $f \;\; \langle X, \vdash_X \rangle \rightarrow \langle Y, \vdash_Y \rangle$ *is a map* $f \;\; X \rightarrow Y$ *satisfying the following condition:*

$$\exists n \in \bar{\lambda} \; \forall x \in X \; \forall p \in \bar{\lambda} \; (p \vdash_X x \Rightarrow (n \;\; p) \vdash_Y f(a))$$

we say that n *tracks* f, *for any morphism* f, *we shall denote a code which tracks it, generically, as* $\hat{f}$

We shall use the symbol $[x \in X]$ to denote the set $\{n \in \bar{\lambda} \mid n \vdash_X x\}$

We would expect that at **ω-Set** would, at the least, have the same kind of closure properties as **PER** This is so and we sketch the argument in the next Theorem

Theorem 7.2.2 *The category* **ω-Set** *is locally cartesian closed*

Proof: The category has the terminal object $\mathbf{1} \equiv \langle 1, \vdash_1 \rangle$ where **1** is the singleton set, and the relation $\vdash_1$ is defined to be $1 \times \bar{\lambda}$ (i.e any code realizes the single element) Given ω-sets $X \equiv \langle X, \vdash_X \rangle$, $Y \equiv \langle Y, \vdash_Y \rangle$, their product is the ω-set $\langle X \times Y, \vdash_{X \times Y} \rangle$ where

$$\langle m, n \rangle \vdash_{X \times Y} \langle x, y \rangle \Leftrightarrow m \vdash_X x \bigwedge n \vdash_Y y$$

for any $\langle x, y \rangle \in X \times Y$. The exponent Y^X is defined as follows

$$Y^X \equiv \{f \mid f \in \hom_{\omega\text{-Set}}(X, Y)\} \qquad n \vdash_{Y^X} f \Leftrightarrow n \text{ tracks } f$$

and we leave the evaluation morphism to the reader

As for cartesian closure in the slices, let us consider morphisms $f \; X \to Z$ and $g \; Y \to Z$ in the slice **ω-Set**$/Z$ their product is obvious, and so is the terminal object in this slice The exponent is constructed in a fashion similar to that for **PER** For any $z \in Z$, define the set $X_z \equiv \{x \in X \mid f(x) = z\}$, we turn this into a ω-set by defining $\forall x \in X_z \; n \vdash_{X_z} x \Leftrightarrow n \vdash_X x$, we may similarly define Y_z Now the ω-set Q is defined as follows

$$Q \equiv \{\langle z, h \rangle \mid z \in Z, \, h \in \hom_{\omega\text{-Set}}(X_z, Y_z)\}$$

$$n \vdash_Q \langle z, h \rangle \Leftrightarrow \pi_0(n) \vdash_Z z \bigwedge \pi_1(n) \text{ tracks the morphism } h$$

and it may be verified that the first projection $Q \to Z$ is the exponent f^g in the slice

We can see the full embeddings of **PER** and **SET** into **ω-Set**

Proposition 7.2 3 *There is a full embedding* ∇_S **SET** $\hookrightarrow$ **ω-Set**

Proof For any set X we define the ω set $\nabla_S(X) \equiv \langle X, \vdash_X \rangle$ with the relation $\vdash_X \equiv X \times \bar{\lambda}$ For any function $f \; X \to Y$ in **SET**, we have the morphism $\nabla_S(f) \; \nabla_S(X) \to \nabla_S(Y)$, which has f as the underlying map, and is tracked by (say) $\lambda x \, x \in \bar{\lambda}$

Proposition 7.2.4 *There is a full embedding* $\nabla_P \cdot$ **PER** $\hookrightarrow$ **ω-Set**

Proof· For any PER R, we define the ω-set $\nabla_P(R)$ as having the underlying set Ξ_R, and with the relation $\vdash$ defined by $n \vdash [x]_R \Leftrightarrow n \in [x]_R$ For a map $[s] \; R \to S$ in **PER**, we define $\nabla_P([s])$ as the map in **ω-Set** having the underlying map $[s] \; \Xi_R \to \Xi_S$ which is obviously tracked by all the codes in $[s]$ Fullness follows easily

We shall denote the full-subcategory of ω-**Set** that is the image of ∇_P by the symbol **MOD** There is an useful characterization of **MOD** which we state below

Proposition 7.2.5 **MOD** *is the full sub-category of* ω-**Set** *consisting of objects* $\langle X, \vdash_X \rangle$ *satisfying the following condition*

$$\forall x, y \in X \quad n \vdash_X x \bigwedge n \vdash_X y \Rightarrow x = y \tag{7 2}$$

Proof: If $R \in$ **PER**, then $\nabla_P(R)$ obviously satisfies this condition (equivalence classes do not intersect) On the other hand, if there is an object X in ω-**Set** satisfying the condition then we may define a PER $\tilde{X}$ as

$$s(\tilde{X})t \Leftrightarrow \exists x \in X \;\; s \vdash_X x \bigwedge t \vdash_X x$$

We may now verify our intuitions concerning ω-**Set** namely that we may define a suitable fibration of PERs over ω-**Set** which is sufficiently complete to be able to model both dependent Types and polymorphism We shall argue that the following fibration suffices

Definition 7.2.6 *We define a fibration* p $\wp \to \omega$-**Set** *The category* $\wp$ *has the following constitution*

Objects· *Objects are* X*-indexed families of PERs for any* $X \in \omega$-**Set** *more formally, an object* R_X, *for* $X \in \omega$-**Set**, *is a family* $R_X \equiv \{R_x\}_{x \in X}$ *such that each* $R_x \in$ **PER**

Morphisms: *For objects* R_X *and* S_Y, *a morphism* $f : R_X \to S_Y$ *consists of a pair* $\langle \bar{f}, f_X \rangle$ *where* $\bar{f}$ $X \to Y$ *in* ω-**Set**, *and* $f_X \equiv \{f_x \cdot R_x \to S_{\bar{f}(x)}\}_{x \in X}$ *is a* X*-indexed family of arrows in* **PER**, *satisfying the condition.*

$$\exists n \in \bar{\lambda} \; \forall x \in X \; \forall p \in |x \in X|.(n \;\; p) \text{ tracks } f_x$$

we would say that such an n *witnesses* f *(or the family* f_X*), or* n realizes f

The fibration p *is defined in the standard way its action on objects is* p $R_X \mapsto X$, *and on arrows* $f \equiv \langle \bar{f}, f_X \rangle \mapsto \bar{f}$

It is pretty straightforward to see that this *is* a fibration we shall not labour the details The important point to check is local smallness The argument is sketched in the next proposition

Theorem 7.2.7 *The fibration* p *in Definition 7 2 6 is locally small*

Proof: Consider an object $X \in \omega$ **Set** and objects R_X and S_X in the fiber $\wp_X$ We define the object $[R_X, S_X] \in \omega$-**Set** as follows

$$
\begin{aligned}
[R_X, S_X] &\equiv \{\langle x, f\rangle \mid x \in X,\ f \in \hom_{\mathbf{PER}}(R_x, S_x)\} \\
\langle n, p\rangle \vdash_{[R_X, S_X]} \langle x, f\rangle &\Leftrightarrow n \vdash_X x \bigwedge p \text{ tracks } f
\end{aligned}
$$

with the "universal map" π $[R_X, S_X] \to X$ simply being the first projection π_0 The representing map $\pi^{R_X}_{S_X}$. $\pi^*(R_X) \to \pi^*(S_X)$ in the fiber above $[R_X, S_X]$ is given by·

$$
\langle \mathrm{id}_{[R_X, S_X]}, \{f\}_{\langle x, f\rangle \in [R_X, S_X]}\rangle
$$

with the code which witnesses the second component being obviously π_1 We shall verify the representing properties of this structure Consider any map α $Y \to X$ in ω-**Set**, and a map u $\alpha^*(R_X) \to \alpha^*(S_X)$ in the fiber over Y, witnessed by the code k. We define the map g $Y \to [R_X, S_X]$ $y \mapsto \langle x, f\rangle$ where $\alpha(y) = x$ and f $R_x \to S_x$ is that map in **PER** that is tracked by k h for all $h \in |y \in Y|$ We can verify that g is tracked by the code $\langle \hat{\alpha}, k\rangle$.

Thus, the fibration has the basic structure needed to interpret dependent Types We shall have to check now if the fibration is (sufficiently) complete. This question, as is well-known by now, is none too straightforward itself As we have mentioned earlier, there is a considerable degree of variation in the criterion of sufficiency, especially when the arguments are carried out in terms of internal categories (*and* in the internal logic of Toposes) The notion of completeness that suffices for the interpretation of polymorphic Types can be summarized in terms of Bènabou's notion of *complete* fibrations that we have stated in Section 5 2, and repeat here

Definition 7.2.8 *A fibration is said to be* complete *if it has*

- *fibered products—i e , for every morphism ϕ in the base, the re-indexing functor ϕ^* has a right adjoint Π_ϕ satisfying the Beck-Chevalley condition*
- *fiberwise finite limits*

Hence this is what we have to establish for our fibration p $\wp \to \omega$-**Set** Let us look at fibered products first Before we do this, we shall state a few lemmas we would need in the argument most of the constructions are standard, and for a more detailed presentation, we refer the reader to [48]

Definition 7.2.9 *For a ω-**Set** A, we may represent an A-indexed collection of objects of **MOD** by a mapping $\phi : A \to$ **MOD**. By the notation $f : A \to \phi$ we mean that f is a (extensional) mapping with domain A, and such that $\forall a \in A\ f(a) \in \phi(a)$. We define an object $\Pi_{a\in A}\phi(a) \in \omega$-**Set** by the following clauses*

$$\Pi_{a\in A}\phi(a) \equiv \{f : A \to \phi \mid \exists n \in \bar{\lambda}\ \forall a \in A\ \forall p \in |a \in A|\ (n \cdot p) \vdash_{\phi(a)} f(a)\}$$

$$n \vdash_{\Pi_{a\in A}\phi(a)} f \Leftrightarrow \forall a \in A\ \forall p \in |a \in A|\ (n \cdot p) \vdash_{\phi(a)} f(a)$$

The significant point is that this object is an object of **MOD**

Lemma 7.2.10 *The object $\Pi_{a\in A}\phi(a)$ defined in Definition 7.2.9 inhabits* **MOD**

Proof. We shall have to show that $\Pi_{a\in A}\phi(a)$ satisfies the condition set out in Equation 7.2 above. Consider a code n such that $n \vdash_{\Pi_{a\in A}\phi(a)} f \bigwedge n \vdash_{\Pi_{a\in A}\phi(a)} g$. But then we would have

$$\forall a \in A\ \forall p \in |a \in A|\ (n \cdot p) \vdash_{\phi(a)} f(a) \bigwedge (n \cdot p) \vdash_{\phi(a)} g(a)$$

and since both $f(a), g(a) \in \phi(a) \in$ **MOD**, (i.e. $\phi(a)$ satisfies the condition in Equation 7.2), we would have that $\forall a \in A\ f(a) = g(a)$, which means that $f = g$ (since they were defined extensionally)

We have the main result

Theorem 7.2.11 *The fibration $p : \wp \to \omega$-**Set** defined in Definition 7.2.6, is complete*

Proof: We have objects $X, Y \in \omega$-**Set**, and a morphism $\phi : X \to Y$. Consider an object R_X in the fiber $\wp_X$, and another S_Y in the fiber $\wp_Y$. We shall construct a functor $\Pi_\phi : \wp_X \to \wp_Y$ and establish a bijection

$$\langle \mu, \nu \rangle : \hom_{\wp_X}(\phi^*(S_Y), R_X) \cong \hom_{\wp_Y}(S_Y, \Pi_\phi(R_X))$$

thus demonstrating the adjunction. We shall overload notation a bit and assume that the X-indexed collection R_X corresponds to a map $R : X \to$ **MOD**^{o}, hence, the PER $R_x = R(x)$. Then we define

$$\Pi_\phi(R_X) \equiv \{\Pi_{x\in\phi^{-1}(y)}R(x)\}_{y\in Y}$$

using the notation of Definition 7.2.9, considering $R(x)$ as an object of **MOD** (*via* the embedding ∇_P). Consider a morphism $u : \phi^*(S_Y) \to R_X$, consisting of a family $\{u_x : S_{\phi(x)} \to R_x\}_{x\in X}$. Its image $\mu(u) : S_Y \to \Pi_\phi(R_X)$ is the family

$$\{u'_y : S_y \to \Pi_{x\in\phi^{-1}(y)}R(x) : [y'] \mapsto f \text{ where } f(x \in \phi^{-1}(y)) = u_x([y'])\}_{y\in Y}$$

where $y' \in \mathrm{dom}(S_y)$ We claim that $\mu(u)$ is witnessed by the code $q \equiv \lambda xyz\,(p\ z\ y)$, where p is the witness for u To see this, note that

$$\begin{aligned} \forall y \in Y\, \forall r \in |y \in Y|\ q\ r &= \lambda yz\,(p\ z\ y) = s \\ \forall y' \in \mathrm{dom}(S_y)\ s\ y' &= \lambda z\,(p\ z\ y') = t \\ \forall x \in \phi^{-1}(y)\, \forall a \in |x \in X|\ t\ a &= (p \cdot a\ y') \vdash_{R_X} u_x([y']) \end{aligned}$$

and hence we can claim that t tracks f (we have used λ-terms directly instead of equivalence classes) Looking at the other part of the bijection, given $u\ \ S_Y \to \Pi_\phi(R_X)$, consisting of the family $u_y \cdot S_y \to \Pi_{x\in\phi^{-1}(y)} R(x)$ we define $\nu(u)\ \ \phi^*(S_Y) \to R_X$ to consist of the family

$$\{u'_x \cdot S_{\phi(x)} \to R_x\ \ [y'] \mapsto (u_y([y']))(x)\}_{x\in X}$$

where $y' \in \mathrm{dom}(S_{\phi(x)})$ We claim that $\nu(u)$ is witnessed by the code $p \equiv \lambda xz\,(q\ r\ x \cdot z)\ x$ where q tracks u and r tracks ϕ. To see this, note that

$$\begin{aligned} &\forall x \in X\ \forall a \in |x \in X|\ \forall y' \in \mathrm{dom}(S_{\phi(x)})\ p\ a\ y' \\ &= (q\ r\ a\ y')\ a \\ &= ((q\ (r\ a))\ y')\ a \\ &= ((q\ e)\ y')\ a \quad \text{for some } e \in |\phi(x) \in Y| \\ &= f\ a \quad \text{for some } f \text{ that tracks } u_y([y']) \\ &\in (u_y([y']))(x) \end{aligned}$$

and hence the proposition It is straightforward though tedious to verify that the maps μ and ν are inverses, and that the naturality conditions hold. Likewise, the Beck-Chevalley can be seen to hold, and we do not labour the details

Fiberwise finite limits follows easily from the fact that **PER** has finite limits (*cf* Theorem 7.1 3) the operation of the re-indexing functors being essentially one of pulling back, they preserve the limits The details are straightforward and we omit them

The fibration p has another remarkable property it has a full and faithful cartesian functor to the codomain fibration cod ω-**Set**$^{\to} \to \omega$-**Set**

Theorem 7.2.12 ([61, Prop 4 3 16]) *There is a full and faithful cartesian functor ϕ $p \to$ cod, where cod . ω-**Set**$^{\to} \to \omega$-**Set** is the codomain fibration*

Proof: The action of q on an object R_X in the fiber over X may be described as follows. We define Y as the ω-set given by the disjoint union

$$\coprod_{x \in X} \equiv_{R_x} \text{ with } |\langle x, [p]\rangle \in Y| = \{\langle k, n\rangle \mid k \in |x \in X|, n \in [p]\}$$

where $[p]$ is the equivalence class of p with respect to the relation R_x Then we define

$$\phi(R_X) = \dot{\pi}_0 \quad Y \to X \quad \langle x, [p]\rangle \mapsto x$$

Now consider an arrow $f \quad R_X \to S_Y$ in $\wp$ The image $\phi(f)$ is the commuting square in ω-**Set** shown if Figure 7-1, with the morphism $f' \cdot \langle x, [p]\rangle \mapsto \langle \bar{f}(x), f_x([p])\rangle$ tracked by the code

$$\lambda z\,\langle n \quad \pi_0(z), (m \quad n \quad \pi_0(z)) \quad \pi_1(z)\rangle$$

where n tracks $\bar{f}$ and m witnesses f Cartesian-ness follows from the basic pullback structure of cartesian liftings, and their conservation under the mapping described above. Fullness and faithfulness are straightforward too and we do not labour the details

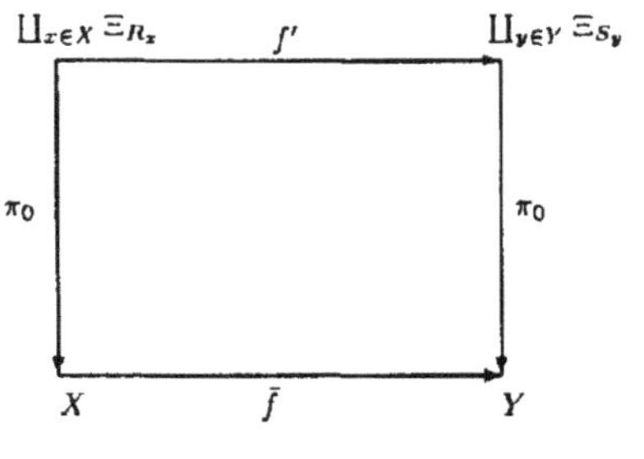

Figure 7-1

Finally, we may establish the fact essential to the interpretation of Polymorphic Types—namely the presence of a generic object

Theorem 7.2.13 *The fibration $p \quad \wp \to \omega$-**Set** defined in Definition 7 2 6, has a generic object*

Proof: We shall denote the set of all partial equivalence relations (over $\bar{\lambda}$ of course) by *PER*. Consider the ω-set $\mathbf{M}_0$ defined as $\langle PER, \vdash_{\mathbf{M}_0}\rangle$ where $\vdash_{\mathbf{M}_0} \equiv \bar{\lambda} \times PER$ The generic object for the fibration can be easily verified to be the object $\{R\}_{R \in \mathbf{M}_0}$ in the fiber over $\mathbf{M}_0$

Hence, Theorems 7.2.13 and 7.2.11 taken together give us the structure adequate for interpreting the polymorphic lambda calculus. We may also remark, that since the fibration p is locally small and has a generic object, it is a small fibration—*i.e.* (equivalent to) the externalization of an internal category in **ω-set**. Obviously, the object of objects of this category is $\mathbf{M}_0$, *viz.* the set of all PERs. Since our ultimate aim in this chapter is to structure our category $\underline{\Lambda}$ (of the previous chapter) too as an internal category in **ω-set**— it behooves us to give a description of it, and we do so in the following proposition (which we state without proof).

Theorem 7.2.14 *The structure* **M** *described by the following data, constitutes an internal category in* **ω-Set**:

M_0 *—the object of objects is as defined in Theorem 7.2.13*

M_1 *—the object of morphisms is defined as* $\langle\{\langle X,f,Y\rangle \mid (f: X \to Y) \text{ in } \mathbf{MOD}\}, \vdash_{\mathbf{M}_1}\rangle$ *and such that* $n \vdash_{\mathbf{M}_1} \langle X,f,Y\rangle \Leftrightarrow n$ *tracks* f

∂_0 *—the domain map, is defined as* $\partial_0 : \langle X,f,Y\rangle \mapsto X$

∂_1 *—the codomain map, is defined as* $\partial_1 : \langle X,f,Y\rangle \mapsto Y$

$\widetilde{\mathrm{id}}_{\mathbf{M}}$ *—the identity map, is defined as* $\widetilde{\mathrm{id}}_{\mathbf{M}} : X \mapsto \langle X,[I],X\rangle$

$\bullet_{\mathbf{M}}$ *—the composition map, is defined as* $\bullet_{\mathbf{M}} : \langle\langle X,f,Y\rangle,\langle Y,g,Z\rangle\rangle \mapsto \langle X,g\circ f,Z\rangle$

The proof is straightforward and we refer the interested reader to any of the standard works on the topic. It is easy to see that our fibration p is nothing but the externalization of **M** (up to isomorphism).

Proposition 7.2.15 *The fibration* $p : \wp \to$ **ω-Set** *is the externalization* $\sum \mathbf{M}$ *of the internal category* **M**.

Proof: We recall that the objects of the total category (of the externalization) $\sum \mathbf{M}$ are pairs $\langle A, f : A \to \mathbf{M}_0\rangle$, which are essentially A-indexed families of PERs for objects $A \in$ **ω-Set**—which is the same as those of the category $\wp$. Morphisms $\langle A, f : A \to \mathbf{M}_0\rangle \to \langle B, g : B \to \mathbf{M}_0\rangle$ are pairs $\langle u,h\rangle$ such that $u : A \to B$ in **ω-Set**, $h : A \to \mathbf{M}_1$ and the following equations hold:

$$\partial_0 \circ h = f \qquad \partial_1 \circ h = g \circ u$$

Thus, morphisms between a A-indexed family of PERS, and a B-indexed family are essentially A-indexed families of **PER** morphisms $\{k_a : A_a \to B_{u(a)}\}_{a\in A}$, with the nuance that, since the map h is in ω-Set, there is a single code n, such that for all $a \in A$ and any $p \in |a \in A|$, $n \cdot p$ tracks k_a. This corresponds exactly to our definition of morphisms in the total category $\wp$.

Thus the "naive" category **PER** may be recovered by taking global sections of the internal category—i.e. the fiber over the terminal in ω-**Set**. Moreover, this result taken in conjunction with Theorem 7.2.12 gives us the following significant fact.

Theorem 7.2.16 *The structure* **M** *is a full internal sub-category of* ω-**Set**.

Proof: From Theorem 7.2.12 and Theorem 7.2.15, we may verify that ϕ is a full comprehension category preserving fibered terminal objects. Also, it is fairly easy to see that ϕ is the internal global sections functor. We omit the details.

It also turns out, that when we take the definition of a limit-as-an-adjunction appropriately relativized to this internal category, the "external" construction of the limit in **PER** (for uniform families) as discussed in the previous section, turns out to yield the true limit. In other words, there exists an internal right adjoint $\Pi : [\mathbf{M_0} \to \mathbf{M}] \to \mathbf{M}$ to the internal diagonal functor $\Delta : \mathbf{M} \to [\mathbf{M_0} \to \mathbf{M}]$, where $\mathbf{M_0}$ is to be understood as the *discrete* category whose object of objects is $\mathbf{M_0}$ as defined above. In fact, the internal category **M** turns out to be *strongly* complete, as defined in Section 5.2[2]: this means that completeness holds (for its externalization) in the fibered sense (that is, for families of diagrams of possibly varying shapes). The proof for that would take as too far afield into the descriptions of internal functors, and internal adjunctions and so forth, and we shall refer the reader to the references ([66, 48, 4, 36, 34]).

Finally there remains a point that could do with some clarification. In the last section we saw that in **PER**, the interpretation of Polymorphic Types was done through the construction of a right adjoint, and the latter was available as an intersection in the category. Yet, in this section, the same thing was done through a right adjoint to re-indexing functors, and the image of this right adjoint—*viz.* $\Pi_\phi(R_\lambda)$ in Theorem 7.2.11 above—did not appear too much like an intersection. Actually, for certain kinds of indexing sets, it turns out that this object *is* (isomorphic to) the intersection: these are essentially ω-sets X for which the relation $\vdash_X$ is the complete cartesian product $\bar{\lambda} \times X$—for instance, the set $\mathbf{M_0}$ (and its sub-objects). We shall prove this as it ties together our intuitions regarding "naive" reasoning in **PER** *vis-a-vis* the fibrational reasoning in this section. The result is taken from [48].

[2]when **M** is considered as an internal category of the realizability topos over $\bar{\lambda}$ (*cf.* next section)

Proposition 7.2.17 *Let $\langle A, \vdash_A \rangle$ be an ω-set, such that $\vdash_A = \bar{\lambda} \times A$, and $\phi : A \to$ **MOD**; then*

$$\Pi_{a \in A}\phi(a) \cong \bigcap_{a \in A} \phi(a)$$

where we have confused the distinction between an object of **MOD** *and one of* **PER**.

Proof: We shall define a map $\mu : \bigcap_{a\in A} \phi(a) \to \Pi_{a\in A}\phi(a) : [x] \mapsto f$, where $f : a \to [x]_{\phi(a)}$. This map is realized by the code **k** (specific to our combinatory algebra $\bar{\lambda}$), since

$$\forall a \in A\, \forall p \in |a \in A| \; (\mathbf{k} \cdot x) \cdot p = x \in f(a)$$

and hence $\mathbf{k} \cdot x$ can be taken to realize f. For the other way around, we define a map $\nu : \Pi_{a\in A}\phi(a) \to \bigcap_{a\in A} \phi(a) : f \to [n \cdot p]$ where p is any code in $\bar{\lambda}$ and n tracks f. This is well-defined since for any such p, and any $a \in A$, we would have that $p \vdash_A a$, and hence $n \cdot p$ must be in the domain of every $\phi(a)$: the image of f then is simply the equivalence class of $(n \cdot p)$ in the intersection, which would not depend on the actual value of p. This map is tracked by the code $\lambda x.(x \cdot 0)$ where the choice of the element 0 is arbitrary. It is easy to verify that the maps μ and ν are mutual inverses.

7.3 The Realizability Topos

As we have stated, the development of the thesis from this chapter onwards is towards the embedding of the constructions of the earlier chapters into a categorical model of Intuitionistic higher-order logic: the ultimate objective being to elucidate the relationship between the semantics of proof-objects and that of denotations (or provability, in the case of propositions). We have remarked that there is a loss of information in the transition from the former to the latter, and it would be insightful to see this transition within an appropriate intuitionistic universe. The latter is salient to our general project since the λ-Types, which we would like to think of as encoding all the functional information in λ-terms, should yield something akin to a program logic—*viz* a framework for reasoning about denotational equivalences. In other words we would like to think of (the denotational spaces of) programs essentially as *(non-standard) sets* (with full (standard) function spaces): thus the standard predicate in denotational semantics, "is less defined than" should be just the subset relation in some non-standard model of Intuitionistic Set Theory. With this objective, we provide a brief sketch of the background on Realizability Toposes. This exposition is not meant to be either rigorous or comprehensive—for which we would refer the reader to any of the references ([61, 58, 33]), (from which is gleaned most of the following discussion).

We shall consider a Topos constructed on the combinatory algebra $\bar{\lambda}$. This algebra provides a model of computation, and we shall construct from it, a set of non-standard propositions The essential idea, which can be traced to Scott and Hyland, is to cast the realizability interpretation ([61, pages 86–92]) in the form of a model for intuitionistic propositions a proposition (truth-value) is conceived as the set of its *realizers*, that is, a set of elements (codes) drawn from the combinatory algebra $\bar{\lambda}$ (putatively, the representation of the proofs of the particular proposition) Hence we have a set of non-standard truth values $2^{\bar{\lambda}}$, which we may turn into Heyting pre-algebra through the following definition

Definition 7.3.1 *For $p, q \subseteq \bar{\lambda}$, we define*

$$
\begin{aligned}
p \bigwedge q &= \{\langle m, n\rangle \mid m \in p,\, n \in q\} \\
p \bigvee q &= \{\langle 0, m\rangle \mid m \in p\} \bigcup \{\langle 1, n\rangle \mid n \in q\} \\
p \longrightarrow q &= \{e \mid \forall n \in p, e\ n \in q\} \\
p \leq q &\Leftrightarrow p \longrightarrow q \neq \emptyset
\end{aligned}
$$

form which it follows that $\emptyset$ is the bottom element, and any non-empty p is a top element We shall denote this structure as Ω

This gives us the basic framework in terms of which we may define, for any set X, the set Ω^X of non-standard predicates on X We structure this set as a Heyting pre-algebra $\langle \Omega^X, \vdash_X\rangle$ through the following operations, noting the nuance in the definition of the order relation $\vdash_X$, which is uniform rather than pointwise

Definition 7.3.2 *For $\phi, \psi \in \Omega^X$ we define the following operations*

$$
\begin{aligned}
(\phi \bigwedge \psi)(x) &= \phi(x) \bigwedge \psi(x) \\
(\phi \bigvee \psi)(x) &= \phi(x) \bigvee \psi(x) \\
(\phi \longrightarrow \psi)(x) &= \phi(x) \longrightarrow \psi(x) \\
(\phi \vdash_X \psi) &\Leftrightarrow \bigcap_{x \in X} \{\phi(x) \longrightarrow \psi(x)\} \neq \emptyset
\end{aligned}
$$

from which it follows that $\lambda x\ \emptyset$ is a bottom element and $\lambda x\ P$ for any $P \neq \emptyset$ is a top element

We may define a quantificational structure on the predicates, these are described below and are a restricted case of a general notion of quantification as adjoints to substitution along arbitrary maps—which are taken to be projections in this case

Definition 7.3.3 *For $\phi \in \Omega^{X \times Y}$ we have the operation of quantification defined by the following rules*

$$(\exists y\, \phi(x,y))(x) = \bigcup_{z \in X \times Y} \{[\pi_0(z) = x] \bigwedge \phi(z)\}$$
$$(\forall y\, \phi(x,y))(x) = \bigcap_{z \in X \times Y} \{[\pi_0(z) = x] \longrightarrow \phi(z)\}$$

where, we define

$$[\pi_0(z) = x] = \begin{cases} \top & \text{if } \pi_0(z) = x \\ \emptyset & \text{otherwise} \end{cases}$$

We have the notion of *validity* (symbolized as $\models$) which is fundamental to the definition and study of the Realizability Topos

Definition 7.3.4 *For a predicate $\phi \in \Omega^X$, we say that ϕ is valid, $\models \phi$ under the following condition.*

$$\models \phi \Leftrightarrow \top \vdash_X \phi$$

By Definition 7 3 2, we have that

$$(\models \phi) \Leftrightarrow \bigcap_{x \in X} \phi(x) \neq \emptyset$$

We may now define the Realizability Topos

Definition 7.3 5 *The Realizability Topos is a category $\Re$, with the following constituents.*

Objects: *An object $X \equiv \langle X, =\rangle$ is a set X with a map $=$ in $\Omega^{X \times X}$ (which essentially represents a non-standard equality) satisfying the following conditions*

$$(\textbf{symmetry}) \models x = y \longrightarrow y = x$$
$$(\textbf{transitivity}) \models x = y \bigwedge y = z \longrightarrow x = z$$

We will write $x \in X$ (or Ex) for the predicate $x = x$, and denote the truth-value $= (x,y)$ as $[x = y]$

Morphisms: *A morphism f $\langle X, =\rangle \to \langle Y, =\rangle$ is an equivalence class of* functional relations, *where a functional relation ϕ is a map in $\Omega^{X \times Y}$ satisfying*

$$(\textbf{relational}) \models \phi(x,y) \bigwedge x = x' \bigwedge y = y' \longrightarrow \phi(x',y')$$
$$(\textbf{strict}) \models \phi(x,y) \longrightarrow Ex \bigwedge Ey$$
$$(\textbf{single-valued}) \models \phi(x,y) \bigwedge \phi(x,y') \longrightarrow y = y'$$
$$(\textbf{total}) \models Ex \longrightarrow \exists y\, \phi(x,y)$$

and the equivalence relation $\sim$ on such functional relations is defined as follows.

$$\phi \sim \psi \Leftrightarrow \models (\phi(x,y) \longleftrightarrow \psi(x,y))$$

We shall overload the symbol Ω and use it to denote both the Heyting pre-algebra defined in Definition 7 3 1 as well as the object $\langle \Omega, \longleftrightarrow \rangle$ in $\Re$ We shall denote an arrow $f \;\; X \rightarrow Y$ in $\Re$ as $[\phi]$, where ϕ is a functional relation representing f, and the square brackets denote the equivalence class of ϕ For any such an ϕ, we shall denote $\phi(x,y)$ as $[y = \phi(x)]$

We record the following standard fact omitting its proof, for which we refer the reader to the references ([33, 37])

Theorem 7.3.6 *The category $\Re$ of Definition 7 3 5, is an elementary Topos*

It would not be difficult to anticipate that the sub-object classifier is the object Ω We shall demonstrate a full embedding of SET into $\Re$[3]

Proposition 7.3.7 *([33, Prop 4 2]) There is a full and faithful functor Δ_S SET $\rightarrow \Re$*

Proof: For any set X, we define an object $\Delta_S(X)$ in $\Re$ as follows $\Delta_S(X) \equiv \langle X, = \rangle$ where, for $x, y \in X$

$$= y] = \begin{cases} \top & \text{if } x = y \\ \emptyset & \text{otherwise} \end{cases}$$

Any arrow $f \;\; X \rightarrow Y$ in **SET**, has as its image under Δ_S, the arrow $\Delta_S(f) \cdot \Delta_S(X) \rightarrow \Delta_S(Y)$ represented by the functional relation (we shall use the same letter f for it) for which

$$[y = f(x)] = \begin{cases} \top & \text{if } y = f(x) \\ \emptyset & \text{otherwise} \end{cases}$$

To see that Δ_S is faithful, suppose there are two arrows $f, g \;\; X \rightarrow Y$ in **SET** such that

$$\begin{aligned} &\models \;\; [y = f(x)] \longleftrightarrow [y = g(x)] \\ &\Rightarrow \;\; [y = f(x)] = \top \Leftrightarrow [y = g(x)] = \top \\ &\Rightarrow \;\; y = f(x) \Leftrightarrow y = g(x) \end{aligned}$$

and hence $f = g$ To see that Δ_S is full, consider an arrow $[\phi] \;\; \Delta_S(X) \rightarrow \Delta_S(Y)$ in $\Re$. This gives us an arrow $\phi \;\; X \times Y \rightarrow \Omega$ (in **SET** of course) We claim that

$$\forall x \in X \, \exists^! y \in Y \; \phi(x,y) \neq \emptyset^4$$

[3]Actually there is a lot more to the story here **SET** is itself a Topos, and the full embedding claimed here has a finite-limit preserving left adjoint—and thus we have have a geometric morphism from **SET** to $\Re$ ([33])

[4]This is *not* an internal language statement!

and this can be seen as follows Consider y and y' such that $\phi(x, y) \neq \emptyset$ and $\phi(x, y') \neq \emptyset$ But then we have the internal validity

$$\models \phi(x,y) \bigwedge \phi(x,y') \longrightarrow y = y'$$

and since $y = y'$ holds exactly in case y is actually identical to y' (from the definition of the embedding Δ_S) we have the proposition This condition (and totality) yields us an obvious arrow $f \; X \to Y$ in **SET**, and we can easily see that ϕ represents $\Delta_S(f)$

We can describe certain objects of $\Re$ in terms of this embedding The terminal object is (up to isomorphism) the object $\Delta_S(1_S)$ where 1_S is the terminal object in **SET** (that is, the singleton set) $\Re$ has a natural numbers object $\Delta_S(\aleph)$ where $\aleph$ is the set of natural numbers

We shall demonstrate now, a full embedding of ω-**Sets** into $\Re$ We define a functor $\Delta_\omega \; \omega$-**Sets** $\hookrightarrow \Re$ as follows

Definition 7 3 8 *The action of Δ_ω on objects may be described as follows $\Delta_\omega \; \langle X, \vdash_X \rangle \mapsto \langle X, = \rangle$ where, for $x, x' \in X$*

$$[x = x'] = \begin{cases} |x \in X| & \text{if } x = x' \\ \emptyset & \text{otherwise} \end{cases}$$

For an arrow $f \; \langle X, \vdash_X \rangle \to \langle Y, \vdash_Y \rangle$ tracked by a code n, we define a function $\phi \; X \times Y \to \Omega$ as follows

$$\phi(x, y) = \begin{cases} \{\langle p, n \; p \rangle \mid p \in |x \in X|\} & \text{if } y = f(x) \\ \emptyset & \text{otherwise} \end{cases}$$

and define $\Delta_\omega(f)$ as the arrow represented by the functional relation ϕ

Of course, we must show that ϕ is indeed a functional relation

Lemma 7.3.9 (*[61, Lemma 4 4 18]*) *The predicate ϕ as defined above, is a functional relation*

Proof: We have to demonstrate the four validities (i e construct realizers) in the definition of a functional relation

Relational: We note that $[x = x'] \neq \emptyset \neq [y = y']$ implies that $x = x'$ and $y = y'$, and hence $\phi(x, y) = \phi(x', y')$ Hence the relationality predicate is realized by the code $\lambda x \; \pi_0(x)$

Strict: From the definition of ϕ, we can see that if $\phi(x, y)$ is non-empty, then the first component of any of its elements give us a realizer for $x = x$, and the second for $y = y$ Hence the strictness predicate is realized by the code for identity

Single-valued: We note that if $\phi(x,y) \bigwedge \phi(x,y') \neq \emptyset$ then by the definition of ϕ we would have that $y = f(x) = y'$ Hence the predicate is realized by the code $\lambda x\ \pi_1(\pi_0(x))$.

Total: Referring to the definition of existential quantification, we have that

$$\begin{aligned}(\exists y\ \phi(x,y))(x) &= \bigcup_{z \in X \times Y} \{[\pi_0(z) = x] \bigwedge \phi(z)\} \\ &= \bigcup_{y \in Y} \{x = x \bigwedge \phi(x,y)\}\end{aligned}$$

Hence, the totality predicate would be realized by the code $\lambda x.\langle x, n\ x\rangle$

Theorem 7.3.10 *([61, Lemma 4 4 18]) There is a full and faithful* $\Delta_\omega : \omega\text{-}\mathbf{Sets} \hookrightarrow \Re$.

Proof: Consider objects $\langle X,=\rangle, \langle Y,=\rangle \in \Re$, which are in the image of ω-sets $\langle X,\vdash_X\rangle, \langle Y,\vdash_Y\rangle$ under the action of Δ_ω, and an arrow $f = [\phi]\ \ \langle X,=\rangle \to \langle Y,=\rangle$ Let p be a realizer for the totality predicate that is

$$\forall x \in X.\forall s \in |x \in X|\ p\ \ n = \langle l,k\rangle,\ \text{where } l \in Ey,\ k \in \phi(x,y)$$

for some $y \in Y$ We define a map $f'\ \ \langle X,\vdash_X\rangle \to \langle Y,\vdash_Y\rangle$ as follows

$$f'\ \ x \mapsto y \text{ where } \exists^! y \in Y\, \forall s \in |x \in X|\ \pi_0(p\ \ s) \in Ey \tag{7 3}$$

We must prove that such a y is unique Consider some other $s' \in |x \in X|$, let us have some other $y' \in Y$, such that $p\ \ s' = \langle l',k'\rangle$ with $l' \in Ey'$ and $k' \in \phi(x,y')$, let $p\ \ s = \langle l,k\rangle$ for s of Equation 7 3 Let the realizer for the single-valuedness predicate be r Then we have that $r\ \ \langle k,k'\rangle \in [y = y']$ which means that $[y = y'] \neq \emptyset$ or $y = y'$ Hence, the embedding is full

As for faithfulness, consider maps $f,g\ \ \langle X,\vdash_X\rangle \to \langle Y,\vdash_Y\rangle$, such that $\Delta_\omega(f) = \Delta_\omega(g) = [\phi]$ where ϕ is a functional relation on $X \times Y$ By the definition of Δ_ω, we would have that

$$\begin{aligned}\phi(x,y) &= \begin{cases} \{\langle p, n\ \ p\rangle \mid p \in |x \in X|\} & y = f(x) \\ \emptyset & y \neq f(x) \end{cases} \\ &= \begin{cases} \{\langle p, m\ \ p\rangle \mid p \in |x \in X|\} & y = g(x) \\ \emptyset & y \neq g(x) \end{cases}\end{aligned}$$

where f is tracked by n and g by n This tells us that $\forall x\ y = f(x)$ iff $y = g(x)$, and hence $f = g$

As we can see from Proposition 7.3.7 and Theorem 7.3.10, the Realizability Topos is a large object: it contains both the category of Sets—which is essentially the universe of classical mathematics, *and* the ω-**Sets**—which is itself a larger universe, and in which a fair amount of constructive math can be done, (it is what is known as a ***quasi-topos***, an excellent reference is [90]). The theory of the Realizability Topos, and the general theory of Toposes is an extensive field of research itself, and much of the discussion is beyond the ambit of our study. What we are interested in primarily, is to see that the category of partial equivalence relations is equivalent to an internal category within the Realizability Topos, and is sufficiently complete to be able to model higher-order Type theories. We have already seen that the category of PERs is a full internal sub-category in ω-**Sets**. Since ω-**Sets** embeds into $\Re$, we would like to think that the PERs would be a full internal sub-category in the latter too, and with all the completeness that it had in ω-**Sets**. Since the structure of a full internal sub-category and its completeness as one, depends on the (locally) cartesian closed structure of the ambient category, we would be able to assert the proposition only if the embedding Δ_ω preserved the locally cartesian closed structure of its domain. This claim and its demonstration is so well-known by now, that we would be justified in describing it as "folklore." The argument is by no means trivial, and is usually derived from a general theory of what are known as j-operators in any Topos. A discussion of this theory would be a digression from the logical development of our thesis, and we would merely sketch a broad picture, leaving the details to the interest of the reader and the standard references on the topic ([33, 34, 36, 42]).

The essential idea is to characterize the objects of $\Re$ in the image of Δ_ω, in the internal logic. This is not difficult and was done by Hyland in his pioneering paper ([33]).

Definition 7.3.11 *An object $\langle X, =\rangle \in \Re$ is said to be $\neg\neg$-separated, if the following condition holds*

$$\models \forall x, x' \in X\ \neg\neg(x = x') \longrightarrow (x = x')$$

This is not the only characterization of the class, nor the primary one (*cf.* [33, §5, page 182]). The class has a number of interesting properties among which we may mention the following.

- The sub-object of a $\neg\neg$-separated object is $\neg\neg$-separated.
- The full-subcategory of $\neg\neg$-separated objects is cartesian closed.
- The full-subcategory of $\neg\neg$-separated objects is locally cartesian closed.

The most significant fact from our point of view is the following.

Theorem 7.3.12 *([33, Prop 6 1][61, Prop 4 5 21]) An object of $\Re$ is $\neg\neg$-separated iff it is isomorphic to one of the form $\langle X, =\rangle$ satisfying*

$$[x = x'] \neq \emptyset \Leftrightarrow x = x'$$

that is, to (the image of) an ω-set

Proof: It is easy to see the "if" part By the definition of Δ_ω, we know that $[x = x'] \neq \emptyset$ exactly when $x = x'$. Moreover it is known that in the Topos, if a formula ϕ is realizable, then any code realizes $\neg\neg\phi$ Hence the proposition For the "only if" part, it can be shown that if an object is $\neg\neg$-separated then it is a sub-object of $\Delta_S(X)$ for some set X, and any such object would be in the required form

Finally we record the fact most significant for our purpose

Theorem 7.3.13 *The full sub-category comprising the separated objects is locally cartesian closed, and the embedding Δ_ω preserves the locally cartesian closed structure of the latter*

Proof: We refer the reader to [33, §5,6,pages 181-188] and [34]

Some more labour is needed to prove that the internal category **M** in ω-**Set** is a full internal sub-category $\Delta_\omega(\mathbf{M})$ within $\Re$, and possessing the relevant completeness structure we refer the reader to the references ([34, 36, 66]) We have alternate characterizations of the image of **PER** and of that of **M** in $\Re$ The former is equivalent to the category of "effective objects," which is essentially a quotient of a *closed* sub-object of $\bar{\lambda}$, by a *closed* equivalence relation (for the precise meaning of this statement, we refer the reader to [34], [33] and [61], and for other characterizations, to [36] and [66]) This (sub-) category of $\Re$ is known as the category of *modest sets*

7.4 λ-Types as Modest Sets

In this chapter, we have have presented so far an account of certain "standard" constructions within the Realizability Topos The culmination of this account has been the demonstration of a full internal subcategory—namely the Modest Sets, which are essentially the (internal version of the) partial equivalence relations on the underlying combinatory algebra In this last section we shall place our own constructions—specifically, the full internal category Δ that we have constructed in the previous chapter—within the framework of the Modest Sets The reader would already have seen that the Basic Types in our system (we shall describe them as λ-Types too) are, in fact partial equivalence relations—namely, restrictions of the relation $\simeq$ to their respective domains This allows us to embed them in the category of modest sets, and explore their properties in this context The constructions are carried out relative to the ω-Sets, since the Theorem 7 3 13 allows us to "lift" the results to the Topos $\Re$ (through the embedding Δ_ω that preserves the LCC structure of the domain) We shall connect the earlier construction—specifically the fibration $p \quad \tilde{\Lambda} \to \mathbf{B}$, to the current one, through a change-of base situation

We shall denote the object of objects and the object of morphisms of the internal category Λ as Λ_0 and Λ_1 respectively We have the following simple result

Proposition 7.4.1 *The small category $\underline{\Lambda}$ is a full sub-category of the category* **PER**.

Proof: A more precise statement of this proposition is that the fiber $(\tilde{\Lambda})_{1_O}$ (over the terminal object 1_O of **B**) is a full sub-category of **PER** (note that the fibration $\tilde{\Lambda}$ is (isomorphic to) the *externalization* of $\underline{\Lambda}$, *cf* Remark 6 2.24) In this form, the proposition is almost obvious Every object of the former (*i e* every Basic Type) is a partial equivalence relation—namely $\simeq$ restricted to an appropriate domain On the other hand, every $\tilde{\Lambda}$-morphism $\alpha \to \beta$ is the $\simeq$ equivalence class $[f]$ of a λ-term f that tracks the corresponding **PER**-morphism Conversely, every **PER**-morphism tracked by a code f, corresponds to a $\tilde{\Lambda}$-morphism tracked by the set of codes in $[f]_{\simeq}$ The only point to note is that the *representation* of any morphism (in terms of its realizers) in the two categories would, in general, differ for $(\tilde{\Lambda})_{1_O}$, the relevant equivalence relation (on the function space) is $\simeq$ in every instance, while for **PER**, it depends on the PERs α and β (*cf* Definition 7 1 2)

We have noted in the previous chapter that **B** is a sub-category of ω-**Sets** (Proposition 6 2 2) In fact it is easy to see that pullbacks, and in general, the relatively cartesian closed structure of the former is preserved by the embedding (which we would denote as $\imath$). We note the fact formally, omitting the easy proof

Lemma 7.4.2 *The embedding $\imath \quad$* **B** $\hookrightarrow$ ω-**Set** *preserves the display map structure, and the relatively cartesian closure of its domain (with respect to the former)*

We can also see that this embedding exhibits $\underline{\Lambda}$ as an internal category in ω-**Sets** We record the fact below

Proposition 7 4 3 *There is an internal category $\imath(\underline{\Lambda})$ in* ω-**Sets**, *for which the relevant sub-structures are the images, under $\imath$ of the corresponding sub-structures of the internal category $\underline{\Lambda}$ in* **B**

Proof: It is straightforward to verify that all the structures and conditions for an internal sub-category in **B** are conserved by the embedding (using Lemma 7.4.2).

Thus we may re-formulate Proposition 7.4.1 as stating that the internal category $\underline{\Delta}$ is (internally) a full sub-category of the internal category of modest sets **M**; we leave the fairly simple proof to the reader.

Proposition 7.4.4 *The internal category $\underline{\Delta}$ is (internally) a full sub-category of the internal category of modest sets* **M**.

Thus, we have a monic $\ell : \imath(\Lambda_0) \rightarrow M_0$, which we shall invoke in the results below.

We have already seen (in Chapter 6) that $\underline{\Delta}$ is a full internal sub-category of **B**. The significant point is that $\imath(\underline{\Delta})$ is a full internal sub-category of ω-**Set**, this is not as trivially established as it may appear and we prove first, two subsidiary results. In the sequel, we shall suppress the notation $\imath(\ )$ for objects in ω-**Sets** in the image of $\imath$, whenever the fact is clear from the context.

We shall establish the change-of base situation between fibration $\tilde{\Lambda}$ and the externalization $\sum(\imath(\underline{\Delta}))$, depicted in Figure 7-2, let $\mathcal{K}$ be the functor given by:

$$\mathcal{K} \quad \begin{cases} \alpha \equiv \{\alpha_x\}_{x\in\phi} & \mapsto \quad \langle \phi, \bar{\alpha} : \phi \rightarrow \Lambda_0 \rangle \\ f \equiv \langle u, \{f_x\}_{x\in} & \mapsto \quad \langle u, \bar{f} : \phi \rightarrow \Lambda_1 \rangle \end{cases}$$

where $\bar{\alpha}$ is as given in the proof of Theorem 6.2.19, and $\bar{f} : x \mapsto f_x$ is tracked by the code $\lambda n.\tilde{f}n$ where $\tilde{f}$ is the realizer of the family f (*cf.* Proposition 6.2.25).

Lemma 7.4.5 *The square indicated in Figure 7-2 (with sides $\mathcal{K}$, $[\imath(\underline{\Delta})]$, and p, $\imath$) is a change-of-base situation.*

Proof: We shall use the fact that $\tilde{\Lambda} \cong \sum(\underline{\Delta})$. We show that the square indicated is a 2-pullback. The vertex of the 2-pullback of $[\imath(\underline{\Delta})]$ along $\imath$ would be denoted as $\mathbf{B} \times_{\omega\text{-}\mathbf{Set}} \sum(\imath(\underline{\Delta}))$, and abbreviated as **K**. Consider any object $b \in \mathbf{B}$; an object in the fiber $\mathbf{K}_b$ can be seen to be of the form $\langle b, f : \imath(b) \rightarrow \imath(\Lambda_0)\rangle$ and this corresponds exactly to the (unique) object $\langle b, f : b \rightarrow \Lambda_0\rangle$ in the fiber $\tilde{\Lambda}_b$ (on account of the embedding). Similarly, any object $\langle b, f : b \rightarrow \Lambda_0\rangle$ in the fiber $\tilde{\Lambda}_b$, would correspond to the unique object $\langle b, \imath(f) : \imath(b) \rightarrow \imath(\Lambda_0)\rangle$ in the fiber $\mathbf{K}_b$. Now consider any map $h : \langle b, f : \imath(b) \rightarrow \imath(\Lambda_0)\rangle \rightarrow \langle c, g : \imath(c) \rightarrow \imath(\Lambda_0)\rangle$ in **K** $(b, c \in \mathbf{B})$: this would consist of a pair $\langle u, h'\rangle$ with $u : b \rightarrow c$, and $h' : b \rightarrow \Lambda_1$, and be over the map u (eliding the $\imath$ notation). Now h' yields a b-indexed family of maps in small category $\underline{\Delta}$ (of the appropriate domains and co-domains), which is precisely a $\tilde{\Lambda}$ morphism between the corresponding objects in the fibers over b and c respectively Conversely, any $\tilde{\Lambda}$ morphism h over the **B**-morphism u corresponds to an b-indexed family of maps of the small category $\underline{\Delta}$ (i e, to a morphism h' $b \to \Lambda_1$) and hence to an unique **K**-morphism $\imath(h')$ over $\imath(u)$ Hence **K** is equivalent to $\tilde{\Lambda}$, and hence the proposition

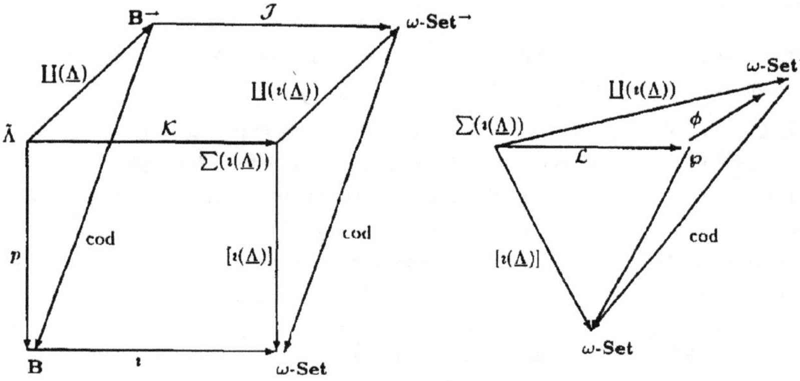

Figure 7-2 Relationships

In the next result we demonstrate that the internal global sections functor $\coprod(\imath(\underline{\Delta}))$ factors through the functor ϕ $\wp \to \omega$-**Set**$^{\to}$ of Theorem 7 2 12 The situation is illustrated in the second diagram of Figure 7-2

Theorem 7.4 6 *There is a full, cartesian functor* $\mathcal{L}$ $\sum(\imath(\underline{\Delta})) \to \wp$ *and we have* $\coprod(\imath(\underline{\Delta})) = \phi \circ \mathcal{L}$

Proof: We shall implicitly make use of the equivalence $\sum(\mathbf{M}) \cong \wp$ We prove first the existence of $\mathcal{L}$ Any object $\langle A, a \;\; A \to \Lambda_0\rangle$ (we have suppressed the $\imath$ as before) in $\sum(\imath(\underline{\Delta}))$ corresponds, from Proposition 7 4 1 above, to a map $\ell \circ a$ $A \to M_0$, and hence to the object [corresponding to the A-indexed family of PERs given by] $\ell \circ a$, we denote the A-indexed family of PERs as $\ell(\bar{a})$ and set $\mathcal{L} : \langle A, a : A \to \Lambda_0\rangle \mapsto \ell(\bar{a})$ Similarly, from Proposition 7 4 1 above, a morphism h $\langle A, a \;\; A \to \Lambda_0\rangle \to \langle B, b \,.\, B \to \Lambda_0\rangle$ given as the pair $\langle u \;\; A \to B, h' \;\; A \to \Lambda_1\rangle$ corresponds to an A-indexed family of **PER**-morphisms (realized by the code $\lambda x\, \check{h} x$, where $\check{h}$ tracks h'), we denote it by $\ell(h')$ (with the appropriate domains and co-domains) and we may set $\mathcal{L}$ $h \mapsto \ell(h')$ Fullness is easy to see any map f $\ell(\bar{a}) \to \ell(\bar{b})$ in $\wp$, is a A-indexed family of **PER**-morphisms (with appropriate domains and co-domains) and corresponds to an unique map $f' \ A \to \Lambda_1$ (once again by Proposition 7 4 1), tracked (essentially) by $\lambda x\ \check{f}x$, where $\check{f}$ realizes the family f We can easily verify that the relevant equations (for a morphism in the externalization) hold for f', and thus f' may be taken to the morphism in $\sum(\imath(\Delta))$ which is mapped by $\mathcal{L}$ to f

It is a bit more difficult to see that $\mathcal{L}$ is cartesian We refer to Figure 7-3 for the reasoning. Consider a cartesian morphism $h \ \langle A, a \ . \ A \to \Lambda_0\rangle \to \langle B, b \ \ B \to \Lambda_0\rangle$ given as the

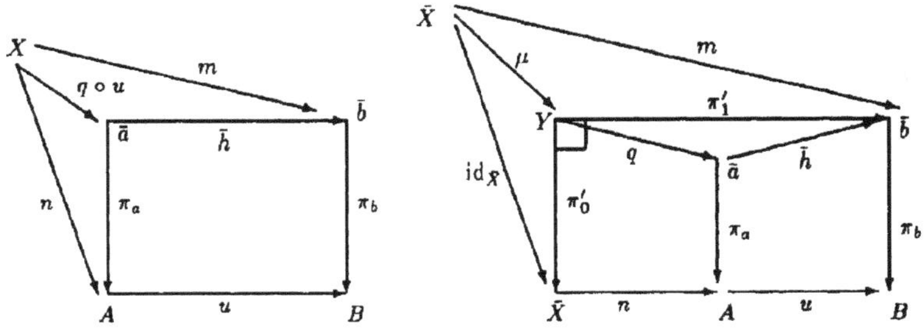

Figure 7-3 $\mathcal{L}$ is cartesian

pair $\langle u \ \ A \to B, h' \ \ A \to \Lambda_1\rangle$, in $\sum(\imath(\underline{\Delta}))$ We take its image in ω-Set$^{\to}$ (composing $\mathcal{L}$ with ϕ) and this is the commuting square shown on the left—$u \circ \pi_a = \pi_b \circ \bar{h}$—with the map $\bar{h}$ obtained from $\ell(h')$ as characterized above We shall claim that $\ell(h')$ is cartesian. Consider any map $m \ \ X \to \ell(\bar{b})$ above u: its image under ϕ is the commuting square shown in the diagram at the left ($\pi_b \circ \bar{m} = u \circ n$). Now pulling back π_b along $u \circ n$ we have the following situation we have morphisms $\mathrm{id}_{\bar{X}} \ \ \bar{X} \to \bar{X}$ and $\bar{m} \ \ \bar{X} \to \bar{b}$, with $\pi_b \circ \bar{m} = \mathrm{id}_{\bar{X}} \circ u \circ n$, and thus, a mediating morphism $\mu \ \ \bar{X} \to Y$ Now the morphism $\pi_1' \ \ Y \to \bar{b}$ yields a corresponding morphism $\widetilde{\pi_1'}$ in $\wp$ (ϕ is full and faithful), we would also note that Y corresponds to an object $\langle \bar{X}, (b \circ u \circ n) \ \ X \to \Lambda_0\rangle$ in $\sum(\imath(\Delta))$ (in the fiber over $\bar{X}$)—and hence $\widetilde{\pi_1'}$ corresponds to a morphism—let us denote it as k—in $\sum(\imath(\underline{\Delta}))$, with co-domain $\langle B, b \ \ B \to \Lambda_0\rangle$ Since h is cartesian, we have an unique morphism q (above n) such that $k = h \circ q$ Taking the image of this system under $\phi \circ \mathcal{L}$ we have the situation shown in the figure to the right, with $\pi_1' = \bar{h} \circ \bar{q}$ ($\bar{q}$ being the image of q) Now we have the following identities

$$\begin{aligned} \pi_a \circ q \circ \mu &= n \circ \pi_0' \circ \mu \\ &= n \circ \mathrm{id}_{\bar{X}} \end{aligned}$$

hence, this tells us that the $\wp$-morphism corresponding to $\bar{q} \circ \mu$ is above the identity id_A (fullness of ϕ invoked here); then again

$$\bar{h} \circ \bar{q} \circ \mu = \pi'_1 \circ \mu$$
$$= \bar{m}$$

and hence, it follows that for an arbitrary m considered as above, there is an unique morphism (given as the $\wp$-morphism corresponding to $\bar{q} \circ \mu$) above the identity id_A, such that m factors through $\ell(h')$, by this unique morphism Hence we may assert that $\ell(h')$ is cartesian, and that $\mathcal{L}$ is a cartesian functor

It's not difficult to see the commutation $\coprod(\imath(\underline{\Lambda})) = \phi \circ \mathcal{L}$. For any object $\langle A, a : A \to \Lambda_0 \rangle$, the image under $\coprod(\imath(\underline{\Lambda}))$ is obtained as the the pullback of the generic family $p : X \to \Lambda_0$ obtained as given in Figure 5-4, (with the category **M** replaced with $\underline{\Lambda}$) along a The reader may easily verify that this is isomorphic to the image under ϕ of the A-indexed family corresponding to the map $\ell \circ a$—or in other words, to the map π_a in Figure 7-3 On the other hand, the image of a morphism $h : \langle A, a : A \to \Lambda_0 \rangle \to \langle B, b : B \to \Lambda_0 \rangle$ given as the pair $\langle u : A \to B, h' : A \to \Lambda_1 \rangle$ is given as the image of the generic morphism s (in the context of Figure 5-4) under the action of the pullback functor derived from h' It is straightforward to verify that this is (isomorphic to) the square shown on the left in Figure 7-3 ($u \circ \pi_a = \pi_b \circ h$)— which is obtained under the action of $\phi \circ \mathcal{L}$ on h Hence the proposition

This allows us to assert the next results quite easily

Theorem 7.4.7 *The internal category $\imath(\underline{\Lambda})$ is a full internal sub-category of ω-***Sets**

Proof: We have to establish that $\coprod(\imath(\underline{\Lambda}))$ is a full comprehension category But we know already that $\phi : \wp \to \omega\text{-}\mathbf{Set}^{\to}$ is a full comprehension category, and that $\mathcal{L}$ is a full cartesian functor, and $\coprod(\imath(\underline{\Lambda})) = \phi \circ \mathcal{L}$ Moreover, preservation of fibered terminal objects is easy it follows from the fact that the λ-Type $\oint[\Omega]$, which is an internal terminal object of the category $\underline{\Lambda}$, is isomorphic to the terminal object **1** of **PER** (and thus of the internal category **M**) described in Theorem 7 1 3 Hence the proposition

Finally, we shall claim that $\imath(\underline{\Lambda})$ is a full internal relatively cartesian closed sub-category of ω-**Sets**, relative to the full sub-category **B** To establish this we use the following lemma.

Lemma 7 4 8 *If $\mathcal{J}$ is the embedding* $\mathbf{B}^{\rightarrow} \rightarrow \omega\text{-}\mathbf{Set}^{\rightarrow}$, *then*

$$\mathcal{J} \circ \coprod(\Delta) = \coprod(\imath(\Delta)) \circ \mathcal{K}$$

where $\mathcal{K}$ is as indicated in Figure 7-2

Proof: As we have seen above, the action of both $\coprod(\Delta)$ and $\coprod(\imath(\Delta))$ have the same characterization on any object $\langle A, a : A \rightarrow \Lambda_0\rangle$ in $\tilde{\Lambda}$ (using the equivalence $\tilde{\Lambda} \cong \sum(\underline{\Delta})$) the former yields the morphism $\pi_a : \bar{a} \rightarrow A$ in $\mathbf{B}$ (and hence in ω-$\mathbf{Set}$), obtained as described in the proof of Theorem 7 4 6 above This is exactly image of $\langle A, a : A \rightarrow \Lambda_0\rangle$ under $\coprod(\imath(\Delta)) \circ \mathcal{L}$ as argued above The same consideration holds for morphisms the image of a morphism $h : \langle A, a : A \rightarrow \Lambda_0\rangle \rightarrow \langle B, b : B \rightarrow \Lambda_0\rangle$ given as the pair $\langle u : A \rightarrow B, h' : A \rightarrow \Lambda_1\rangle$ is given as the image of the generic morphism s (in the context of Figure 5-4) under the action of the pullback functor derived from h' As argued in the proof of Theorem 7 4 6 above, this is (isomorphic to) the commuting square (in $\mathbf{B}$, and hence in ω-$\mathbf{Set}$) shown on the left in Figure 7-3 ($u \circ \pi_a = \pi_b \circ \bar{h}$), and once again this is precisely the case for the image under $\coprod(\imath(\Delta)) \circ \mathcal{L}$ Hence the proposition

We have finally the main result

Theorem 7.4.9 *$\imath(\Delta)$ is a full internal relatively cartesian closed sub-category of ω-**Sets**, relative to the sub-category* $\mathbf{B}$

Proof: Follows immediately from Lemma 7 4 8 we have already demonstrated that $\coprod(\Delta)$ (which is but the comprehension category $\mathcal{P}$ of Chapter 6) is a closed comprehension category, and this is preserved by the embedding $\mathcal{J}$ (the reader might like to step through the details involved in this verification) The change-of base situation of Figure 7-2 has already been established in Lemma 7 4 5 above Preservation of fibered terminal objects follows on the same consideration as suggested in the proof of Theorem 7 4 7

This brings to a close the first part of our effort to see the category of λ-Types structured as a full internal sub-category within the Realizability Topos[5] In the next chapter we shall see that the small category $\underline{\Delta}$ admits the notion of a partial order, and hence may be completed into domains However, we can already notice an interesting fact the completeness properties of our category get progressively weaker in the process of the embedding While Δ had an internal relative cartesian closure in $\mathbf{B}$ it remains merely so, *relative* to the latter when

[5]Though we have demonstrated the relevant conditions for the case of ω-**Sets**, by virtue of Theorem 7 3 13, this structure is preserved by the embedding into $\mathfrak{R}$

embedded into ω-**Set** In fact we shall note this process throughout the next chapter: as we move from the semantics of proof towards that of denotation, the corresponding structures lose much of their Type-theoretic completeness, and admit only domain theoretic properties. This is reminiscent to some extent of the parallel situation for propositions—whereby in a Topos, all proofs are collapsed into a single arrow We shall have occasion to comment on this in the sequel

Chapter 8

Internal Domain Theory

This final chapter is concerned with the relation between the Heyting-semantics of λ-terms—the semantics of *proofs* (or proof-objects, to be precise)—and the traditional semantics of the denotational kind We have already mentioned that the development of our thesis has been oriented along a course parallel to that of a Heyting-semantics for propositions The epitome of this latter development is, as we know, a constructive theory of Types—the simplest example of which is perhaps Girard's System F, or the (second-order) polymorphic λ-Calculus We have remarked that the move from proofs (in fact, any representation of intensional information) to denotations would in general entail a loss of information In the context of propositions, this is easily seen in a categorical model for intuitionistic higher-order logic—which is an elementary topos—the proofs are collapsed into a single morphism, that simply tokens *provability* In other words, the object of propositions (truth values) in a topos is a Heyting algebra object, and the Type structure of constructive proofs is lost

The hiatus between denotations and proofs shows itself especially with respect to the denotational semantics of the *Types* themselves We have remarked earlier that such a semantics, in terms of an adequately complete full sub-category of the classical (or boolean) topos of Sets is ruled out on cardinality considerations ([65]) The resolution, as we have remarked earlier, was to interpret the theory in an elementary topos—which had an intuitionistic internal logic This was done by A M Pitts (through a generalization of an earlier construction of D S Scott on cartesian closed categories with a reflexive object, *cf* [74]), by embedding a Hyperdoctrine model of the polymorphic λ-Calculus into its presheaf topos through the Yoneda functor ([62]) The presheaf topos was shown to contain a full internal sub-category, *closed* under certain limits that could interpret the Type-theoretic operations, and hence could interpret the object of Types The constructive information in the proofs could thus be conserved by embedding the category of Types as an adequately complete internal sub-category of the classifying topos The remarkable conceptual gain in this is that the Types could now be understood as essentially *sets* and reasoned about within a full intuitionistic logic

There was a more subtle aspect to this problem if the Type theory was rich enough to allow the construction of *recursive* terms (and Types)—as would be the case for (the Curry-Howard Types of) certain logical theories with induction principles (*cf* [52, 13])—the semantics would have a natural domain-theoretic formulation Domains have fix-points, however, and it had been known for some time that fix-points do not sit well inside a topos (more specifically, any cartesian closed category with equalizers) the objects degenerate ([32]) This was in fact the reason why display map categories were formulated in the first place–as the generalization of locally cartesian closed categories ([85]) The resolution of *this* problem is still an active field of research the general principle is to construct adequately complete *internal* categories of order-theoretic objects (which could interpret recursive constructs as fix-points) in a topos—and this may be done in more ways than one ([1, 22, 13, 3, 58, 59, 86, 35, 68]). A particularly elegant method is to *induce* the order *synthetically*, on the basis of recursively enumerable sub-objects classified by an object of *computable* truth-values ([35, 68, 86, 58]) This has the virtue of intrinsically relating general recursion theory and its denotational semantics in a single foundational framework—and without any *ad hoc* notion either of coding or of order—a conceptual possibility that had been unrealized since Scott and Strachey's first attempts towards a semantics of computable functions ([71, 75])

In this chapter, we would attempt to formalize our intuitions regarding the constitution of the denotations of terms from the sets of their proof-objects We would see that the problems and their resolutions, discussed above–whereby the constructive information in the proofs is conserved within suitable internal categories—have a fairly close correspondence with the situation in the case of λ-terms We would see that the proof-objects admit an order-theoretic structure and denotational semantics may be formulated through a process of *completion* (into dcpos) The resulting collection of objects constitute an internal category of dcpos, and moreover one that may be conceived as a category of *synthetic* objects The analogy with propositions would be complete if this object of denotations—which is the object of truth-values in the former case—could be shown to have analogous properties specifically, one might be led to expect that since the object of truth-values is a Heyting-algebra object, the corresponding denotational objects for the λ-terms would, at the least, be (internally) cartesian closed

The denotational semantics of programs is based, traditionally, on the notion of a Domain. There are variants of this notion, but the essential requirements and the structure that fulfills them are reasonably clear The most important condition is the ability to give a semantics to recursive functions, and the structure that can do this economically is the directed complete partial order, with a least element (abbreviated cpo hereafter, *cf* [64]) The requirement of directed completion comes from another (computational) direction· denotations of λ-terms is epitomized in the set of its *approximate normal forms* (essentially, our *residues*), such a set is always directed (*cf* Lemma 2 2 6) and its least upper bound corresponds to the Bohm tree of the λ-term in question ([5, Chapter 14 §3]) The category of cpos (and continuous functions) has another important virtue it is cartesian closed, (and closed under a variety of other Type operations) and hence sustains an interpretation of a simply typed programming system Most significantly, it is possible to construct in this category, objects that are isomorphic to their function space, and hence can interpret the untyped λ-calculus ([80]) Thus, the notion of a cpo evidently furnishes a general idea of a domain for denotational semantics This relatively simple notion may be refined in several ways One is to endow it with the additional property of *algebraicity* essentially, the idea of equipping a cpo with a base of compact elements, and such that any element is the supremum of the set of compact elements below it ([73, 29]). The resulting class of objects are known as algebraic complete partial orders, or *Domains* These objects have significant advantages over the cpos when considered as spaces, their topology is determined by their lattice structure, and the topology of certain objects constructed from of them through Type-theoretic operations relates simply to the topologies of the initial objects ([72]) Hence, the topological construction of spaces homeomorphic to their function space is greatly simplified The category of Domains (and continuous maps) is, however not cartesian closed, so it is usual to consider maximal sub-categories which are Two such sub-categories are well known the class of the *SFP*-objects, and that of the *L*-domains ([79, 43]) The former is known to be complete under most commonly used Type-theoretic operations, including simple non-deterministic constructs (power-domains, *cf.* [63])

Thus, we shall complete the analogy between propositions and programs (closed λ-terms) by structuring our Types as Domains We have already remarked the existence of an (partial) order on the λ-Types The move towards denotations is essentially one of *completing* this incipient order structure under directed joins The idea we have is essentially this in the case of propositions and in the transition to their denotations (truth-values) in the context of an elementary Topos, all proofs were collapsed into a single arrow that tokened entailment, in the case of programs, we will collect the information in the residues ***into the least upper bounds of directed sets*** Thus, we shall essentially *complete* the λ-Types by closure under the least upper bounds of directed sets, suitably defined Remarkably, under a certain constraint on these directed sets (essentially, that they be recursively enumerable) the resulting class of directed complete partial orders is still contained within the sub-category of modest sets. These objects sustain an interpretation of λ terms as directed completions of their approximations (proof-objects). They are demonstrated to be dcpos (some of them do not posses a least element)—and most significantly, *synthetic* objects. By this we mean that the order defined extrinsically on the λ-Types is shown to coincide with an intrinsic notion of order derived from the structure of what may be conceptualized as *recursively enumerable sub-objects*. This demonstration is achieved through methods recently conceived in the study of what are called *Synthetic Domains*. Moreover, the internal category of pre-domains is demonstrated to be a sub-category of a certain canonical (internal) category of objects known as the *replete* objects ([35, 86]).

With this rather long preamble, which in our view was important in order to understand the motivation behind the constructions in this chapter, we turn to the concept of internal Domains.

8.1 An Internal Category of Domains

We shall tackle first, the question of obtaining from the (internal) category of λ-Types, a category of objects that have most of the standard Domain theoretic properties. We have already suggested, though never formally, that any λ-Type α admits a notion of an ordering. This partial order is essentially the Bohm tree η subsumption order ([5, Chapter 10 §3 & 4, Chapter 19 §2]), well-known in the theory of separability and the local structure analysis of λ-models. After establishing this order, we apply a form of the directed-completion technique (suitably modified for the internal logic) to obtain a class of what may be be described as *ω-directed complete partial orders* (abbreviated as ω-dcpos): these have least upper bounds of recursively enumerable directed sets, and in particular, least upper bounds of ω chains. In this section, the constructions will have a "naive" flavor—meaning thereby, that they would be straightforward translations of "external" constructions into the internal structure of the Realizability Topos. In the next section, we shall reformulate them in "synthetic" terms.

We review a few concepts from the theory of Bohm Trees and Solvability. The set of all Bohm-like trees would be denoted by the symbol BT. The Bohm tree of any λ-term x would be denoted by $BT(x)$. A fundamental relation among such trees is the relation of η-expansion, denoted by the symbol $\leq_\eta$; it is essentially the transfinite transitive closure of the operation of making a single η-expansion at any node. For a comprehensive account of the operation and its properties, we refer the reader to [5, Chapter 10 §2].

Definition 8.1.1 *For Böhm-like trees m, n, we define the binary relation $m \preceq n$, and then* *by correspondence, for λ-terms x, y, by the following equations*

$$m \preceq n \iff \exists m', n' \in \mathcal{BT}\ m \leq_\eta m' \bigwedge n \leq_\eta n' \bigwedge m' \subseteq n'$$
$$x \preceq y, \iff \mathcal{BT}(x) \preceq \mathcal{BT}(y)$$

It follows easily that the relation $\preceq$ is a pre-order on both $\mathcal{B}$ and λ. The corresponding partial order is defined in the usual way

Definition 8 1.2 *For $m, n \in \mathcal{BT}$, we have the relation $\simeq$ defined as follows.*

$$m \simeq n \iff m \preceq n \bigwedge n \preceq m$$

The relation $\simeq$ is defined on λ-terms on the basis of the corresponding relation on the Böhm trees, as before

We have the easy conclusion the relation $\simeq$ is an equivalence on both $\mathcal{B}$ and λ We shall also be using the Bohm tree order $\sqsubseteq$ on the set of λ-terms, that is

$$x \sqsubseteq y \iff \mathcal{BT}(x) \subseteq \mathcal{BT}(y)$$

for $x, y \in \lambda$ For a set of λ-terms X, if there exists a λ-term $\hat{x}$ such that

$$\mathcal{BT}(\hat{x}) = \bigcup\{\mathcal{BT}(x) \mid x \in X\}$$

then we consider that the least upper bound of the set X in the $\sqsubseteq$ order exists, and we write $\hat{x} = \bigsqcup X$

We have the important and well-known result in the theory of Solvability, which we state below for reference For the proof, which is by no means trivial, the reader is referred to [5, Chapter 19 §2]

Proposition 8 1.3 *The following equivalences obtain*

$$x \simeq y \iff \forall C[\ ]\ (C[x] \textit{ is solvable} \Leftrightarrow C[y] \textit{ is solvable})$$
$$x \preceq y \iff \forall C[\ ]\ (C[x] \textit{ is solvable} \Rightarrow C[y] \textit{ is solvable})$$

where x, y are λ-terms

Thus, the relation $\simeq$ defined in Definition 8 1 2 and that used earlier in Chapter 6 for the construction of the proof-objects, coincide With these preliminaries, we can define the partial order on the modest set $\oint[\alpha]$ for any Basic Type $[\alpha]$ For any element x of the underlying combinatory algebra λ (which is itself an equivalence class with respect to the β-equivalence), we denote by $[x]$, the equivalence class of x with respect to the relation $\simeq$. Note that the relation $\preceq$ on λ-terms is compatible with β-equivalence, i.e. for

$$m =_\beta m' \bigwedge n =_\beta n \bigwedge m \preceq n \Leftrightarrow m' \preceq n'$$

and also (obviously) the relation $\simeq$ *contains* the relation $=_\beta$. For $x, y \in \bar{\lambda}$, we shall abuse notation and write $x \preceq y$ to mean that for any $m \in x$ and $n \in y$, $m \preceq n$, and generally confuse terms with their β-equivalence classes.

Definition 8.1.4 *For any* $[\alpha] \in \Lambda_0$, *we define the binary relation* $\preceq$ *on* $\oint[\alpha]$ *as follows*

$$[x] \preceq [y] \Longleftrightarrow x \preceq y$$

This is obviously a partial order, and hence, any Basic Type denotes a partially ordered set. Also, from Proposition 8.1.3 we have the following

Proposition 8.1.5 *For any* $[\alpha] \in \Lambda_0$, *and* $[x], [y] \in \oint[\alpha]$, *we have*

$$[x] \preceq [y] \Longleftrightarrow \forall C[\;]\ (C[x] \text{ is solvable} \Rightarrow C[y] \text{ is solvable})$$

Proof: Immediate, from Proposition 8.1.3.

The considerations which led up to the characterization of the partial order $\preceq$ can be cast in an appropriate internal form, whereby we have the sub-object $\preceq \rightarrowtail \Xi^2_\alpha$, for any α that is (the denotation of) a Basic Type. Thus, the internal category Δ may be structured as an internal category of posets in the Realizability Topos. In much of the subsequent constructions, we would argue in the standard "external" universe (keeping the reasoning sufficiently constructive), and then indicate the points at which they could be internalized. From this category of posets, we may obtain an equivalent category of internal domain-theoretic objects by an appropriate kind of completion. The standard ideal completion does not appear to be suitable since we would want the resulting category of domains to be an internal sub-category of the modest sets: arbitrary ideals (or directed sets) would not admit of disjoint sets of realizers. On the other hand, *recursively enumerable* directed sets (in a sense to be made precise) would be more suitable candidates. We have the following formulation, wherein the symbol $[\alpha]$ would always refer to an expression in the set of Basic Types, unless otherwise stated.

Definition 8.1.6 *A subset* χ *of* $\oint[\alpha]$ *is called* ω*-directed iff there is a recursively enumerable set* $\underline{\chi}$ *such that*

$$\chi = \{[x] \mid x \in \underline{\chi}\}$$

with $\underline{\chi}$ *directed in the* $\sqsubseteq$ *order*

Thus, an ω-directed set is directed in the $\preceq$ order We shall say that $\underline{\chi}$ is the *presentation* of the ω-directed set χ The precise reason for requiring that the presentation be recursively enumerable is as follows it is well known that the the poset of Bohm-like trees, $\langle BT, \subseteq \rangle$ is an algebraic cpo Hence the least upper bound of any ideal, such as $\underline{\chi}$ exists in B, however, it might not be the Bohm tree of any λ-term The condition for this to be so is also known and we record it for reference

Theorem 8 1.7 (*[5, Theorem 10 1 23]*) *The necessary and sufficient condition for a Böhm-like tree A to be the Böhm tree of a term, is that the set of variables free in A be finite, and that A, considered as a function on the set of finite sequences of natural numbers, be recursive*

Thus, if $\underline{\chi}$ is a recursively enumerable set of closed terms, its least upper bound would satisfy the conditions of the Theorem

Proposition 8.1.8 *The least upper bound of the Böhm trees of any recursively enumerable directed set of closed terms (in the partial order $\sqsubseteq$) is the Bohm tree of a λ-term*

Proof. It is quite straightforward to see that there is a recursive function that computes the label at each node of the lub if the node occurs at a depth k, it enumerates successively the Bohm trees of the terms up to a depth k—and it does so in the standard interleaving manner, that is (informally)

```
2 steps in the computation of the tree of term 0
1 step in that of the tree of term 1
3 steps in that of the tree of term 0
2 steps in that of the tree of term 1
1 step in that of the tree of term 2
4 steps in that of the tree of term 0
3 steps in that of the tree of term 1
2 steps in that of the tree of term 2
1 step in that of the tree of term 3
```

and so on—and till it hits the first tree that has a value for the label of the node This must be the label for the node in the lub, since the set is directed Such a function is (Turing) computable, and hence must be recursive Also since all the terms in the set are closed, the condition on free variables is trivially satisfied

This result allows us to define the least upper bound of ω-directed subsets

Definition 8.1.9 *For any ω-directed subset χ of some object in $\oint[\alpha]$, we define the least upper bound as $[\hat{\chi}]$ where*

$$\hat{\chi} = \bigsqcup\{x \mid x \in \chi\}$$

The preceding constructions give us the means by which we may *ω-complete* the Types and Orders, by adding to them, the least upper bounds of ω-directed subsets The idea is stated formally

Definition 8.1.10 *For any set $X \equiv \oint[\alpha]$, we define the ω-completion of X, denoted as $\Omega(X)$, as follows*

$$\Omega(X) = \{[x] \mid \exists \chi \subseteq X \ \chi \neq \emptyset \bigwedge \chi \text{ is } \omega\text{-directed} \bigwedge x = \hat{\chi}\}$$

We can easily see that $X \subseteq \Omega(X)$ and that $\Omega(\Omega(X)) = \Omega(X)$ The final idea that we borrow from the theory of Bohm trees is the following, which we state without proof (which may be looked up in the reference cited)

Theorem 8.1.11 *([5, Corollary 14 3 21]) For any λ-context $C[\,]$, the map defined by the term $\lambda x\ C[x]$ on λ, is continuous with respect to the order $\sqsubseteq$*

This is an extremely significant and useful result, and will underlie many of the propositions in the sequel

From this process of completion we can proceed to define the internal category of domains, for which we shall use the symbol $\mathbf{L}$

Definition 8 1.12 *The internal category $\mathbf{L}$ in ω-**Set** is defined as follows*

L_0: The object of objects is given as the ω-set

$$\{\langle X, \Omega(\oint(X))\rangle \mid X \in \Lambda_0\}$$

(where Λ_0 is the object of objects of the internal category $\underline{\Lambda}$) with the realizability relation $n \vdash l \Leftrightarrow n \simeq \Omega$, for any $l \in L_0$ Note that this gives us a isomorphism $\Omega(\ )\ \Lambda_0 \rightleftharpoons L_0\ \ [\alpha] \mapsto \langle[\alpha], \Omega(\oint[\alpha])\rangle$ We shall suppress this isomorphism in the sequel, whenever its clear from the context

L_1: The object of morphisms is given as $L_1 \equiv \Lambda_1$ where Λ_1 is the object of morphisms of the internal category $\underline{\Lambda}$

The rest of the components, viz, the domain and co-domain maps, and the internal identity and composition are isomorphic to the corresponding morphisms for the internal category $\underline{\Lambda}$

The relevant components of the internal categories **L** and $\underline{\Lambda}$ being isomorphic, it follows immediately that the former satisfies the conditions for being an internal category. It is also evident that L_0 is a sub-object of M_0, the object of object of the internal category of modest sets, and in fact that there is a internal inclusion $\mathbf{L} \hookrightarrow \mathbf{M}$, however, it is also clear that the former is *not* a full internal sub-category. In the sequel, we shall use the fact that **L** is an internal sub-category of **M**.

We state two lemmas that are important for verifying that the category **L** is internally cartesian closed. For $A \equiv [\alpha]$ and $B \equiv [\beta]$ in Λ_0, we shall use the symbols $A \times B$ and $A \Rightarrow B$ for the expressions $[\Sigma x \quad \alpha\ \beta]$ and $[\Pi x \quad \alpha\ \beta]$ in Λ_0.

Lemma 8.1.13 *For objects $A \equiv [\alpha]$, $B \equiv [\beta] \in \Lambda_0$, we may assert that*

$$\Omega(\oint(A \times B)) = \Omega(\oint(A)) \times \Omega(\oint(B))$$

where the latter occurrence of $\times$ denotes the cartesian product in **MOD**

Proof: Consider any element $[\langle a,b\rangle] \in \Omega(\oint(A \times B))$ as may be easily seen, for any such element, there would exist a ω-directed set $C \equiv \{[\langle a_i, b_i\rangle] \mid i \in I, [a_i] \in \oint(A), [b_i] \in \oint(B)\}$, for some indexing set I, such that $a = \bigsqcup_I \{a_i\}_{i\in I}$ and $b = \bigsqcup_I \{b_i\}_{i\in I}$. Since the sets $\{a_i\}_{i\in I}$ and $\{b_i\}_{i\in I}$, are ω-directed subsets of $\oint(A)$ and $\oint(B)$ respectively, we may assert that $a \in \Omega(\oint(A))$ and $b \in \Omega(\oint(B))$, hence $[\langle a,b\rangle] \in \Omega(\oint(A)) \times \Omega(\oint(B))$

On the other hand, it's not difficult to see that any element of $\Omega(\oint(A)) \times \Omega(\oint(B))$ is of the form $[\langle a,b\rangle]$ with $[a] \in \Omega(\oint(A))$ and $[b] \in \Omega(\oint(B))$. We would thus have indexing sets I, J such that $a = \bigsqcup_I \{a_i\}_{i\in I}$ and $b = \bigsqcup_J \{b_j\}_{j\in J}$, where the sets $\{[a_i] \mid i \in I\}$ and $\{[b_j] \mid j \in J\}$ are ω-directed in $\oint(A)$ and $\oint(B)$ respectively. This gives us the following (double) lub in $\Omega(\oint(A \times B))$ namely, $\bigsqcup_I \bigsqcup_J \{[\langle a_i, b_j\rangle]\}$; the relevant sets may be seen to be ω-directed in $\oint(A \times B)$ and thus the least upper bound exists in $\Omega(\oint(A \times B))$; and hence $[\langle a,b\rangle] \in \Omega(\oint(A \times B))$

Lemma 8.1.14 *For objects $A \equiv [\alpha]$, $B \equiv [\beta] \in \Lambda_0$, every element $[f] \in \Omega(\oint(A \Rightarrow B))$ tracks a morphism $\Omega(\oint(A)) \to \Omega(\oint(B))$ (in* **MOD***)*

Proof: Consider a general element $[f] \in \Omega(\oint(A \Rightarrow B))$, given by the condition $f = \bigsqcup\{f_i \mid i \in I, f_i \in \oint(A \Rightarrow B)$, for some indexing set I (and the relevant set being ω-directed). For a general element $[a] \in \Omega(\oint(A)$ given by the condition $a = \bigsqcup\{a_j \mid j \in J, a_j \in \oint(A)\}$ for some indexing set J (and the relevant set being ω-directed), we may represent the action of the morphism tracked by f on $[a]$ as $[\bigsqcup_J \{f a_j\}_{j\in J}]$ (by continuity, cf

Theorem 8 1.11) Again by continuity, we can write this as the double lub

$$f \quad [a] \mapsto [\bigsqcup_I \bigsqcup_J \{f_i a_j \mid i \in I, j \in J\}]$$

and the relevant sets being directed in $\oint(B)$, the lub exists in $\Omega(\oint(B))$, and hence the proposition

Corollary 8 1.15 *For objects $A \equiv [\alpha]$, $B \equiv [\beta] \in \Lambda_0$, if f tracked a morphism $\oint(A) \to \oint(B)$ (in* **MOD***), then f tracks a valid morphism $\Omega(\oint(A)) \to \Omega(\oint(B))$*

We shall use the preceding group of results to establish that certain $\underline{\Delta}$-morphisms remain valid when we reason in the context of $\mathbf{L}$

We demonstrate now that the category $\mathbf{L}$ is internally cartesian closed The relevant clauses in the definition use the notion of an internal adjunction (and internal natural transformations) rather heavily and we recall the definition of the former

Definition 8.1 16 *Given internal categories $\mathbf{C}$ and $\mathbf{D}$ (in some ambient category), and internal functors $F \ \mathbf{C} \to \mathbf{D}$ and $G \ \mathbf{D} \to \mathbf{C}$, and natural transformations $\eta \cdot \mathbf{id}_{\mathbf{C}} \to GF$ and $\epsilon \ \mathbf{id}_{\mathbf{D}} \to FG$ (where $\mathbf{id}_{\mathbf{X}}$ denotes the identity functor on the internal category $\mathbf{X}$), we say that F is a left adjoint G, or G is a right adjoint to F, or that $\langle F, G\ \eta, \epsilon\rangle$ constitutes an adjunction between $\mathbf{C}$ and $\mathbf{D}$ if and only if the following commutations obtain*

$$G \xrightarrow{\eta G} GFG \xrightarrow{G\epsilon} G = \mathbf{id}_G$$
$$F \xrightarrow{F\eta} FGF \xrightarrow{\epsilon F} F = \mathbf{id}_F$$

where $\mathbf{id}_X$, for a internal functor X denotes the identity natural transformation on X, and the relevant composition of natural transformations is the vertical composition

With this definition, we claim the subsequent set of results We shall use a few notational conventions: objects of $\mathbf{L}$ that have been defined to be of the general form $\langle X, \Omega(\oint(X))\rangle$ for $X \equiv [\alpha] \in \Lambda_0$ would be denoted simply as α to keep the notation simple We would denote an expression of the form $\Sigma x \ \ \alpha\ \beta$ as $\alpha \times \beta$ and $\Pi x \ \ \alpha\ \beta$ as α^β With these conventions, a typical element of L_1 may be represented as $\langle\langle\alpha, \beta\rangle, [f]\rangle$—meant to represent the (unique) morphism from α to β tracked by $[f]$ (this follows from the form of the elements of Λ_1); we would frequently use simply f rather than its equivalence class, and drop the domain and co-domain components whenever clear from the context We shall generically denote the functors constituting an adjunction as F and G (with the former being the left adjoint to the latter) We would also not be explicit, in the proofs below, about the codes tracking the particular morphisms that are mentioned· in all cases, the codes are obvious constant terms and may be easily constructed by the reader

Theorem 8.1.17 *The (unique) internal functor $1_{\mathbf{L}}$ $\mathbf{L} \to \mathbf{1}$, where $\mathbf{1}$ is the discrete category on the terminal object 1 in ω-Set, has an internal right adjoint T $\mathbf{1} \to \mathbf{L}$*

Proof: We shall take the terminal object 1 as given by the set $\{\star\}$ This is, of course the object of objects 1_0 of the internal category $\mathbf{1}$, the object of morphisms 1_1 is given as the identity id_1 of the terminal object The object and morphism parts of the functor $1_{\mathbf{L}}$ are obvious and we shall not labour the details. The functor T is given as follows·

$$\begin{array}{lll} T_0 & 1_0 \to L_0 & \star \mapsto \Omega \\ T_1 & 1_1 \to L_1 & id_1 \mapsto id_\Omega \end{array}$$

where id_Ω denotes the internal identity morphism on the object Ω (the λ-Type of the standard unsolvable term) The conditions of functoriality may be easily verified The natural transformations η $\mathbf{id_L} \to GF$ and ϵ $FG \to \mathbf{id_1}$ (with $F \equiv 1_{\mathbf{L}}$ and $G \equiv T$) are given as the morphisms

$$\begin{array}{lll} \eta : & L_0 \to L_1 . & \alpha \mapsto \langle\langle\alpha, \Omega\rangle, \lambda x\ \Omega\rangle \\ \epsilon & 1_0 \to 1_1 & \star \mapsto id_1 \end{array}$$

respectively, and the conditions for a natural transformation may be easily verified We explicate the following compositions

$$\begin{array}{llll} F\eta = F_1 \circ \eta & L_0 \to 1_1 & \alpha \mapsto id_1 \\ \epsilon F = \epsilon \circ F_0 : & L_0 \to 1_1 & \alpha \mapsto id_1 \\ \eta G = \eta \circ G_0 \cdot & 1_0 \to L_1 : & \star \mapsto id_\Omega \\ G\epsilon = G_1 \circ \epsilon & 1_0 \to L_1 \cdot & \star \mapsto id_\Omega \end{array}$$

where we have used id_Ω to denote the L_1-element representing the identity on the object Ω With these the relevant identities may be verified

$$\begin{array}{ll} (\epsilon F) \circ (F\eta) & \alpha \mapsto id_1 \circ id_1 = id_1 \\ (G\epsilon) \circ (\eta G) & \star \mapsto id_\Omega \circ id_\Omega = id_\Omega \end{array}$$

and hence the proposition

We would claim, next, that the category $\mathbf{L}$ has internal cartesian products This property too is framed in terms of an internal right adjunction We have the notion of an internal product category $\mathbf{L} \times \mathbf{L}$ its object of objects is predictably $L_0 \times L_0$, while that of its morphisms is $L_1 \times L_1$, the product of internal categories is defined exactly in the same way as the product of "external" categories. The rest of the components of $\mathbf{L} \times \mathbf{L}$ follow easily from this consideration and we shall not labour the details. We have the internal diagonal functor, $\Delta : \mathbf{L} \rightarrow \mathbf{L} \times \mathbf{L}$: we can verify its components given below

$$\Delta_0 \quad L_0 \rightarrow L_0 \times L_0 \quad \alpha \mapsto \langle \alpha, \alpha \rangle$$
$$\Delta_1 \quad L_1 \rightarrow L_1 \times L_1 \quad \langle\langle \alpha, \beta \rangle, [f] \rangle \mapsto \langle \langle\langle \alpha, \beta \rangle, [f] \rangle, \langle\langle \alpha, \beta \rangle, [f] \rangle \rangle$$

We shall drop the annotations of domain and co-domain whenever clear from the context. We have the main result.

Theorem 8.1.18 *The internal diagonal functor $\Delta : \mathbf{L} \rightarrow \mathbf{L} \times \mathbf{L}$ has an internal right adjoint ∇.*

Proof: The functor ∇ is given as follows

$$\nabla_0 \quad L_0 \times L_0 \rightarrow L_0 \quad \langle \alpha, \beta \rangle \mapsto \alpha \times \beta$$
$$\nabla_1 : \quad L_1 \times L_1 \rightarrow L_1 \quad \langle \langle\langle \alpha, \beta \rangle, [f] \rangle, \langle\langle \gamma, \delta \rangle, [g] \rangle \rangle \mapsto$$
$$\langle\langle \alpha \times \gamma, \beta \times \delta \rangle, [\lambda x \, \langle f\pi_0(x), g\pi_1(x) \rangle] \rangle$$

The conditions of functoriality may be easily verified. The relevant morphisms may be seen to be well-defined on the basis of Lemma 8.1.13 and Corollary 8.1.15: this would also be the case for the morphisms defined subsequently, and we shall take this as a general condition entailing validity without mentioning it explicitly every time. The natural transformations $\eta : \mathbf{id_L} \rightarrow GF$ and $\epsilon : FG \rightarrow \mathbf{id_{L \times L}}$ (with $F \equiv \Delta$ and $G \equiv \nabla$) are given as the morphisms

$$\eta \quad L_0 \rightarrow L_1 \quad \alpha \mapsto \langle\langle \alpha, \alpha \times \alpha \rangle, [\lambda x \, \langle x, x \rangle] \rangle$$
$$\epsilon \quad L_0 \times L_0 \rightarrow L_1 \times L_1 \quad \langle \alpha, \beta \rangle \mapsto \langle \langle\langle \alpha \times \beta, \alpha \rangle, \pi_0 \rangle, \langle\langle \alpha \times \beta, \beta \rangle, \pi_1 \rangle \rangle$$

respectively, and the conditions for a natural transformation may be easily verified. We explicate the following compositions

$$F\eta = F_1 \circ \eta \quad \alpha \mapsto \langle \langle\langle \alpha, \alpha \times \alpha \rangle, [\lambda x \, \langle x, x \rangle] \rangle, \langle\langle \alpha, \alpha \times \alpha \rangle, [\lambda x \, \langle x, x \rangle] \rangle \rangle$$
$$\epsilon F = \epsilon \circ F_0 \quad \alpha \mapsto \langle \langle\langle \alpha \times \alpha, \alpha \rangle, \pi_0 \rangle, \langle\langle \alpha \times \alpha, \alpha \rangle, \pi_1 \rangle \rangle$$
$$\eta G = \eta \circ G_0 \quad \langle \alpha, \beta \rangle \mapsto \langle\langle \alpha \times \beta, (\alpha \times \beta) \times (\alpha \times \beta) \rangle, [\lambda x \, \langle x, x \rangle] \rangle$$
$$G\epsilon = G_1 \circ \epsilon \quad \langle \alpha, \beta \rangle \mapsto \langle\langle (\alpha \times \beta) \times (\alpha \times \beta), \alpha \times \beta \rangle, [\lambda x \, \langle \pi_0\pi_0(x), \pi_1\pi_1(x) \rangle] \rangle$$

With these the relevant identities may be verified

$$(\epsilon F) \circ (F\eta) \quad \alpha \mapsto \mathrm{id}_\alpha \tag{8.1}$$
$$(G\epsilon) \circ (\eta G) \quad (\alpha \times \beta) \mapsto \mathrm{id}_{\alpha \times \beta} \tag{8.2}$$

where Equation 8 1 follows from the fact

$$(\pi_0 \circ \lambda x\ \langle x, x\rangle)(a) \quad = \quad a$$

for any $[a] \in \alpha$, and Equation 8 2 from the fact

$$\begin{aligned}
&(\lambda x\ \langle \pi_0\pi_0(x), \pi_1\pi_1(x)\rangle \circ \lambda x\ \langle x, x\rangle)(a, b) \\
&= \ (\lambda x\ \langle \pi_0\pi_0(x), \pi_1\pi_1(x)\rangle)(\langle\langle a, b\rangle, \langle a, b\rangle\rangle) \\
&= \ \langle a, b\rangle
\end{aligned}$$

for any $[\langle a, b\rangle] \in \alpha \times \beta$ Hence the proposition

In the next and final result, we shall claim that the category $\mathbf{L}$ has exponents the definition, as earlier, is couched in terms of an internal right adjoint We recall that $|L_0|$ denotes the discrete (internal) category defined on L_0, the object of objects of $\mathbf{L}$ This category has L_0 as both the object of objects and the object of morphisms The internal identity is then simply the identity id_{L_0}, which is obviously an isomorphism We have the product category $|L_0| \times \mathbf{L}$, and we shall denote it as χ We have the (internal) functor $P\ \ \chi \rightarrow \chi$ defined as follows

$$\begin{aligned}
&P_0 \cdot \ \ \chi_0 \rightarrow \chi_0 \cdot \ \ \langle \alpha, \beta\rangle \mapsto \langle \alpha, \alpha \times \beta\rangle \\
&P_1 \ \ \ \chi_1 \rightarrow \chi_1 \ \ \ \langle\langle\langle \alpha, \alpha\rangle, I\rangle, \langle\langle \beta, \gamma\rangle, [f]\rangle\rangle \mapsto \\
&\qquad\qquad \langle\langle\langle \alpha, \alpha\rangle, I\rangle, \langle\langle \alpha \times \beta, \alpha \times \gamma\rangle, [\lambda x\ \langle \pi_0(x), f\pi_1(x)\rangle]\rangle\rangle
\end{aligned}$$

The conditions of functoriality may be easily verified The relevant morphisms may be seen to be well-defined on the basis of Lemma 8 1 13 and Corollary 8 1 15 as before We have the main result

Theorem 8.1.19 *The internal functor $P\ \ \chi \rightarrow \chi$ has an (internal) right adjoint E*

Proof. The functor E is given as follows

$$\begin{aligned}
&E_0 \ \ \ \chi_0 \rightarrow \chi_0 \ \ \ \langle \alpha, \gamma\rangle \mapsto \langle \alpha, \alpha^\gamma\rangle \\
&E_1 \ \ \ \chi_1 \rightarrow \chi_1 \cdot \ \ \langle\langle\langle \alpha, \alpha\rangle, I\rangle, \langle\langle \beta, \gamma\rangle, [f]\rangle\rangle \mapsto \langle\langle\langle \alpha, \alpha\rangle, I\rangle, \langle\langle \beta^\alpha, \gamma^\alpha\rangle, [\lambda n x. f(n(x))]\rangle\rangle
\end{aligned}$$

The conditions of functoriality may be easily verified The relevant morphisms may be seen to be well-defined on the basis of Lemma 8 1 13, Lemma 8.1 14 and Corollary 8 1 15, as earlier The natural transformations $\eta\ .\ \mathbf{id}_\chi \rightarrow GF$ and $\epsilon\ \ FG \rightarrow \mathbf{id}_\chi$ (with $F \equiv P$ and $G \equiv E$) are given as the morphisms

$$\begin{aligned}
&\eta \ \ \ \chi_0 \rightarrow \chi_1 \ \ \ \langle \alpha, \beta\rangle \mapsto \langle\langle\langle \alpha, \alpha\rangle, I\rangle, \langle\langle \beta, (\alpha \times \beta)^\alpha\rangle, [\lambda x y\ \langle y, x\rangle]\rangle\rangle \\
&\epsilon \ \ \ \chi_0 \rightarrow \chi_1 \ \ \ \langle \alpha, \gamma\rangle \mapsto \langle\langle\langle \alpha, \alpha\rangle, I\rangle, \langle\langle \alpha \times \gamma^\alpha, \gamma\rangle, \mathrm{ev}\rangle\rangle
\end{aligned}$$

respectively, where ev is the evaluation combinator, tracked by $\lambda x\ (\pi_1(x))(\pi_0(x))$ The conditions for a natural transformation may be easily verified We explicate the following compositions

$$\begin{array}{ll} F\eta = F_1 \circ \eta & \langle\alpha,\beta\rangle \mapsto \langle\langle\langle\alpha,\alpha\rangle, I\rangle, \langle\langle\alpha\times\beta, \alpha\times(\alpha\times\beta)^\alpha\rangle, [g]\rangle\rangle \\ & \text{where } g \equiv \lambda z\ \langle\pi_0(z), f\pi_1(z)\rangle \text{ with } f \equiv \lambda xy\ \langle y, x\rangle \\ \epsilon F = \epsilon \circ F_0 & \langle\alpha,\beta\rangle \mapsto \langle\langle\langle\alpha,\alpha\rangle, I\rangle, \langle\langle\alpha\times(\alpha\times\beta)^\alpha, \alpha\times\beta\rangle, \mathrm{ev}\rangle\rangle \\ \eta G = \eta \circ G_0 & \langle\alpha,\beta\rangle \mapsto \langle\langle\langle\alpha,\alpha\rangle, I\rangle, \langle\langle\beta^\alpha, (\alpha\times\beta^\alpha)^\alpha\rangle, [\lambda xy\ \langle y, x\rangle]\rangle\rangle \\ G\epsilon = G_1 \circ \epsilon & \langle\alpha,\beta\rangle \mapsto \langle\langle\langle\alpha,\alpha\rangle, I\rangle, \langle\langle(\alpha\times\beta^\alpha)^\alpha, \beta^\alpha\rangle, [\lambda nx\ \mathrm{ev}(n(x))]\rangle\rangle \end{array}$$

With these the relevant identities may be verified

$$(\epsilon F)\circ(F\eta) \qquad \langle\alpha,\beta\rangle \mapsto \mathrm{id}_{\langle\alpha,\alpha\times\beta\rangle} \tag{8 3}$$

$$(G\epsilon)\circ(\eta G) \qquad (\alpha\times\beta) \mapsto \mathrm{id}_{\langle\alpha,\beta^\alpha\rangle} \tag{8 4}$$

where Equation 8 3 follows from the fact

$$\begin{aligned} (\mathrm{ev}\circ g)\langle a,b\rangle &= \mathrm{ev}(\langle a, \lambda y\ \langle y,b\rangle\rangle) \\ &= (\lambda y\ \langle y,b\rangle)a \\ &= \langle a,b\rangle \end{aligned}$$

for any $[\langle a,b\rangle] \in \alpha\times\beta$, and Equation 8 4 from the fact

$$\begin{aligned} &(\lambda nx\ \mathrm{ev}(n(x)) \circ \lambda xy\ \langle y,x\rangle) f \\ &= (\lambda xy\ \langle y,x\rangle)(\lambda y\ \langle y,f\rangle) \\ &= \lambda x\ (\lambda x\ (\pi_1(x))(\pi_0(x)))((\lambda y\ \langle y,f\rangle)(x)) \\ &= \lambda x.fx \\ &\simeq f \end{aligned}$$

for any $[f] \in \beta^\alpha$, and hence the proposition

Theorems 8 1 17, 8 1 18 and 8 1 19 yield that **L** is an internal cartesian closed category, and thus epitomizes the program we have been developing It generalizes the analogous condition for the Heyting semantics of propositions, which gave us a Heyting-algebra object as the object of its Tarskian semantics However, we may still note that the internal category **L** is a fairly impoverished object For one, it is not a full internal sub-category of **MOD** thus, the computation of its limit properties would be quite a complex matter, as the proofs of the last three theorems would have shown Second, it is far from complete as an internal category· that too diminishes the serious possibility of its functioning as an internal category of domains, capable of yielding solutions of recursive domain equations Third, the category is really one of dcpos and not of domains many of its objects do not have a bottom element, and that limits its potential for yielding unitary solutions of functions defined by recursion at all Types Finally, it loses the rich fibered structure of the Types. in fact, such a structure would have been preserved under the completion if the following property could have been shown to hold

Property 8.1.20 *If in* $\oint[\Sigma x\ \ \alpha\ \beta]$ *there is a directed set*

$$\{[\langle a_i, b_i\rangle] \mid i \in I, a_i \in \oint[\alpha], b_i \in \oint[\beta(a_i/x)]\}$$

and $\langle a, b\rangle = \bigsqcup\{\langle a_i, b_i\rangle \mid i \in I\}$, *then* $[a] \in \oint[\alpha]$ *and* $[b] \in \oint[\beta(b/x)]$

This property is violated principally by the product Types, which in fact, are the ones that lack a bottom element Of course, we would expect that there would be a loss of information—and thereby of structure in the transition to denotations, and fiberwise structure would predictably be a casualty in this process Yet, the deficiency in respect of the first three points listed above does limit the theoretical significance of the construction—especially with regard to the possibility that the latter might be a concrete instance of a canonical category of domains in the topos that we would describe in the next section (the *replete* objects) Perhaps this indicates that some more sophisticated form of completion is needed to yield the desired properties, and this is a matter for further investigation

8.2 Towards a Synthetic Theory

Perhaps the most challenging question in the last two and a half decades of formal semantics, has been the possibility of treating the domains of the denotations of programming languages as sets, *with full function spaces* Perhaps this makes more sense to a logician than to a computer scientist, but the advantages of being able to reasoning about (the semantics) of Programming language Types, using standard (perhaps intuitionistic, higher-order) logic is undeniable We have remarked upon the impossibility of being able to do this in the classical universe of sets, the resolution was, as we have seen, embedding the theory (category) within a non-standard (intuitionistic) universe—which essentially meant an elementary Topos—usually through a pre-sheaf construction (*cf* [74, 62]). The outcome was in general, an internal category in the Topos, with enough completeness to support the standard Type constructions. A lacuna in this approach was the systematic exploration of the properties of such internal categories, especially with a view to supporting the standard constructions within programming language semantics For instance, it was known that cartesian closed categories, having fix-points of endomorphisms and equalizers, were degenerate Hence, it was important to demonstrate the viability of such basic semantic constructions within the internal categories obtained by the general method

At this juncture, a need was felt to formulate this general program within an axiomatic framework· that is, systematically build up the theory of a (complete) category of domains, *internal* to a Topos The suggestions had already made by Scott, and taken up by Hyland, to have theory of Domains formulated completely and axiomatically within the internal language of a Topos As we have indicated earlier, the minimal requirement of such a theory was to support the fix-points of functions, and the limit-colimit coincidence structure for the solution of recursive domain equations ([80]) Rosolini ([68, 67]) and Mulry ([54]) constructed most of the initial scaffolding the basic abstraction was the concept of a partial map classifier within a Topos, and of a classifier of recursively enumerable sub-objects Such a class of sub-objects could provide the basic topology, the specialization order (or the *intrinsic* order) with respect to which could give us the basic (pre-) domains There were alternative ways to look at this which would not emphasize the intrinsic order, but start with some other basic considerations relating to the structure of the recursively enumerable sub-objects (for instance, the "external" inclusion order amongst such sub-objects) The great virtue of this general technique was that it gathered into a single general framework the notions of continuity and effectivity that had been known for almost three decades to be foundational to the concept of computability· and this framework was *a priori* in that it invoked no *ad hoc* notion of codings or Godel numberings

The essential consideration in all the variants of this theory was the concept of a partial maps within a Topos, and a classifier of the sub-objects of the domains of such partial maps, which could be thought of (in a suitably qualified sense) as *computable* Since the development of this thesis draws to an end, we shall have to abbreviate our account to simply providing a sketch of the foundational notions on which this theory can be developed, and situate the constructions of the previous section in its context As we just mentioned, the cornerstone of the theory is the notion of a classifier Σ of the domains of those partial maps in the Topos, that we would like to consider as computable Recall that in the external universe, the domains of general recursive functions are precisely the recursively enumerable sets Hence the classifier Σ could be thought of as the classifier of recursively enumerable sub-objects Certain general considerations on the nature of the computable maps give us the basic axioms which we would have this object obey (*cf* [86, 35]) A significant principle is that it should be, in fact, a sub-object of the usual sub-object classifier Ω of the Topos Hence Σ should be thought of as the object of "computable" truth-values We elucidate the basic axiom upon which we base the object Σ below It is essentially an adaptation from Hyland's essay ([35]) on the topic.

Axiom 8.2.1 *We have a sub-object Σ of the (usual) sub-object classifier Ω, equipped with the sub-object $\top\ 1 \to \Sigma$. The pullbacks of arbitrary maps $f . X \to \Sigma$ along $\top$ are called the Σ-subsets (denoted by the symbol $\subseteq_\Sigma$), we assume that $\top$ is a generic Σ-subset, in the sense that every Σ-subset $\check{f}$ of an object X, is obtained by pulling back an unique (classifying) map $f\ X \to \Sigma$ along $\top$ We would also require that $A \subseteq_\Sigma B$ and $B \subseteq_\Sigma C$ implies $A \subseteq_\Sigma C$*

A number of consequences follow from this axiom those significant for our purpose are

1. for any object X, we have that $X \subseteq_\Sigma X$,
2. the pullback of a Σ-subset is a Σ-subset, and
3. the collection of Σ-subsets of an object is closed under finite intersection

The actual theory goes on to posit a number of other axioms, some of which we shall mention as and when required

The conditions of Axiom 8 2 1 are usually presented in a form convenient for reasoning in the internal logic The first and last conditions of the axiom are summed up in an internal logic statement which we present below

$$\top \in \Sigma \tag{8.5}$$

$$p \in \Sigma \bigwedge [(p = \top) \Rightarrow (q \in \Sigma)] \Rightarrow (p \bigwedge q) \in \Sigma \tag{8 6}$$

An object with these properties is known as a *dominance* ([68]) A number of such objects have been used in the study of internal domains We mention one due to Rosolini ([68]), existing within the Effective Topos and defined by the following internal language statement.

$$\Sigma = \{p \in \Omega \mid \exists f\ N^N\ (p \Leftrightarrow \exists n\ N\ f(n) = 0)\}$$

Note that it is defined *a priori* as a sub-object of Ω.

We shall use two different kinds of dominances in this section The first one is due to Phoa ([58]), and we demonstrate how we may use it in a fairly straightforward manner to "secure" the partial order on the objects of our category **L**.

Definition 8.2.2 *The object Σ is defined to be the modest set having as its underlying set $\{\top, \bot\}$ with $\top$ realized by the set $\{I\}$ and $\bot$ by the set $\{\Omega\}$ (where $\Omega \equiv [(\lambda x\ xx)(\lambda x.xx)]_\beta$)*

The first step in establishing this as a dominance would be to formulate its definition as a sub-object of Ω, the sub-object classifier The reader may verify, that Σ as defined is (isomorphic to) the following sub-object of Ω

$$\{p \in \Omega \mid \exists x \in \bar{\lambda}\, (\neg p \Leftrightarrow (x = I)) \bigwedge (p \Leftrightarrow (x = \Omega))\}$$

The actual proof that this object is indeed a dominance is quite complicated and we refer the reader to [60] for the details

Given a sub-object of Ω that is a dominance, we may take the sub-objects (of any object) classified by it, as a set of recursively enumerable predicates, and define on their basis an (intrinsic) pre-order on the object X In very much the same fashion that a specialization order is defined in a Topology, we have the following definition.

Definition 8.2.3 *For any object X in the Topos $\Re$, and $x, y \in X$, we write*

$$x \ll y \Leftrightarrow \forall \phi\ \ \Sigma^X\ \phi(x) \Rightarrow \phi(y)$$

This can be easily seen to be a pre-order We would of course be interested in those objects for which this is a partial order Such objects are known as Σ-spaces, and may be defined as an object satisfying the following statement

$$\textit{The natural map } X \to \Sigma^{\Sigma^X} \textit{ is a mono,}$$

or equivalently

$$\forall x, y\ \ X\, (\forall \phi\ \ \Sigma^X.\phi(x) \Leftrightarrow \phi(y)) \Rightarrow x = y$$

Paul Taylor calls this the Weak Leibnitz principle, which essentially asserts that any pair of elements which satisfy the same set of recursively enumerable properties, are in fact the same ([86])

The dominance defined in Definition 8 2 2 would not be very useful, but it is instructive to see exactly why not

Theorem 8 2.4 *For every object $\alpha \in$ L the relation $\ll$ is entailed by the internal order $\preceq$.*

Proof: We know that α is (essentially) a modest set, consider any map $\phi\ \ \alpha \to \Sigma$ since both domain and co-domain are modest sets, this is essentially a map in **PER** Suppose it is tracked by the code f—which is the same thing as saying that f realizes that the functional relation representing ϕ is total Consider any elements $[a] \preceq [b] \in \alpha$. From the definition of maps in **PER** we know that for all $x \in [a]$, $(f\ x) \vdash \phi([a])$ Now if for any $x \in [a]$, $(f\ x) = I$ we would have that for any $y \in [b]$, $(f\ y) = I$—since we have that for any context $C[\ ]$, if $C[a]$ is solvable, then so is $C[b]$, (and in fact both have the same head normal form, *cf* Proposition 8.1.3). Hence we have that for any map $\phi\ \alpha \to \Sigma$, $\phi([a]) \Rightarrow \phi([b])$, and thus

$$[a] \preceq [b] \Rightarrow [a] \ll [b]$$

which is our proposition Note that the converse may not hold, since the space of morphisms $\phi\ \ \alpha \to \Sigma$ would in general be (properly) contained in the space of all λ-contexts, and it is precisely for this reason too that we may not assert that the $\ll$ pre-order is an order

Hence, we would be justified in looking around for a dominance with respect to which we *would* have in **L**, a category of Σ-spaces In the next series of definitions we work towards such an object We shall denote by the symbol σ, the unary predicate of solvability on the object $\bar{\lambda}$ Recall that a term is solvable if and only if it has a head normal form, or equivalently, if the head reduction sequence of the term terminates There is an effective procedure (i e a partial Turing computable function) for this, which terminates if the term has a (principal) head normal form, and diverges otherwise Hence we may assert that the solvability predicate is recursively enumerable We make the following claim

Lemma 8.2.5 *The binary predicate $\bar{\sigma}([x],[y])$ on $\bar{\lambda}$, defined by the statement*

$$\bar{\sigma}([x],[y]) \Leftrightarrow \sigma([x]) \bigwedge \sigma([y])$$

is recursively enumerable Hence there is a λ-term ϑ such that $\vartheta\ \langle x, y\rangle$ is solvable if and only if x and y are both solvable

Proof: This is fairly straightforward Given the partial Turing computable function for σ, we simply run it first on x and then, if it terminates, on y This gives us the required partial Turing computable function—call it f—and demonstrates that $\bar{\sigma}$ is recursively enumerable But then, by the equivalence of (partial) Turing computable functions, and the functions encoded as λ-terms, we would have a λ-term ϑ which computes the same function f Hence the proposition

We shall write $\vartheta(x, y)$ for the term $\vartheta\ \langle x, y\rangle$, and confuse terms with their β-equivalence classes in the sequel Hence, by the result above we have that

$$\models \sigma(\vartheta(x,y)) \Leftrightarrow \sigma(x) \bigwedge \sigma(y) \tag{8 7}$$

for arbitrary elements x, y in λ

Definition 8.2.6 *We shall denote by $\tilde{\lambda}$, the quotient of the object λ by the equivalence relation $\simeq$. We define the following sub-object of the classifier Ω*

$$\Sigma \equiv \{p \in \Omega \mid \exists X \in \tilde{\lambda}\, (p \Leftrightarrow \exists x \in X\, \sigma(x))\}$$

Note that X, in the context of this definition is a (closed) sub-object of the object λ of $\Re$ the latter is an object which has the underlying set $\tilde{\lambda}$, and with the equality defined by

$$[m = n] = \begin{cases} \{m\} & \text{if } m = n \\ \emptyset & \text{otherwise} \end{cases}$$

where $m, n \in \tilde{\lambda}$, thus X inherits this equality from $\tilde{\lambda}$ This remark is important for the application of the axiom of countable choice in Theorem 8 2 7 below We claim that Σ is a dominance

Theorem 8.2.7 *The object Σ defined in Definition 8 2.6 above, is a dominance*

Proof: Let us establish the validity of the two defining properties of a dominance set out in Equations 8 5 and 8 6 First, we may set $\top$ to be the specified element $[I]_{\simeq}$ of $\tilde{\lambda}$. This would secure us our first property As for the second we have the following argument in the internal logic Suppose $p \in \Sigma$ this means that for some X, an equivalence class in $\tilde{\lambda}$, we have that $p \Leftrightarrow \exists x \in X\, \sigma(x)$ Now the clause $(p = \top) \Rightarrow (q \in \Sigma)$ translates as the (internal logic) statement·

$$\exists x \in X\, \sigma(x) \Rightarrow \exists Y \in \tilde{\lambda}\, (q \Leftrightarrow \exists y \in Y\, \sigma(y)) \tag{8.8}$$

$$\Leftrightarrow \quad \forall x \in X\, \exists Y \in \tilde{\lambda}\, (\sigma(x) \Rightarrow (q \Leftrightarrow \exists y \in Y\, \sigma(y)))$$

since $\sigma(x)$ is (semi-) decidable

$$\Leftrightarrow \quad \forall x \in X\, (\sigma(x) \Rightarrow (q \Leftrightarrow \exists y \in \kappa(x)\, \sigma(y)))$$

using the axiom of countable choice for a choice function $\kappa \quad X \to \tilde{\lambda}$

hence,
$$(p \wedge q) \Leftrightarrow \exists x \in X\, \exists y \in \kappa(x)\, \sigma(x) \wedge \sigma(y) \tag{8 9}$$

Now note that both X and $\tilde{\lambda}$ are modest sets, hence we may take the function $\kappa \cdot X \to \tilde{\lambda}$ as essentially one between PERs Let it be tracked by the code f (as before, this is the same as saying that f realizes the predicate that the functional relation representing κ is total) From the modest set structure of the domain and co-domain—namely that any $x \in X$ is realized by the set $\{x\}$ and any equivalence class $Y \in \tilde{\lambda}$ is realized by the set of all the codes in Y we have that $\forall x \in X\ (f \cdot x) \in \kappa(x)$ Consider the set Z' defined as follows.

$$Z' \equiv \{\vartheta(x,y) \mid x \in X,\ y \in \kappa(x)\} \tag{8 10}$$

we claim that any pair $\vartheta(x,y)$, $\vartheta(x',y') \in Z'$ are in the equivalence relation $\simeq$. We have the following argument Consider any context $\mathcal{C}[\cdot]$, we have that

$$\begin{array}{lll} & \sigma(\mathcal{C}[\vartheta(x,y)]) & \\ \Rightarrow & \sigma(\mathcal{C}[\vartheta(x, f \cdot x)]) & \text{since } y \simeq f \cdot x \\ \Rightarrow & \sigma(\mathcal{C}[\vartheta(x', f \cdot x)]) & \text{since } x \simeq x' \\ \Rightarrow & \sigma(\mathcal{C}[\vartheta(x', f \cdot x')]) & \text{since } (x \simeq x') \Rightarrow (f \cdot x \simeq f \cdot x') \\ \Rightarrow & \sigma(\mathcal{C}[\vartheta(x', y')]) & \text{since } y' \simeq f \cdot x' \end{array}$$

and by symmetry of the argument the claim is established Now define Z to be the closure of Z' under the equivalence relation $\simeq$: that is, Z is defined by the following internal language comprehension scheme

$$Z \equiv \{z \in \dot{\lambda} \mid \exists z' \in Z'\ \forall \mathcal{C}[\,]\ \sigma(\mathcal{C}[z]) \Leftrightarrow \sigma(\mathcal{C}[z'])\}$$

Now we claim the following

$$(\exists x \in X\ \exists y \in \kappa(x)\ \sigma(x) \bigwedge \sigma(y)) \Leftrightarrow \exists z \in Z\ \sigma(z)$$

The argument in the direction $\Rightarrow$ is obvious (recall Equation 8 7) The other way is also straightforward by the definition of Z we have

$$\begin{array}{lll} & \exists z \in Z\ \sigma(z) & \\ \Rightarrow & \exists z' \in Z'\ \sigma(z') & \\ \Rightarrow & \exists x \in X\ \exists y \in \kappa(x)\ \sigma(\vartheta(x,y)) & \text{cf Equation 8.10} \\ \Rightarrow & \exists x \in X.\exists y \in \kappa(x)\ \sigma(x) \bigwedge \sigma(y) & \text{cf Equation 8.7} \end{array}$$

and hence the claim Thus we have from Equation 8 9 that

$$p \bigwedge q \Leftrightarrow \exists z \in Z\ \sigma(z)$$

with $Z \in \dot{\lambda}$, and hence $(p \bigwedge q) \subset \Sigma$

We shall see that taking Σ as our dominance, allows us to derive some significant canonical properties of our category **L** In fact, Σ has some interesting features apparent *prima facie*

It is a sub object of the classifier Ω, containing the distinguished element $\top$ which we have defined as $[I]_{\simeq}$; it has a bottom element $\perp$ which is essentially the empty set $\emptyset$ corresponding to the $\simeq$ equivalence class of all unsolvable terms In fact Σ is a modest set, and isomorphic to the modest set $\tilde{\lambda}$ we may make its modest presentation explicit as follows

$$\begin{array}{ccc} \text{for } p \in \Sigma & \text{such that} & \exists X \in \tilde{\lambda}\ (p \Leftrightarrow \exists x \in X\ \sigma(x)) \\ \text{we have } x \vdash p & \Longleftrightarrow & x \in X \end{array}$$

and obviously $\emptyset$ is realized by the set of unsolvable terms Also, Σ has a pleasing relation to the objects of $\mathbf{L}$: namely, every object of the category is a sub-object of Σ We shall see that this has important consequences for $\mathbf{L}$ We note another significant fact in the next lemma

Lemma 8.2.8 *For any code* $[f] \in \tilde{\lambda}$, *and for any* $X \in \mathbf{L}$, *there is a morphism* $\phi : X \to \Sigma$ *tracked by* f

Proof: We have abused the language in the statement of the lemma, in implicitly considering a $\Re$-morphism between any $X \in \mathbf{L}$ as equivalent to one between the corresponding PERs A more precise statement would be that any code f realizes the totality condition on the functional relation representing some morphism between any $X \in \mathbf{L}$ and Σ. We shall go by the abused version since it simplifies the proof Consider any code f, and any X as before We know that for any $x, y \in \lambda$, $x \simeq y$ implies that $(f\ \ x) \simeq (f\ \ y)$. hence, we define the map ϕ as follows ϕ $[a] \mapsto p$ where $p \Leftrightarrow \exists y \in Y \sigma(y)$ with $Y = [f \cdot a]_{\simeq}$ it requires a slight re-formulation to write this in terms of a functional relation in $\Re$ and we leave that to the reader

With this we would not have much difficulty in establishing the fact that with respect to Σ, we have in $\mathbf{L}$, a category of Σ-spaces

Theorem 8.2.9 *Any object in the category* $\mathbf{L}$ *is a* Σ*-space, with the internal order* $\preceq$ *coinciding with the intrinsic order* $\ll$

Proof: Consider any $X \in \mathbf{L}$; since both X and Σ are modest sets, we shall consider maps in $\Re$ between as between PERs Suppose for $[a], [b] \in X$, and all $\phi \cdot X \to \Sigma$, we have $\phi([a]) = \phi([b])$, by Lemma 8 2 8, this implies that $\forall f \in \lambda\ (f\ \ a) \simeq (f\ \ b)$ which means that for all contexts $C[\ ]$, $C[a] \simeq C[b]$, which is to say that $a \simeq b$ or that $[a] = [b]$ Hence X is a Σ-space

As for the coincidence of the orders, note that $\preceq \Rightarrow \ll$ is easy since if $[a] \preceq [b]$ then for any code f, if $f\ \ a$ is solvable then so is $f\ \ b$ Hence for any ϕ $X \to \Sigma$, $\phi([a]) \Rightarrow \phi([b])$

For the converse, suppose we have that $\forall \phi \; X \to \Sigma \; \phi([a]) \Rightarrow \phi([b])$ By Lemma 8 2 8, this would mean that for any code f (and thus, for any context $C[\;]$), if $f \; a$ (respectively $C[a]$) is solvable, then so is $f \; b$ (respectively $C[b]$); but this is precisely to say that $a \preceq b$ or that $[a] \preceq [b]$ Hence the proposition

Thus the choice of the dominance is extremely important in establishing the desired properties of our category

In the last part of this section, we shall touch briefly upon a canonical property that the category **L** exhibits. A comprehensive discussion on the precise significance of this canonical property is beyond the scope of this thesis that would require too deep an excursion into Topos theory We shall merely indicate that our category satisfies this property and hence is, in some sense, canonical

Over the last few years of research into the topic of internal domain theory, there has emerged some agreement upon the internal category of domains that one would like to consider as canonical, and that, in some sense has the greatest theoretical economy We have seen that our category satisfies the property of being a Σ-space, *and* is complete with respect to countable sequences increasing with respect to the intrinsic order Such things were called *complete Σ-spaces* by Phoa ([58, 59]), and considered as an appropriate category of domains Likewise Freyd et al considered a class of objects known as ***extensional PERs***, as an appropriate category of domains ([22]) A common concept emerges in Taylor ([86]) and Hyland ([35]) about such a category As the latter remarks, two considerations should inform the choice of the appropriate category first, that we should generalize the weak Leibnitz principle to (semi-decidable) *properties* (a precise statement of this would be given in the sequel), and second, that the category should have "sufficient" internal completeness to handle the standard semantics of constructive Types Hyland demonstrates that both considerations converge on a single characterization namely that of the category of *replete* objects, which is the least internally full reflective sub-category (of the Topos) which contains the object Σ

As we have said, a precise formulation of this theory is beyond the scope of this work We shall merely indicate a few of the principles underlying its development. The generalization of the weak Leibnitz principle mentioned above, takes the following form, which we excerpt from Taylor ([86])

Definition 8.2 10 (The Strong Leibnitz Principle) *If a morphism $p \; X \to Y$ induces a bijection between semi-decidable predicates, with Y satisfying the weak Leibnitz principle, then p is an isomorphism*

Hence, as Hyland remarks, this principle essentially ordains that objects are determined by their Σ-sub-objects. The precise definition of the category of such objects can be arrived at in different ways. Taylor considers a kind of a epi-mono factorization of the natural map $\varepsilon_X : X \to \Sigma^{\Sigma^X}$, to arrive at a characterization. We shall use Hyland's definition ([35]).

Definition 8.2.11 *A map $g : P \to Q$ is said to be* **Σ-equable** *if the induced map $\hat{g} : \Sigma^Q \to \Sigma^P$ is an isomorphism. A map $f : A \to B$ is said to be* **Σ-replete** *if for any Σ-equable map $g : P \to Q$, the (induced) diagram in Figure 8-1 is a pullback. The internal full sub-category*

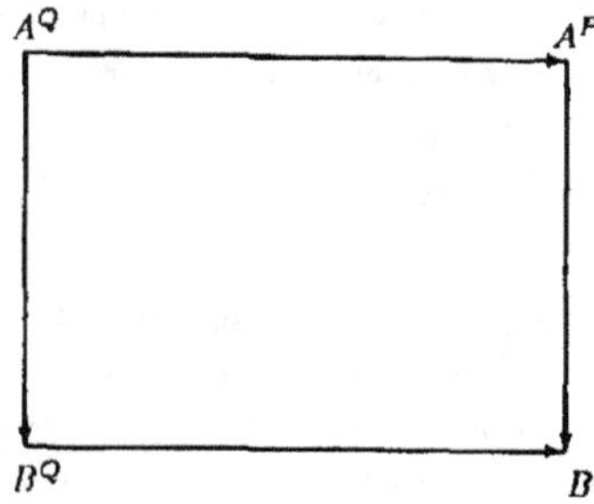

Figure 8-1: Σ-replete Morphisms

of all objects A such that the unique map $A \to 1$ is Σ-replete, is known as a category of replete *objects. We shall say that any object A for which the map $A \to 1$ is Σ-replete, satisfies the* repleteness condition.

In the internal logic, and as set out in [35], this characterization assumes the following intuitive form: replete objects are objects A, such that for any Σ-equable map $P \to Q$, every commutative square of the form shown in Figure 8-2 has an unique diagonal fill-in $s : Q \to A$. We shall use this characterization and show that our category **L** is a sub-category of the internal category of replete objects. We note the following fact about the map $\hat{f} : \Sigma^Q \to \Sigma^P$ induced from an arbitrary map $f : P \to Q$.

Lemma 8.2.12 *For the canonical map $\hat{f} : \Sigma^Q \to \Sigma^P$ induced by a map $f : P \to Q$, we have, in the internal logic:*

$$\models \forall H : \Sigma^Q\, \forall G : \Sigma^P\, \hat{f}(H) = G \Rightarrow G = H \circ F$$

where we use $\hat{f}(H) = G$ as an abbreviation for $[\hat{f}](H, G) = \top$, $[\hat{f}]$ being the functional relation representing $\hat{f}$, and the formula $G = H \circ F$ stands for

$$\forall p : P \forall s : \Sigma\, G(p, s) \Leftrightarrow \exists q : Q\, F(p, q) \bigwedge H(q, s)$$

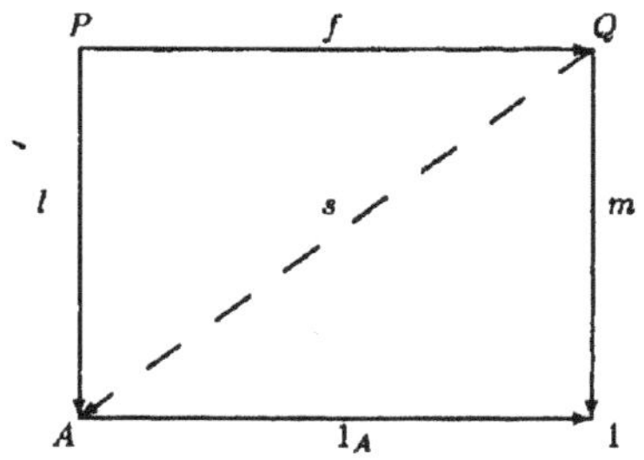

Figure 8-2 Replete Objects

where upper-case letters denote the functional relations representing the corresponding morphisms in lower-case

Proof: In the internal logic, the situation is pretty much as in the category of Sets We sketch the argument in the internal logic, the basic validities used in the proof can be checked up in [37] We note first the structure of the exponent Σ^Q, as set out in [37], it has the general structure of exponents in the Realizability Topos, which has the set of maps $\hom_{\mathrm{Sets}}(Q \times \Sigma, \Omega)$ as its underlying set, with equality defined as follows:

$$\begin{aligned} [F = F] &= [\text{'}F \text{ is a functional relation'}] \\ [F = G] &= [EF \bigwedge EG \bigwedge \forall q \cdot Q\ \forall s\ \ \Sigma\,(F(q,s) \Leftrightarrow G(q,s))] \end{aligned}$$

We shall use lower-case letters to denote morphisms, and (corresponding) upper-case letters or enclosing square brackets to denote the representing functional relations Since we have a map $f\ \ P \to Q$, we have a map $\langle \mathrm{id}, f\rangle\ \ \Sigma^Q \times P \to \Sigma^Q \times Q$, for which, in the internal logic

$$\models \forall H \cdot \Sigma^Q\ \forall p \in P\ \forall H'\ \ \Sigma^P\ \forall q\ \ Q\ [\langle \mathrm{id}, f\rangle](\langle H,p\rangle,\langle H',q\rangle) \Leftrightarrow H = H' \bigwedge F(p,q)$$

Composing with the canonical evaluation morphism $\epsilon\ \ \Sigma^Q \times Q \to \Sigma$ we have $\epsilon \circ \langle \mathrm{id}, f\rangle \cdot \Sigma^Q \times P \to \Sigma$, for which we have the validity

$$\begin{aligned} \models \forall H\ \ \Sigma^Q\ \forall p \in P\ \forall s\ \ \Sigma\ [(\epsilon \circ \langle \mathrm{id}, f\rangle)](\langle H,p\rangle,s) \Leftrightarrow \\ \exists H'\ \ \Sigma^Q\ \exists q\ \ Q\ [\langle \mathrm{id}, f\rangle](\langle H,p\rangle,\langle H',q\rangle) \bigwedge H'(q,s) \end{aligned} \quad (8\ 11)$$

Now for any map $j\ \ A \times B \to C$ we have the exponential transpose $j^*\ \ A \to C^B$, for which we have the validity

$$\models \forall a \in A\ \forall F\ \ C^B\ J^*(a,F) \Rightarrow (\forall b\ \ B\ \forall c\ \ C\ F(b,c) \Leftrightarrow J(\langle a,b\rangle,c))$$

Hence, taking the transpose of the map $\epsilon \circ \langle \mathrm{id}, f \rangle$, we have the validity

$$\models \forall H \cdot \Sigma^Q \; \forall G \cdot \Sigma^P \; [(\epsilon \circ \langle \mathrm{id}, f \rangle)^*](H,G) \Rightarrow$$
$$(\forall p \cdot P \; \forall s \cdot \Sigma \; G(p,s) \Leftrightarrow [\epsilon \circ \langle \mathrm{id}, f \rangle](\langle H,p \rangle, s))$$

But then, from Equation 8.11 we have that

$$\begin{aligned} &\forall H \cdot \Sigma^Q \; \forall p \in P \; \forall s : \Sigma \; [\epsilon \circ \langle \mathrm{id}, f \rangle](\langle H,p \rangle, s) \\ \Leftrightarrow \;& \exists H' \cdot \Sigma^Q \; \exists q \cdot Q \; [\langle \mathrm{id}, f \rangle](\langle H,p \rangle, \langle H',q \rangle) \bigwedge H'(q,s) \\ \Leftrightarrow \;& \exists H' \cdot \Sigma^Q \; \exists q \cdot Q \; H = H' \bigwedge F(p,q) \bigwedge H'(q,s) && (8.12) \\ \Leftrightarrow \;& \exists q \cdot Q . F(p,q) \bigwedge H(q,s) && (8.13) \end{aligned}$$

where the last statement can be seen to hold on the following grounds the implication 8.12 $\Rightarrow$ 8.13 follows from the definition of $=$ on the object Σ^Q, the converse implication follows from the fact that $\models H = H' \Rightarrow EH \bigwedge EH'$ by the same definition. Thus we have

$$\models \forall H \cdot \Sigma^Q \; \forall G \cdot \Sigma^P \; [(\epsilon \circ \langle \mathrm{id}, f \rangle)^*](H,G) \Rightarrow$$
$$(\forall p \cdot P \; \forall s \cdot \Sigma \; G(p,s) \Leftrightarrow \exists q \cdot Q \; F(p,q) \bigwedge H(q,s))$$

But the transpose is precisely the functional relation representing $\hat{f}$, hence the proposition.

We also note that any object of the internal category **L** is a sub-object of the object Σ, and hence that any morphism $l \cdot P \to A$, from an arbitrary object P to an object $A \in \mathbf{L}$ can be considered as a map $l' \cdot P \to \Sigma$. We state this formally

Lemma 8.2.13 *Any object $A \in \mathbf{L}$ is a sub-object of the object Σ, and hence, for any morphism $f \cdot P \to A$ from an arbitrary object P, we have a corresponding (unique) morphism $\imath \circ f \cdot P \to \Sigma$, where $\imath \cdot A \rightarrowtail \Sigma$, is the obvious monic*

Proof: Considering both $A \in \mathbf{L}$ and Σ as modest sets, we can easily see that A is a sub-object of Σ; we have the monic $\imath \cdot A \rightarrowtail \Sigma$, which has the following description for any element X of A, realized by the class $[x]_\simeq$ of codes, we have that $\imath(X) = p$ where $p \equiv \exists y \in [x]_\simeq \sigma(y)$ (we have confused descriptions of morphisms in **PER** with those between modest sets). This can be easily seen to be a monic. Now any morphism $f \cdot P \to A$, extends to $\imath \circ f \cdot P \to \Sigma$ and the property of monics tells us that if, for any $g \cdot P \to A$, we have $\imath \circ f = \imath \circ g$, then we would have that $f = g$. Hence the uniqueness of the extension

Remark 8 2 14 *By virtue of this proposition, we would, in the sequel, confuse maps l $P \to A$ (with $A \in \mathbf{L}$, and P arbitrary), with the map $\imath \circ l \cdot P \to \Sigma$*

Theorem 8.2.15 *Every object in the (internal) category* $\mathbf{L}$ *satisfies the repleteness condition.*

Proof· We refer to Figure 8-2, and consider any Σ-equable map f $P \to Q$, and commutative square comprising maps l . $P \to A$, m $Q \to 1$ and 1_A $A \to 1$ We define a map S $Q \times A \to \Omega$ (note that this is a morphism in the category of Sets, and not in the Topos $\Re$) by the following statement

$$[S(q,a)] = [\exists p \in P\ F(p,q) \bigwedge L(p,a)]$$

where we have used the letters F and L to denote the functional relations representing the morphisms f and l respectively We claim that the map S is a functional relation, and verify the defining properties

Relational· From the relationality of the functional relations F and L we have the following validities

$$\begin{aligned} F(\langle p,q\rangle) \bigwedge q = q' &\Rightarrow F(\langle p,q'\rangle) \\ L(\langle p,a\rangle) \bigwedge a = a' &\Rightarrow L(\langle p,a'\rangle) \end{aligned}$$

whence,

$$S(\langle q,a\rangle) \bigwedge q = q' \bigwedge a = a' \Rightarrow S(\langle q',a'\rangle)$$

Strict: From the strictness of F and L we have the following validities

$$\begin{aligned} F(\langle p,q\rangle) &\Rightarrow Ep \bigwedge Eq \\ L(\langle p,q\rangle) &\Rightarrow Ep \bigwedge Ea \end{aligned}$$

whence,

$$S(\langle q,a\rangle) \Rightarrow Eq \bigwedge Ea$$

Single-valued· We shall need the Σ-equableness of f to prove this Suppose we have that $S(q,a) = \top \wedge S(q,a') = \top$, then we could have two possibilities:

Case $F(p,q) \wedge L(p,a) \wedge L(p,a')$· then, from the single-valuedness of L we would immediately have $a = a'$, proving the proposition

Case $F(p,q) \wedge F(p',q) \wedge L(p,a) \wedge L(p',a')$· from Lemma 8 2 13, we may confuse the map l $P \to A$ with the map $\imath \circ l$ $P \to \Sigma$ From the Σ-equableness of

$f : P \to Q$ we have a bijection $\hat{f} : \Sigma^Q \to \Sigma^P$, let L be the image of H under this bijection—that is, $\hat{f}(H) = L$ in the notation of Lemma 8.2.12. We have from Lemma 8.2.12 and arguing in the internal logic,

$$F(p,q') \bigwedge H(q',a) \bigwedge F(p',q'') \bigwedge H(q'',a')$$

for elements $q', q'' \in Q$, but then, from the hypothesis, and single valuedness of F we would have that $q = q' = q''$; relationality of H would yield us $H(q,a) \bigwedge H(q,a')$ and single-valuedness $a = a'$.

Total: We claim (in the meta-theory) that for every $q \in Q$, such that $\models Eq$, there is some $p \in P$ such that $F(p,q) = \top$. Now suppose our claim is false. Let us designate by q, the element of Q, such that there exists no $p \in P$ such that $F(p,q) = \top$. Let a denote a specified element of Σ, define a functional relation $H : Q \times \Sigma \to \Omega$ as follows

$$H(x,a) = \begin{cases} \top & \text{if } x = q \\ \emptyset & \text{otherwise} \end{cases}$$

The bijection $\hat{f}$ must assign some element $G \in \Sigma^P$ to H, and we would have from Lemma 8.2.12 that $G = H \circ F$ as explicated in the Lemma. But then looking at the formulae defining composition, and the definition of H we see that $\forall p : P\ \forall s : \Sigma\ G(p,s) = \emptyset$, which violates the condition of Totality: thus G cannot be a functional relation, but then, if $\hat{f}(H) = G$ then we must have that EG which means that G must be a functional relation. Thus we have a contradiction, which implies the premise cannot be true. Thus our claim stands vindicated. Now we claim the following validity

$$\models Eq \Rightarrow \exists a : A\ S(q,a)$$

for which the realizer is the code $\lambda x.y$ where y realizes $\models Ep \Rightarrow \exists a : A\ L(p,a)$, and p is an element such that $F(p,q) = \top$.

This completes the argument that S is a functional relation. As for uniqueness, suppose we had another fill-in represented by the functional relation S'. From the commutation condition, and the fact that f is surjective, we would have the proposition. More explicitly, we have the following logic (in the metatheory). First note that for any $q \in Q$ for which there is some $p \in P$ such that $F(p,q) = \top$, we must have that $S(q,a) = \top = S'(q,a)$ where a is an element of A, such that $L(p,a) = \top$. This holds because both S and S' are fill-ins But we have argued above that for every $q \in Q$ there is some $p \in P$ such that $F(p,q) = \top$. Hence we have, that $\forall q \in Q. \forall a \in A. S(q,a) = \top \Leftrightarrow S'(q,a) = \top$ From this it is easy to claim the validity

$$\models S(q,a) \Leftrightarrow S'(q,a)$$

for which the realizer is simply the (code for the) identity.

Hence our category $\mathbf{L}$ is a sub-category of the category of replete objects relative to the dominance Σ—which is itself not an object of this category With this thought, we conclude this chapter, leaving to the Conclusion, the reflections and conjectures on the results thus far

Chapter 9

Conclusion

If there is in the history of semantics, any one concept which can be made out, even if indistinctly, to be at the back of every epochal moment, it is the concept of *structure*. To my understanding, the greatest insight in Frege's philosophy was that the analytical theory of meaning can proceed rigorously only on the basis of an adequate conception of structure: it was only thus that the former may attain a completely objective status. The theory of meaning has a history to the precise extent that the notion of structure was never determinately conceived. Much of the intellectual ferment around the theory of truth—and subsequently, the extensional theories of meaning—was founded in an unnecessary mistrust of Frege's perceived intensionalism. If it was true that Frege's theory was intensionalist—which it was—it was equally true that intensions were never meant to be mysterious "internal" objects: they were conceived in the first place as completely analytical and objectively presented entities. The lacuna was that they were never thus presented, and from that, truth-theorists decided to do away completely with them. We have seen that *a fortiori* such a theory may never be complete: the burden may only be shifted to a meta-language, and the resulting theory establishes application only through the declaration as illegitimate of an entire class of perfectly meaningful expressions (semantic paradoxes).

It is only in the latter half of this century, that the notion of structure revealed an opening from another direction: namely, the concept of *information*. The general insight, available across a number of disciplines, was that entities were informative to the extent that they were structured, and that the information content of such entities was amenable to formal analysis; a number of measures of information were formulated at varying levels of abstraction and from diverse theoretical perspectives. In the specific context of formal semantics, seminal abstractions came from within Intuitionism. The first was the formulation of intuitionistic validity in terms of sheaf interpretations of higher-order logic ([45, 87, 28, 19]), the second was the theory of constructive proofs of A. Heyting ([87, 27]). The essential insight in the first was that the information content of objects was only incompletely represented in their global elements (corresponding to complete evaluations), in general, *local* sections (corresponding to partial evaluations) had to be taken into account. The essential insight in the second was that information embedded in the structure of expressions could be represented in the class of its *proofs*—that is, transformations and analyses according to the inference rules of the language, moreover, such information could be extracted as effective procedure provided the rules of inference were formulated in a certain finitistic (and effective) way.

The essay into constructive semantics in this dissertation is animated by the perception that a truly general semantic framework should take every linguistic system (formal or otherwise) as its field, and that such a framework should be formulated as an abstract theory of information. The question was whether constructive type theory could furnish such an abstract and general framework. The scope of this question extends considerably beyond what can be, and has been attempted within this thesis. in the general context of the question, it should be viewed perhaps as a prolegomenon. As stated in the introduction, it initiates a certain application of an available theory, and argues for the validity of the generalization. The argument accepted, its success as a sufficiently foundational framework has to be judged on the ground of the necessity of its logic—the extent to which its basic constructs are free from the *ad hoc*. We are perfectly aware that all the information constituting semantics is contained within syntax. the point is how economically the redundancies of the latter—what Girard characterizes as "taxonomy" ([25])—are factored out. It is here that the inherent limitations of the constructive paradigm become apparent.

The *ad hoc* appears at several points in the construction of our CC-Category in Chapter 6. The syntax of the Types and Orders is almost trivially induced from that of the basic Theory of Constructions. The intimate relation with the ω-**Sets** and the PER model is practically forced on to the constructions—the requirement of having a name for every ω-**Set** morphism in the syntax being a particularly awkward technical symptom—and the justification for this can only be provided *a posteriori*. Moreover, the Types are constructed so as to correspond to *equivalence classes* of terms. this is a choice forced by the formalism and while semantically equivalent terms *should* have isomorphic Types (as argued in the Introduction) this should be a *conclusion* of the theory and not an initial choice. Finally, the Types of the *pure* λ-terms form only a small part of the induced theory—even if we ignore the sums and products representing quantification over Orders, the sum and product Types do not, in general, correspond to the Type of any λ-term. This is a significant divergence from the propositional

These are symptomatic, perhaps, of a certain hesitation in the formulation of constructive type theory itself. As pointed out by Girard ([25]), the intuitionistic sequent calculus suppresses the basic symmetries of logic: it forbids weakening and contraction on the right-hand side of sequents (intuitionistic sequents may have only a single formula on the right). The logical extension of this is to restore the arity of sequents, but forbid weakening and contraction throughout—and this gives us Linear Logic. At a deeper level, we perceive the lack of a relation between the two critical abstractions within the Intuitionistic thinking on semantics stated earlier: the concept of partiality and the pre-eminence of *local* notions fundamental to the conception of sheaf semantics, seems difficult to relate to the finitism of constructive proofs. In fact, the conception of a proof itself, as a mathematical object, lacks a sufficiently abstract formal description. We are reminded persistently that proofs are fundamentally *geometric* objects and represent the *finite dynamics* of the system of inference ([25, 26])—yet both geometry and dynamics, as conventionally understood in mathematics, remain elusive within the theory. The situation is even more provocative as sheaf formulations and local notions in the other strand of the abstraction are fundamentally geometric notions. Hence, there is ground to question the legitimacy of constructive type theory as a foundation for the semantics of information. For that matter one might question the claim of every proposed system of proofs to such a foundational role (Linear Logic too)—and we see here genuine lack of clarity: for unless we have a formalism-independent and abstract mathematical characterization of the dynamics of information, there may be no ground for stopping at any specific proof-calculus as foundational.

The lack of a relationship between the local formulations in sheaf semantics, and the finitary formulations of constructive type theories is underscored all the more in our work, since the basic notion of a proof-object comes from that of a residue—which is really a representation of a partial evaluation. The partiality is under-emphasized in the construction of the theory of constructions, and only weakly revived in the embedding within the Realizability Topos: genuine partiality should be captured in terms of *local sections* of the Type-objects—while in our case, all proof-objects turn out to be global—a consequence of going via **ω-Set**. In fact the lack of sensitivity to the partial is especially pronounced in the categorical construction, where no special terminal property attaches to the Type $\{\perp\}$ corresponding to the completely undefined term Ω: it shares the terminal property with any other singleton Type—even that of normal form terms!

Some of the considerations above lead us to question the critical role given to the ω-Sets and the partial equivalence relations in our work. We may recall that this was justified *a posteriori* on the ground of an elegant topos-theoretic framework within which the theory of constructive types and that of denotational domains could be related—specifically one in which the least upper bound constructions of canonical denotations (of terms) could be reconstructed The remarkable benefit was that the denotational objects could be given a synthetic formulation through an appropriate dominance The specific advantage of embedding in a topos is that the types (or their completions) could be conceived of logically as (intuitionistic) sets—and we would have a higher-order theory at our disposal This was aesthetically satisfying in our case, since the Types were constructed basically from denotations, and thus we could, starting from the latter, arrive at a rudimentary and abstract (higher-order) logic of program denotations. An attempt had been made earlier by Abramsky ([2]) in this direction on the basis of the Stone Duality, where the logic was essentially a weak second-order one

Topos-theoretic models of impredicative type theories are traditionally obtained in two ways. the first is through the classifying topos of the theory category ([62, 21])—which has the advantage of yielding a conservative extension of its logic (appropriately conceived); the second is through the construction of a small complete category in the Realizability Topos ([34])—of which the internal category of the modest sets is the best-known instance Other models are known, though not very frequently invoked ([38, 86]) The precise relationship or its lack, between the two model constructions is not well-understood in fact the realizability topos is not even a grothendieck topos We know that the ω-sets is the sub-category of sheaves with respect to the $\neg\neg$-topology in the former ([33]), but we do not understand how the topology comes to play such a canonical role in the world of effective mathematics· the Godel translation, or considerations on decidability that prompt the double negation offers no deep insight in the nature of effective objects, especially form the point of view of the dynamics of information Thus, in order to free the constructions from the contrived character of the ω-sets, or alternatively, to give a logical justification for using it within our general program, we need to deepen the embedding framework—keeping in mind, of course, that we need a justifiable notion of an abstract logic of programs in the topos, and not lose the synthetic character of the objects Perhaps in this more general framework, we could obtain stronger completeness properties of the internal domain-theoretic objects, perhaps even full repleteness This is then, the speculative ground of further research

Bibliography

[1] M Abadi and G Plotkin A PER model of polymorphism and recursive types In *Proceedings of the Fifth IEEE Symposium on Logic in Computer Science* IEEE Computer Society Press, 1990

[2] S Abramsky Domain theory in logical form Technical Report DOC 88/15, Imperial College of Science and Technology, London, September 1988

[3] R. Amadio Recursion over realizability structures *Information and Computation*, 91 55–85, 1991

[4] A Asperti and G Longo *Categories, Types and Structures An introduction to category theory for the working computer scientist* Foundations of Computing MIT Press, Cambridge, Massachusetts, 1991

[5] H Barendregt *The Lambda Calculus Its Syntax and Semantics* North-Holland, Amsterdam, 1984

[6] H Barendregt Introduction to generalised type systems Technical Report 90-8, Dept of Informatics, University of Nijmegen, May 1990

[7] M Barr and C Wells *Toposes, Triples and Theories* Springer-Verlag, Berlin, 1985

[8] M B Beeson *Foundations of Constructive Mathematics* Springer-Verlag, 1985

[9] J. Bénabou Fibered categories and the foundations of naive category theory *Journal of Symbolic Logic*, 50(1) 10–37, 1985

[10] G Berry, P-L Curien, and J.-J. Levy Full abstraction for sequential languages the state of the art In M Nivat and J Reynolds, editors, *Algebraic Methods in Semantics* Cambridge University Press, Cambridge, 1985.

[11] G Boudol Computational semantics of term rewriting systems In M Nivat and J Reynolds, editors, *Algebraic Methods in Semantics*, chapter 5, pages 170–236 Cambridge University Press, Cambridge, 1985

[12] J A Coffa *The Semantic Tradition from Kant to Carnap To the Vienna Station.* Cambridge University Press, Cambridge, 1991

[13] R. L. Crole and A M Pitts New foundations for fixpoint computations. FIX-hyperdoctrines and the FIX-logic *Information and Computation*, 98(2).171–210, 1992.

[14] P-L Curien *Categorical Combinators, Sequential Algorithms and Functional Programming* Pitman, London, 1986

[15] N Dershowitz, S Kaplan, and D A Plaisted Rewrite, rewrite, rewrite, rewrite, rewrite, ...*. *Theoretical Computer Science*, 83, 1991.

[16] J. Dugundji. *Topology* Universal Book Stall, New Delhi, third indian reprint edition, 1993.

[17] M Dummett *Frege Philosophy of Language*. Duckworth, London, second edition, 1981

[18] T Erhard A categorical semantics of constructions In *Proceedings of the Third IEEE Symposium on Logic in Computer Science* IEEE, Computer Society Press, 1988

[19] M P Fourman Continuous truth I. Nonconstructive objects In G Lolli *et al*, editor, *Logic Colloquium '82*, pages 161–180 North-Holland, Amsterdam, 1984

[20] M P Fourman and D S Scott Sheaves and logic In *Applications of Sheaves Lecture Notes in Mathematics 753*, pages 302–401 Springer-Verlag, Berlin, 1979

[21] M P Fourman and S Vickers Theories as categories. In *Lecture Notes in Computer Science 240*, pages 434–448. Springer-Verlag, Berlin, 1985.

[22] P Freyd, P Mulry, G Rosolini, and D Scott Extensional PERs. *Information and Computation*, 98.211–227, 1992.

[23] P Geach and M. Black *Translations from the Philosophical Writings of Gottlob Frege.* Oxford, second revised edition, 1960 Specifically, translation of *Über Sinn und Bedeutung*

[24] J-Y Girard *Interprétation Fonctionelle et Elimination des Coupures de l'Arithmetique d'ordre supérieur* PhD thesis, Université Paris VII, 1972

[25] J-Y Girard Towards a geometry of interaction In J W Gray and A Scedrov, editors, *Categories in Computer Science and Logic* American Mathematical Society, 1987

[26] J-Y Girard Geometry of interaction 1 Interpretation of system F In Ferro, Bonotto, Valentini, and Zanardo, editors, *Logic Colloquium '88*, pages 221–260. Elsevier Science Publishers B V (North-Holland), 1989

[27] J-Y Girard, P Taylor, and Y Lafont *Proofs and Types* Cambridge University Press, 1989

[28] R. Goldblatt *Topoi The Categorial Analysis of Logic*, volume 98 of *Studies in Logic and the Foundations of Mathematics* North-Holland, 1979.

[29] C A Gunter and D S Scott Semantic domains In J van Leeuwen, editor, *Handbook of Theoretical Computer Science*, chapter 12, pages 635–674 Elsevier Science Publishers B. V., 1990.

[30] J R Hindley and J P Seldin *Introduction to Combinators and λ-Calculus*, volume 1 of *London Mathematical Society Student Texts* Cambridge University Press, Cambridge, 1986.

[31] G Huet and D Oppen Equations and rewrite rules: a survey Technical report, SRI, 1979

[32] H Huwig and A. Poigne A note on inconsistencies caused by fixpoints in cartesian closed categories *Theoretical Computer Science*, 73:101–112, 1990. Note

[33] J M E Hyland The effective topos. In A S Troelstra and D van Dalen, editors, *The L E J Brouwer Centenary Symposium* North-Holland, 1982

[34] J M E Hyland A small complete category *Annals of Pure and Applied Logic*, 40, 1988

[35] J M. E Hyland. First steps in synthetic domain theory *Lecture Notes in Mathematics*, 1488, 1991

[36] J. M E Hyland and G Rosolini E P Robinson The discrete objects in the effective topos *Proceedings of the London Mathematical Society*, 60 1–36, 1990

[37] J M E Hyland, P T Johnstone, and A M Pitts Tripos theory *Mathematical Proceedings of the Cambridge Philosophical Society*, 88, 1980

[38] J M E Hyland and A M Pitts The theory of constructions Categorical semantics and topos-theoretic models. In J W. Gray and A Scedrov, editors, *Categories in Computer Science and Logic* American Mathematical Society, 1987

[39] B Jacobs, E Moggi, and T. Streicher Relating models of impredicative type theories. In D H Pitt *et al*, editor, *Category Theory and Computer Science. Lecture Notes in Computer Science 530*, pages 197–218, Berlin, 1991 Springer-Verlag

[40] B. P. F Jacobs *Categorical Type Theory* PhD thesis, Univ Nijmegen, 1991

[41] B P F Jacobs Comprehension categories and the semantics of type dependency Technical report, Univ Nijmegen, 1991

[42] P T. Johnstone. *Topos Theory*, volume 10 of *L M S Monographs* Academic Press, London, 1977.

[43] A. Jung Cartesian closed categories of algebraic cpos *Theoretical Computer Science*, 70 233–250, 1990

[44] J Lambek Cartesian closed categories and typed lambda calculi In G Cousineau, P -L Curien, and B Robinet, editors, *Combinators and Functional Programming Languages Lectures Notes in Computer Science 242* Springer-Verlag, Berlin, 1985

[45] J Lambek and P J Scott *Introduction to Higher-Order Categorial Logic*, volume 7 of *Cambridge Studies in Advanced Mathematics* Cambridge University Press, Cambridge, 1986

[46] F W Lawvere Adjointness in foundations *Dialectica*, 23 281–296, 1969

[47] F W Lawvere Equality in hyperdoctrines and the comprehension schema as an adjoint functor In A Heller, editor, *Proceedings of the New York Symposium on Applications of Categorical Logic*, pages 1–14 American Mathematical Society, 1970

[48] G Longo and E Moggi Constructive natural deduction and its ω-set interpretation Technical Report LIENS-90-21, LIENS, DMI, Ecole Normale Superieure, October 1990

[49] S MacLane *Categories for the Working Mathematician* Springer-Verlag, New York, 1971

[50] P Martin-Lof An intuitionistic theory of types. Predicative part In H E Rose and J C Shepherdson, editors, *Logic Colloquium, '73*, pages 73–118 North-Holland, Amsterdam, 1973

[51] P Martin-Lof Constructive mathematics and computer programming In *Proceedings of the 6th International Congress for Logic, Methodology, and Philosophy of Science*, pages 153–175, Amsterdam, 1982 North-Holland

[52] P Martin-Lof Notes on the domain theoretic interpretation of type theory In *Proceedings of the Workshop on Semantics of Programming Languages* Chalmers University, 1983

[53] P Martin-Lof *Intuitionistic Type Theory* Bibliopolis, Napoli, 1984

[54] P Mulry Generalized banach-mazur functionals in the topos of recursive sets *Journal of Pure and Applied Algebra*, 26 71–83, 1981.

[55] C R Murthy *Extracting Constructive Content from Classical Proof* PhD thesis, Department of Computer Science, Cornell University, 1990

[56] M Nivat On the interpretation of recursive polyadic program schemes *Symposia Mathematica*, 15 255–281, 1975

[57] D Pavlović *Predicates and Fibrations* PhD thesis, Faculteit der Wiskunde en Informatica, Rijksuniversiteit Utrecht, May 1990

[58] W. Phoa *Domain Theory in Realizability Toposes* PhD thesis, Oxford, 1986

[59] W Phoa Effective domains and intrinsic structure In *Proceedings of the Fifth IEEE Symposium on Logic in Computer Science* IEEE Computer Society Press, 1990

[60] W Phoa From term models to domains In *Proceedings of the Symposium on Theoretical Aspects of Computer Software Lecture Notes in Computer Science 526* Springer-Verlag, 1991

[61] W Phoa An introduction to fibrations, topos theory, the effective topos and modest sets Technical report, LFCS Univ. of Edinburgh, April 1992

[62] A M Pitts Polymorphism is set theoretic, constructively In D H Pitt *et al*, editor, *Category Theory and Computer Science Lecture Notes in Computer Science 283*, Berlin, 1987 Springer-Verlag

[63] G Plotkin A powerdomain construction *SIAM Journal on Computing*, 5 452–488, 1976

[64] G Plotkin The category of complete partial orders a tool for making meanings In *Proceedings of the Summer School on Foundations of Artificial Intelligence and Computer Science* Instituto di Scienze dell'Informazione, University of Pisa, 1978

[65] J C Reynolds Polymorphism is not set-theoretic In G Kahn *et al*, editor, *Semantics of Data Types Lecture Notes in Computer Science 173*, pages 145–156. Springer-Verlag, Berlin, 1984

[66] E Robinson How complete is PER? In *Proceedings of the Fourth IEEE Symposium on Logic in Computer Science* IEEE Computer Society Press, 1989

[67] G Rosolini *Continuity and Effectiveness in Topoi* PhD thesis, Carnegie-Mellon University, 1986

[68] G Rosolini Categories and effective computations *Lecture Notes in Computer Science*, 283, 1987

[69] G Rosolini About modest sets *International Journal of Foundations of Computer Science*, 1(3) 341–353, 1990

[70] D S Scott Lattice-theoretic models for the λ-calculus Princeton University, 1969.

[71] D S Scott Outline of a mathematical theory of computation In *Proceedings of the Fourth Annual Princeton Conference on Information Science and Systems*, 1970

[72] D S. Scott Continuous lattices In F W Lawvere, editor, *Toposes, Algebraic Geometry and Logic Lecture Notes in Mathematics 274* Springer-Verlag, Berlin, 1972

[73] D S Scott Data types as lattices *SIAM Journal on Computing*, 5 522–587, 1976

[74] D S Scott Relating theories of the lambda calculus In J R Hindley and J P Seldin, editors, *To H B Curry essays on combinatory logic, lambda calculus and formalism*, pages 403–450 Academic Press, London, 1980

[75] D S Scott Lectures on a mathematical theory of computation Technical Report PRG-19, Oxford University, Oxford, 1981

[76] R A G Seely Hyperdoctrines, natural deduction and the Beck condition. *Zeitschrift fur Math Logik und Grundlagen der Math* , 29 505–542, 1983

[77] R A G Seely. Locally cartesian closed categories and type theory. *Mathematical Proceedings of the Cambridge Philosophical Society*, 95·33–48, 1984

[78] R A G Seely Categorical semantics for higher order polymorphic lambda calculus. *The Journal of Symbolic Logic*, 52(4).969–989, December 1987

[79] M B Smyth The largest cartesian closed category of domains *Theoretical Computer Science*, 27 109-119, 1983

[80] M B Smyth and G Plotkin The category-theoretic solution of recursive domain equations. *SIAM Journal on Computing*, 11(4) 761–783, 1982

[81] A Stoughton *Fully Abstract Models of Programming Languages* Pitman, London, 1988

[82] T Streicher Dependence and independence results for (impredicative) calculi of dependent types Technical Report MIP 9015, Universitat Passau, Fakultat für Mathematik und Informatik, October 1990

[83] A Tarski The semantic conception of truth and the foundations of semantics *Philosophy and Phenomenological Research*, 4, 1944.

[84] A. Tarski. *Logic, Semantics, Metamathematics. Papers from 1923 to 1938* Hackett Publishing Co., Indianapolis, second edition, 1983

[85] P Taylor *Recursive Domains, Indexed Category Theory and Polymorphism* PhD thesis, Mathematics Department, University of Cambridge, 1987

[86] P. Taylor. The fixed point property in synthetic domain theory. In *Proceedings of the Sixth IEEE Symposium on Logic in Computer Science* IEEE Computer Society Press, 1991

[87] A Troelstra and D van Dalen *Constructivism in Mathematics An Introduction*, volume 121, 123 of *Studies in Logic and the Foundations of Mathematics* North-Holland, Amsterdam, 1988

[88] S. Vickers. *Topolgy via Logic*. Cambridge Tracts in Theoretical Computer Science Cambridge University Press, Cambridge, 1989

[89] C P Wadsworth The relation between computational and denotational properties for Scott's D^{∞} model *SIAM Journal on Computing*, 5(3) 488–521, September 1976

[90] O Wyler *Lecture Notes on Topoi and Quasitopoi*. World Scientific, Singapore, 1991

www.ingramcontent.com/pod-product-compliance
Lightning Source LLC
LaVergne TN
LVHW012203040326
832903LV00003B/84
* 9 7 8 1 0 1 9 9 6 2 6 7 1 *